90 02

WITHDRAWN
FROM
UNIVERSITY OF PLY
LIBRARY SERVICES

D0421485

A TIME TO CHANT

A TIME TO CHANT

The Sōka Gakkai Buddhists in Britain

BRYAN WILSON
and
KAREL DOBBELAERE

CLARENDON PRESS · OXFORD
1994

Oxford University Press, Walton Street, Oxford OX2 6DP
Oxford New York Toronto
Delhi Bombay Calcutta Madras Karachi
Kuala Lumpur Singapore Hong Kong Tokyo
Nairobi Dar es Salaam Cape Town
Melbourne Auckland Madrid
and associated companies in
Berlin Ibadan

Oxford is a trade mark of Oxford University Press

Published in the United States
by Oxford University Press Inc., New York

© Bryan Wilson and Karel Dobbelaere 1994

All rights reserved. No part of this publication may be reproduced,
stored in a retrieval system, or transmitted, in any form or by any means,
without the prior permission in writing of Oxford University Press.
Within the UK, exceptions are allowed in respect of any fair dealing for the
purpose of research or private study, or criticism or review, as permitted
under the Copyright, Designs and Patents Act, 1988, or in the case of
reprographic reproduction in accordance with the terms of the licences
issued by the Copyright Licensing Agency. Enquiries concerning
reproduction outside these terms and in other countries should be
sent to the Rights Department, Oxford University Press,
at the address above

British Library Cataloguing in Publication Data
Data available

Library of Congress Cataloging in Publication Data
Wilson, Bryan R.
A time to chant: the Sōka Gakkai Buddhists in Britain/Bryan
Wilson and Karel Dobbelaere.
Includes bibliographical references.
ISBN 0-19-827915-9
1. Sōka Gakkai—Great Britain. 2. Sōka Gakkai Buddhists—Great
Britain. I. Dobbelaere, Karel. II. Title.
BQ8412.G7W55 1994 294.3'928'0941—dc20 93-24507

1 3 5 7 9 10 8 6 4 2

Typeset by J&L Composition Ltd, Filey, North Yorkshire

Printed in Great Britain
on acid-free paper by
Biddles Ltd, Guildford and King's Lynn

PREFACE

ONE of the most successful of new religious movements in Western countries, with respect to both rapid growth and the recruitment of a stable membership, is Sōka Gakkai International, yet, in Europe at least, it has commanded relatively little attention from scholars. The authors, both of whom have previously had some acquaintance with the movement in Japan, its country of origin, have observed its growth in Western Europe for some time, and when Dobbelaere spent some months as a Visiting Fellow of All Souls College, Oxford, the opportunity presented itself for us to collaborate in a study of the SGI membership. The idea of such a study was put to the leader of the movement in Britain. He accepted the proposal readily, and, at our request, put at our disposal a membership list (as it stood in the late summer of 1990) from which we were able to draw a random sample of members to whom we distributed a postal questionnaire. Without the co-operation of SGI headquarters in Britain, our study would have taken a very different shape, and might not have been possible at all.

In a period when ancient families, large business concerns, and even city councils not infrequently commission scholars to undertake research into their history, we should make it clear that, although we received ready co-operation from the subjects of our study, our work was an entirely independent operation. It was not undertaken at the invitation of Sōka Gakkai, and was neither sponsored nor commissioned by that organization. The financial research support for our work was provided more or less equally by All Souls College, Oxford, and by the Catholic University of Leuven (Louvain, Belgium). That funding covered the cost of producing and distributing the 1,000 postal questionnaires; the expenditure on travel entailed in conducting interviews (in London, Bristol, and Gloucester, as well as in Oxford); and the cost of coding and computer analysis.

In an ideal world, the sample of respondents might have been compared with a control group matched for at least age, sex, geographic distribution, and perhaps educational attainment. To organize such a comparative exercise would, however, have been intrinsically difficult, and would certainly have been far beyond the financial means at our disposal. We have sought to obtain some of the advantages of comparison by use of the United Kingdom sample of the European Value Study (1990), and this brings out in some measure the extent to which the members of SGI differ in their dispositions and orientations both from the general public, and from a section of that public which we have matched for age. Where appropriate, we have also alluded to other new religious movements operating in Britain to bring out the particular characteristics of the SGI membership.

The basic source of our material was derived from the questionnaire, which had a response rate of some 62 per cent from the 1,000 members invited to respond. The questionnaire is reproduced as an appendix, and the interested reader will learn from it the categories of response that were provided. Many of our respondents felt free to add comments on the questions and were not constrained by the categorical choices that were provided. We have been able to make use of many of these comments. Our questionnaire survey was augmented by some thirty interviews with members whom we invited to tell us how they first encountered Nichiren Buddhism, about their general life circumstances at that time, and of their experiences since joining the movement. The interviews were wide-ranging and loosely structured. Members were encouraged to tell us their stories in their own way. We interposed further questions only to fill in lacunae or to clarify the sequence of events. The interview material is copiously cited alongside the comments elicited by the questionnaires. Those whom we interviewed were mainly well-established members, though a few were relative newcomers. We obtained their names from national or local leaders, and, in the nature of the case, those who were willing to spend between one and a half and two hours being interviewed were all enthusiastic members. All those whom we invited to be interviewed readily accepted, and no one refused to answer any of our questions. Indeed, several members said afterwards how much they had enjoyed the experience, just as some of those who filled in a questionnaire said that they had found the experience exhilarating and thought-provoking.

The authors collaborated closely in producing the questionnaire, and in the mechanical tasks of preparing it for distribution.
Dobbelaere supervised the initial computer analysis, and he produced
the tables and a preliminary commentary on them. Wilson then
reworked the draft and suggested points for further elaboration. The
interview schedule was jointly produced and the interviews themselves were conducted separately and equally by us both. Wilson
selected the material to be cited from both interviews and questionnaires, and provided a first draft of the introductory chapter on the
history and the organization of the movement. Chapters were
subsequently revised in the light of further discussion between the
authors.

Grateful acknowledgement is due to various people who rendered
assistance in our work. The members of SGI gave us their fullest
co-operation, and in particular we should like to express our thanks
to Mr Richard Causton, the Director-General of the movement, to
Mr John Delnevo, leader of the Youth division, and to Mr Mike
Yeadon, Oxford Chapter leader, for their assistance in helping us to
arrange interviews and to attend meetings. Needless to say, we are
also grateful to the hundreds who filled in questionnaire forms and
the thirty members who allowed us to conduct interviews. To
Professor L. Halman of the Catholic University of Brabant, Tilburg,
The Netherlands, we are indebted for his calculations of the United
Kingdom sample adapted for age. Professor Jaak Billiet provided
statistical advice, and Miss Anne Van Meerbeeck is owed a special
debt of thanks for her work on the computer analysis.

-4. NOV. 1994   Z

UNIVERSITY OF PLYMOUTH
LIBRARY SERVICES

Item No.	900 2066476
Class No.	294.392808092 WIL
Contl. No.	0198279159

CONTENTS

FIGURES

TABLES

I

Introduction

THE Japanese lay Buddhist organization Sōka Gakkai (Value Creation Society) is today one of the world's most rapidly expanding religious movements. Members are to be found in virtually every country in Europe, the Americas, and Australasia, in most Asian countries, and in several parts of Africa. Yet, fifty years ago, Sōka Gakkai was a tiny organization of a few hundred people, all of them in Japan. The laymen and -women who constituted this society were devotees of the version of Buddhism which had been propounded by Nichiren in the thirteenth century, who in particular attached themselves to the priestly sect Nichiren Shōshū, which expounded one of the numerous variants of his teaching as handed down by his disciple Nikkō. Nichiren Shōshū had—and still has—other lay adherents whose allegiance antedated the formation of Sōka Gakkai, and who have remained separate from it. But with millions of followers in Japan, and hundreds of thousands overseas, Sōka Gakkai members (Sōka Gakkai International—SGI—as it has more recently styled itself) far exceed in number the other devotees of Nichiren Shōshū. Furthermore, when many Japanese migrated overseas, as permanent settlers (in the United States and in Latin America) or as expatriate business people, they carried with them their religion, and SGI acquired a following overseas. By dint of vigorous proselytizing, which their faith explicitly enjoined on members, foreigners were converted until, in various countries, the movement adapted more fully to local culture and became somewhat less explicitly Japanese. Today, the overseas branches cultivate their own national traditions whilst continuing, of course, to draw exclusively on Nichiren's teaching, as SGI interprets it, as their sole source of religious enlightenment.

Today, SGI is an increasingly well-publicized movement. Its sponsorship of the cause of international peace; its promotion of ecological concerns; its educational commitments and benefactions;

and its cultural promotions of music and dance, ensure that it enjoys conspicuous public recognition. Perhaps even more telling than anything else, however, has been the role assumed by its current president, Daisaku Ikeda, in effecting meetings with statesmen and politicians—from Mr Major and President Mitterrand to Zhou Enlai and Mr Gorbachev. For the wider public, all these activities establish a high profile for SGI, while for its own members they sustain the sense of the movement's relevance, influence, and potency in world affairs.

The public presence which SGI has attained stands in sharp contrast to what, for Westerners, might be perceived as the obscure and perhaps arcane temple rituals of the priests of the Nichiren sect. The central and essential requirements of Nichiren's Buddhism, however, the chanting of an invocation of the *Lotus Sutra*, and the worship of a sacred mandala, the *Gohonzon*, are fervently espoused by SGI members, and in this priests and laity are one: but in style, worldly involvement, and perhaps general philosophical orientation, the lay Buddhists of SGI are far removed from any sort of monkish image. They are thoroughly engaged in the workaday world, see their Buddhist practice as the best possible support for that engagement, and reject entirely the idea of world-renouncing asceticism. The outgoing style of members, and the movement's vigorous programme of activities, belies much of what is expected of 'Buddhists' by the man in the street. His stereotype might well be much closer to the projected ideal of priests of Nichiren Shōshū than to the lay people of SGI, who represent Buddhism adapted to, and practised in, the modern world.

Given this divergence from expectable Buddhist belief and practice as Westerners traditionally might conceive of it, the relation of Sōka Gakkai to Nichiren Shōshū must in itself be a subject of some interest and importance, both for the sociologist and for the student of comparative religion, but that is not the burden of the present study, which is less controversial, and which depends for the most part on interviews and on a questionnaire survey of a random sample of Sōka Gakkai's following in the United Kingdom. A growing religious movement of foreign provenance, appealing, as it does, to what might be considered a somewhat atypical public, is an intrinsically significant social phenomenon. A profile of the movement and an endeavour to trace the source of its attraction and its pattern of growth are the focus of our concern. Just how such a religion becomes established and how it flourishes in modern Britain opens the way for tentative analysis of how a contemporary movement is related to the conditions and circumstances of our times. First, however, it is necessary to set out the history of this form of Buddhism, the course of its development in Britain, and the claims made for the efficacy of its practice.

Nichiren and the Lotus Sutra

Nichiren Shōshū Buddhism—a variant of the Japanese Mahayana tradition which traces its origins to the monk Nichiren (1222–82)—was introduced into Britain in the early 1960s by members of Sōka Gakkai, a movement of lay adherents, since which time it has become a thriving British religious movement. The British devotees, although all recruited by Sōka Gakkai, the lay association attached to the original Japanese priestly sect, were, until recently, organized under the designation Nichiren Shōshū UK, taking the name of the priestly sect, rather than the name of the lay association. In 1991 the British adherents began proceedings to change the name of their movement to Sōka Gakkai International UK, thus making apparent its essential identification with the lay organization, which had arisen in post-war Japan to disseminate Nichiren's teachings as purveyed by Nichiren Shōshū, but which in 1991, had been expelled *en bloc* by the Nichiren Shōshū High Priest. An account of that dramatic schism and the difficulties arising between on the one hand, (most) priests, and, on the other, the (vast majority of) laymen is provided in Appendix A below. Our immediate purpose, however, is to trace briefly the Japanese origins of the movement, to provide an indication of its doctrines, as the background for understanding the appeal, consequences, and the social significance of this growing movement in Britain.

Mahayana Buddhism, which Japan received from China, is regarded by its votaries, including Nichiren, as the so-called 'greater vehicle' because it claims to be intrinsically more compassionate than the tradition of Buddhism found in Burma, Thailand, Cambodia, and Sri Lanka, which, because it is concerned primarily with salvation for monks, they label *Hinayana* (the lesser vehicle). Whereas Mahayana Buddhism generally extends the possibility of early salvation to all, Hinayana is perceived by the Mahayana school as embodying a complex set of precepts, the maintenance of which is required for salvation, and which are so exacting that only those who withdraw from the world as monks are likely to be capable of meeting them. According to the Mahayana tradition, these precepts had their purpose for a certain audience at a particular time, but were superseded by the Gautama Buddha (Shakyamuni) in his later teachings. This interpretation of the evolution of the Buddha's doctrines found vigorous expression in the work of T'ien-t'ai, the Chinese exegete of the various *sutras* attributed to Shakyamuni, who gave his name (Japanese: *Tendai*) to a dominant sect in Japanese Buddhism. In particular, T'ien-t'ai maintained that the last *sutra* attributed to Shakyamuni, the *Lotus Sutra*, contained a definitive statement of his teachings. Shakyamuni is held to have modified his teachings as the circumstances of his audiences changed: he could not reveal his ultimate teachings at an earlier time since they would have been incomprehensible to those who heard them. However, the Mahayanaists maintain that because he devoted his life to teaching people how to attain enlightenment, and postponed his own entry into nirvana in order to do so, Shakyamuni, even when teaching precepts espoused by the Hinayana school, was in fact behaving in the spirit of a more compassionate manifestation of Buddhism, that of the Mahayana tradition.

That many modern Buddhologists dispute the contention that the *Lotus Sutra* is in fact the work of Shakyamuni, attributing it to a much later period, does not alter the fact that it retains a powerful influence on those who regard it as the highest expression of the Buddha's mission when it is enlarged by the universalizing tendency of Mahayana conceptions of salvation. In the *Muryōgi Sutra*, a prelude to the *Lotus Sutra*, Shakyamuni is held to have promised that readers and reciters of the Law who strove to save others would thus 'attain the supreme enlightenment quickly' and would 'receive all the benefits of the six *pāramitās* without having to practice [sic] them'.[1] (The *pāramitās* were six ways of salvation—by alms; observance of the precepts; forbearance; assiduousness; meditation; and attaining wisdom—which were to be practised for ten aeons of time). Yet the law to which Shakyamuni alluded was not at that point

[1] *Buddhism and the Nichiren Shoshu Tradition* (Tokyo: Nichiren Shōshū International Centre, 1986), 33.

revealed. Its revelation, even in the *Lotus Sutra*, was only partial: its final exposition was to await the appearance of Nichiren.

Nichiren's teaching was that the whole point of the *Lotus Sutra* was to wean people from dependence on Buddha's mercy and to make them reliant on 'the unsurpassed wisdom latent within themselves'.[2] This doctrine challenged the central doctrine of the Jōdo (Pure Land) sect, an earlier and widely popular variant of Japanese Mahayana Buddhism, which emphasized dependence on the mercy of Amida Buddha for salvation (in a pure land, after death), thus denying the individual's own power and responsibility. Nichiren's followers assert that 'the land of true happiness described in Buddhism is not to be found anywhere apart from this world. It can only be created within the realitites of actual society, after people have firmly established an awareness of the True Law within their own lives.'[3]

The focus of Shakyamuni's purported last teaching was to enable all people to attain buddhahood; all were capable of becoming Buddhas, and this was to be achieved not by rational means but by faith. The *Lotus Sutra* 'is the only one which teaches that *all* people—be they good or evil, men or women, intellectuals or simple peasants—have the inherent potential for enlightenment and can become Buddhas in their present lifetimes'.[4] Thus, all earlier Buddhist teaching is seen as merely preparatory or provisional, and hence less than appropriate for the modern age, since this is the time designated as the predicted Latter Day of the Law, and the *sutra* is powerful enough to save even these people 'who are tainted with the three poisons of greed, anger, and stupidity'.[5]

According to the Nichiren tradition, what the *Juryō* (sixteenth) chapter of the *Lotus Sutra* reveals is that Shakyamuni attained buddhahood for the first time, not in India in Guatama's own lifetime, but in the remote past; but what the *sutra* does not reveal is the law by which he acquired that enlightenment. The revelation of that law was left for a later reincarnation, identified as that of Jōgyō, the supreme leader of the bodhisattvas of the earth. Since Nichiren claimed to make this revelation, he identified himself as Jōgyō by declaring the Law 'concealed in the depths of the *Juryō* chapter as the Mystic Law, or *Nam-myōhō-renge-kyō*'. The phrase is

[2] Ibid. 43.   [3] Ibid. 61.
[4] Richard Causton, *Nichiren Shoshu Buddhism; An Introduction* (London: Rider, 1988), 26.   [5] *Buddhism and the Nichiren Shoshu Tradition*, 51.

the invocation (*daimoku*) of the *sutra*. It had not been revealed earlier
because people 'would be able to perceive it themselves when they
practiced [*sic*] exactly as the *Lotus Sutra* taught. . . . [To] have
correctly practiced [*sic*] all of Shakyamuni's teachings requires a
certain extraordinary quality which few people are endowed with.
In the Latter Day of the Law, people with this quality will cease to
appear.'[6] Therefore, by revealing this law so that all people might
attain buddhahood, Nichiren revealed himself as the Buddha of the
Latter Day, a long-prophesied time of general social decay.

The phrase *Nam-myōhō-renge,kyō*, which invokes the *Lotus Sutra*,
is referred to as the Mystic Law, but the term True Law is also
applied to the true object of worship, the *Gohonzon*, a scroll (or
mandala) inscribed with many Chinese and two Sanskrit characters,
the names of Buddhas, and a summation of the law of enlightenment. The basic practice of Nichiren Shōshū Buddhism thus
consists of chanting the invocation *Nam-myōhō-renge-kyō* to the
Gohonzon. This practice is the law which is the particular means of
attaining enlightenment in the modern age. Nichiren was, then, the
Buddha who enabled 'all people in the Latter Day, when Shakyamuni's
Buddhism had become inappropriate, to attain enlightenment'.[7]
This Buddhism was held to be complete in both doctrine and
practice. 'Any person who believes in this object of worship and
chants Nam-myōhō-renge-kyō to it, can expiate all negative karma
and attain Buddhahood. The most essential point in Nichiren
Shōshū Buddhism, therefore, was the establishment of the object of
worship'—the *Gohonzon*.[8]

Nichiren held that, in inscribing the *Gohonzon*, he had also
inscribed his own life, leading to the teaching of 'the oneness of the
person and the law'.[9] The most important object of the Nichiren
movement is not a god, but rather an object which draws forth from
the worshipper qualities of his Buddha nature: it is held to present
what is already within the individual. Thus, it is often said that it is
like a mirror, reflecting the buddhahood within. To it is applied the
phrase *kanjin no honzon*, 'an object of worship for observing one's
mind (or life)'.[10] What is said of it is:

---

  [6] Ibid. 59–60.   [7] Ibid. 160.   [8] Ibid. 157.
  [9] The personalization of abstract qualities is by no means unusual in religion; one
need only recall that Christ proclaimed himself as the light and the way, to see distinct
parallels with the claims made by Nichiren.
  [10] Causton, *Nichiren Shoshu Buddhism*, 231.

Were it not for the 'mirror' of the Gohonzon, it would be impossible for us to change our karma and attain Buddhahood. This is because, although chanting Nam-myōhō-renge-kyō by itself creates good fortune in the form of conspicuous benefit, unless we can first see that there are fundamental karmic tendencies within ourselves which cause us to suffer, we will never summon up the desire to challenge and change them. For example, chanting Nam-myōhō-renge-kyō by itself may bring you a wonderful partner, but if you still have a very jealous nature, say, it is likely that your new relationship will quickly sour . . . In this ever-changing world, it is only by being able to refer constantly to the unchanging state of Buddhahood embodied in the Gohonzon that we can draw forth our own Buddhahood, again and again, to reflect on the deep underlying causes of our actions.[11]

This quotation already describes the role of the *Gohonzon* in the modern movement. From this exposition can be recognized the importance attached by believers to the opportunity to obtain an authenticated copy of this scroll before which to engage in chanting. Until the great schism of 1990–1, a smaller copy of the *Gohonzon*, inscribed by the High Priest of the Nichiren Shōshū sect, was made available to all who committed themselves to protect it and to practise chanting before it. Those who obtained such a copy enshrined it in a Buddhist altar (*butsudan*) in their own homes, which then became virtual sanctuaries. A copy of the *Gohonzon* is a powerful focus for chanting, even though it has never been regarded as indispensable, since chanting might be undertaken anywhere and at any time.

There is a third 'Great Secret Law' derived from the *Lotus Sutra* and promulgated by Nichiren Buddhism in addition to the invocation and the object of worship, and that is the sanctuary (*Kaidan*), the place in which the original *Gohonzon* is enshrined. The invocation was first chanted by Nichiren in 1253. The *Gohonzon* was inscribed in 1279. It was much later that a suitable sanctuary was constructed for this object, however, and that construction was claimed as its own special achievement by the lay organization, the Sōka Gakkai, which, in 1972, built a new structure, the *Shō-Hondō* at Taiseki-ji, Mount Fuji, the ancient seat of Nichiren Shōshū. The movement also identifies three treasures of the law, one of these being *Nam-myōhō-renge-kyō* of the Great Secret Law itself, and the others being the Buddha (Nichiren), and the priest (and in particular the second High Priest, Nikkō, who maintained what is held to

[11] Ibid. 232.

be Nichiren's true teaching in the face of the defection of his contemporaries).

Nichiren promoted his doctrine combatively in his own time, excoriating other Japanese variants of the Mahayana tradition. The persecutions that he faced were all seen as confirming the predictions of the *sutras*, and as legitimizing his status as the eternal Buddha. Japanese Buddhism generally had made the prospects of salvation more widely and more readily available than had previously been vouchsafed in the Buddhist tradition. The doctrines expounded by Shakyamuni were often abstruse and the requirements of the precepts heroically exacting. Nichiren was in the stream of Japanese popularizers of the faith, and he went further than his predecessors and contemporaries in proclaiming the immediate availability of salvation and its instant benefits. His advocacy of the *daimoku* of the *sutra*, the simple phrase, *Nam-myōhō-renge-kyō*, amounts to the claim that saving power is concentrated in this one formula and that this power amounts to a universal law. Chanting is believed to release the individual's buddhahood, a higher state of consciousness, which puts him into harmony with the laws governing the universe and the rhythms of life. Indeed, since this is held to be a practical exercise, actual study of the *sutra* is seen to be, at least initially, unnecessary for lay people. All that is needed is commitment to the chanting of the *daimoku*. As the English-language organ of the British movement has expressed it, 'In practising Nichiren Daishonin's teachings . . . the study of the Lotus Sutra is unnecessary for us to deepen our faith and help us to attain Buddhahood in this lifetime. Rather it should be studied only once we have been able to master Nichiren Daishonin's teachings and can thus view the Lotus Sutra from the correct historical perspective.'[12] The authority of Nichiren is invoked to sustain this position, since he himself wrote, 'Now, in the Latter Day of the Law, neither the Lotus Sutra nor other sutras lead to enlightenment. Only Nam-myōhō-renge-kyō can do so. And this is not merely my own opinion. Shakyamuni, Tahō, and all other buddhas of the ten directions have so determined. To mix other practices with Nam-myōhō-renge-kyō is a grave error.'[13]

---

[12] *UK Express*, 233 (Nov. 1990), 13.
[13] *The Major Writings of Nichiren Daishonin*, iii (Tokyo: Nichiren Shōshū International Centre, 1981), 266.

Soka Gakkai and the Diffusion of Nichiren Shōshū

The Nichiren Shōshū sect was one of some thirty-one variants of Nichiren's teachings which quickly proliferated among those who succeeded him, and was not even the largest among these. In the early years following the Meiji restoration in Japan (1868), the sect was threatened with compulsory amalgamation with other Nichiren movements, and although successful in resisting the more extensive version of the government's intentions, it was for some years forced into association with other sects that claimed succession from the second High Priest, Nikkō. It took the name Nichiren Shōshū in 1912.[14] The sect experienced further government pressure in 1940, when the government again sought to impose amalgamation on the various Nichiren groups. By this time, however, the movement had acquired a new lay following and, although at that time small, that following was destined to affect profoundly its history.

In the 1920s a Japanese teacher and educationalist, Tsunesaburō Makiguchi (1871–1944), who had already propounded some radical educational ideas, was converted to Nichiren Shōshū Buddhism. His biographer believes that by the time of his conversion his

basic concepts and ideas had been formulated. It is my conclusion . . . that not until several years after his conversion, during the mid-1930s, did Nichiren Shōshū doctrine come to be an important element in his thought . . . [and] had not significantly influenced Makiguchi's thought during the time he compiled and edited his major work *Sōka Kyōikugaku Taikei*, roughly from 1929 to 1933 . . . In fact, the basic concepts of [his] system, the philosophy of value and value creation, are present in embryonic form in *Jinsei Chirigaku* which he published in 1903.[15]

Makiguchi stressed three cardinal values: benefit, beauty, and goodness (the satisfaction, respectively, of material, spiritual, and altruistic desires). He substituted the concept of benefit for the Kantian ideal of truth, since he considered the 'true' to be merely factual reality, which in itself might not promote happiness, which was the supreme goal. These ideas were to become significant in the teachings drawn from Nichiren in the formation of the laymen's

---

[14] *UK Express*, 234 (Dec. 1990), 23.
[15] Dayle M. Bethel, *Makiguchi the Value Creator* (New York: Weatherhill, 1973), 42–3.

Buddhist educational association which Makiguchi founded as an adjunct to the Nichiren Shōshū sect.

Makiguchi's organization, Sōka Kyōiku Gakkai, was formally established in 1937, and was originally very much an educational reform society, concentrating on the need to make the creation of value a primary aim of education. It had, at its beginnings, only sixty members, but its number increased to between 300 and 400 at its meeting in 1940. In the following year the movement produced a magazine, *Kachi Sozo* (The Creation of Value), revealing a commitment, much wider than the purely pedagogic, to the ideals of Nichiren Shōshū, testimonies to the healing power of which now appeared in its pages, including those of mothers who claimed to have experienced painless childbirth.[16] Ordered, in 1943, by the wartime government to enshrine a Shinto talisman of the Sun Goddess Tensho Daijin, Makiguchi, seeing this as a derogation from his Buddhist faith, refused and was in consequence arrested.[17] Together with his disciple Jōsei Toda (1900–58), who was to be his successor in the organization he had founded, Makiguchi was imprisoned. He died in prison in 1944.

After the Second World War Toda took over the leadership of the reconstituted movement, now known as Sōka Gakkai (Value Creation Society), as an organization of lay followers of Nichiren Shōshū Buddhism. Although there was some friction between the priestly sect and this growing lay organization, these problems appear to have been resolved at the time of Toda's death in 1958. During his presidency, by vigorous methods of proselytization, Toda had built the organization from some 500 families in 1951 to his acclaimed goal of 750,000 families. Sōka Gakkai had become a highly visible force in Japanese affairs and had reinvigorated the Nichiren Shōshū movement. The growth of the movement was largely the result of the theory of conversion which Toda endorsed—*shakubuku* (often translated as 'break and subdue'). This policy was not an innovation introduced by Soka Gakkai: 'historically there are within Buddhist teachings two principal methods of propagating the faith . . . *shōju* and *shakubuku*.'[18] *Shakubuku* was an

---

[16] Ibid. 97.   [17] *Buddhism and the Nichiren Shoshu Tradition*, 217.

[18] Bethel, *Makiguchi*, 103, *Shōju* was a method of 'propogating Buddhism without refuting misconceptions, gradually leading others to supreme Buddhist teachings'. Nichiren, *The Major Writings*, in (1979), 335. One of the issues raised in the arguments affecting the schism between Nichiren Shōshū and Sōka Gakkai was the charge made by the priests that Sōka Gakkai had abandoned the practice of *shakubuku* in favour of the softer methods of *shōju*.

uncompromising method of recruitment which Nichiren said would be necessary in Buddhist countries in the Latter Day of the Law, 'where there are many persons of perverse views who slander the Law',[19] that is in Japan. Otherwise, *shōju*, a more moderate and conciliatory approach through dialogue and example, would be appropriate, in particular in non-Buddhist countries. There can be no doubt that Nichiren endorsed an uncompromising approach in order to win adherents to his cause. He was 'militant in his insistence that his interpretation of Buddhism and the Lotus Sutra was the only true belief'.[20] All other forms of Buddhism were false, corrupt, and evil. Toda appears to have endorsed this orientation. He frequently reminded his followers of the earthly benefits they would receive from conducting shakubuku. On August 3, 1951, he told an audience: 'You carry on shakubuku with conviction. If you don't do it now, let me tell you, you will never become happy.' On September 1, 1954, he gave the following explanation to members: 'Let me tell you why you must conduct shakubuku. This is not to make Sōka Gakkai larger, but for you to become happier . . . There are many people in the world who are suffering from poverty and disease. The only way to make them really happy is to shakubuku them. You might say it is sufficient for you to pray at home, but unless you carry out shakubuku you will not receive any divine benefit. A believer who has forgotten to shakubuku will receive no such benefit.'[21]

Under its third president, Daisaku Ikeda (b. 1928), Sōka Gakkai continued to grow until, by 1990, it claimed more than eight million families of adherents in Japan, and hundreds of thousands overseas, with an increasing presence world-wide. Ikeda also promoted the extension of a wide range of cultural activities by the movement, such as the creation of two art museums; the development of sponsorship for classical music and other live arts performances; the founding of schools and of a thriving university in Tokyo, with overseas campuses; and, not least, the establishment of an autonomous political party, Kōmeitō (Clean Government Party), which quickly became the third largest party in the Japanese parliament.[22] As easily the biggest of the many new religious movements in Japan, Sōka

---

[19] Nichiren, *Major Writings*, ii (1981), 208. [20] Bethel, *Makiguchi*, 103.
[21] Ibid. 105.
[22] In 1964 Ikeda declared that Kōmeitō was to be entirely separate from the religious organization: no Kōmeitō politician could be a leader in Sōka Gakkai. Sōka Gakkai members have, of course, supported Kōmeitō in elections since, wherever possible, its policies have been based on the principles of Nichiren Buddhism.

Gakkai became a powerful force on the national scene, evoking, it must be said, some considerable hostility in the country's media, particularly for its methods of *shakubuku*, a practice which Ikeda somewhat modified.

Nichiren Shōshū Buddhism was introduced to Western countries largely through the activities of Japanese adherents who emigrated temporarily or permanently after the Second World War. The Japanese brides of American servicemen were undoubtedly significant in the case of the United States, but in Britain and Europe these Japanese carriers of the faith were more typically employees of Japanese companies who had been seconded to Britain, or the Japanese wives of British businessmen who had worked in Japan. The migration of adherents from Japan was almost certainly of greater significance in the growth of Sōka Gakkai in the West than the interest stimulated in the early years of the century by converts and missionaries of various other types of Buddhism. Those various incursions were initially of Theravada Buddhism, and later of Tibetan, Tantric, and Zen traditions, the first being disseminated by the leaders of the Theosophical Society.[23] Theosophy and the Maha Bodi Society (in 1926 the first direct Buddhist missionary body established in Britain[24]) and the development of a British Buddhist organization by Christmas Humphreys are scarcely to be regarded as precursors of Nichiren Buddhism, so different were they in mood, teachings, and general orientation. But in the years after the Second World War, the Western devotees of the different schools of Buddhism displayed an increasing eclecticism, and their divisions tended to melt as Western Buddhism 'rejected the escape into Nirvana and concentrated more and more on enlightenment breaking through here and now'.[25] This accommodative response to Western culture, although not directly associated with the incursion of Nichiren Shōshū into Britain, in some measure indicated the prospects for it, and certainly a few of those who found their eventual satisfaction in Nichiren's Buddhism had experienced one or another of these other Buddhist variants.

[23] For an account, see Bruce F. Campbell, *The Ancient Wisdom Revived: A History of the Theosophical Movement* (Berkeley, Calif.: University of California Press, 1980).
[24] John Snelling, *The Buddhist Handbook* (London: Century, 1987), 233.
[25] Ernst Benz, 'Buddhism in the Western World', in H. Dumoulin and John C. Maraldo (eds.), *Buddhism in the Modern World* (New York: Collier, 1976), 316.

SGI in Britain: Organization and Activities

Sōka Gakkai is almost certainly the school of Buddhism with the largest body of support in Britain, and the one experiencing the fastest rate of growth. The American branch had led the way, inaugurated in 1960 by Daisaku Ikeda, soon after he became president. In the following year Ikeda visited nine European countries, and the movement began in Britain with just two members. Within a decade American membership was in tens of thousands, and by 1988 a quarter of a million American members were claimed.[26] By this time, in Europe, some 20,000 were attending meetings, of which 4,000 were in Britain. The number has increased since 1988. Whereas earlier studies in Japan indicate that members there have cited healing as a primary benefit achieved through their faith, occidental members are reported as regarding the acquisition of a sense of direction as the major blessing experienced by virtue of their practice.[27] In an American survey, members declared that Nichiren Shōshū attracted them because it taught that the individual could change his own destiny by ritual practice, in contrast to the teachings of Christianity, in which the individual's destiny was in the hands of God; because Buddhism was realistic and compatible with scientific thinking; because its logic was inductive rather than, as in the case of Christianity, deductive; and because it emphasized the here and now rather than the afterlife.[28] Hitherto, there has been no research to suggest the nature of the appeal of this oriental religion to its British adherents, and the present work is intended to illuminate some of these same issues.

[26] Daniel Metraux, *The History and Theology of Soka Gakkai* (Lewiston, NY: Edwin Mellen Press, 1988), 115, reports 'Inoue Nobutaka, a Japanese scholar who studied Nichiren Shoshu in America in the early and mid-1980s, concedes that while there may be over 200,000 believers in the United States, the actual hard-core membership must number half that. See Inoue Nobutaka *Umi o Watatta Shukyo*, (Tokyo, 1985), p. 156.' In 1992 Sōka Gakkai International claimed 1,260,000 members in 115 nations in addition to 8,030,000 *families* in Japan: *Nikkei Weekly*, 30/1,530 (15 Aug. 1992).

[27] James W. White, *The Sōka Gakkai and Mass Society* (Stanford, Calif.: Stanford University Press, 1970), 85–6; Metraux, *History and Theology*, 59, 61, 74, citing Inoue, *Umi o Watatta Shukyo*.

[28] Nobutaka Inoue, 'NSA and Non-Japanese Members in California', in Kei'ichi Yanagawa (ed.), *Japanese Religions in California: A Report of Research within and without the Japanese-American Community* (Tokyo: Dept. of Religious Studies, University of Tokyo, 1983), 123–4.

From its early days, the British Sōka Gakkai drew a disproportionate part of its following from London, and for a few years there
were very few adherents in the provinces, but slowly, mainly by
direct inter-personal contacts, the movement spread. Beginning in
Southampton, converts were made in Portsmouth, Bristol, Glasgow,
Edinburgh, Birmingham, Liverpool, Oxford, Brighton and Leeds,
in more or less that order, and so to other cities and smaller towns,
until the movement attained the distribution indicated in the
following chapters. Organizationally, local groups are linked in
somewhat larger districts, and several district groups are associated
in chapters. The chapters, which are perhaps the core unit, are
associated in a (regional) headquarters, and the various headquarters
are under the direction of the national centre, now located at Taplow
Court, Berkshire. Members participate at all the levels of the lower
echelons up to chapter level, the chapter usually consisting of
between fifty and 100 people. Thus, although the organization may
readily be represented as constituting a hierarchy, this relates to
numbers rather than to patterns of authority. Members associate
easily and freely at group, district, and chapter level, and although
there is a readily evinced respect for national leaders, a pattern of
relaxed and informal sociation prevails.

Members are also encouraged to draw together in response to
common interests and vocation, as well as in accordance with the
basic locality principle. There are a number of professional cultural
groups. Thus, there are distinct groups for lawyers, scientists,
teachers, business people, and chefs, and there is a health division
for members who are doctors, nurses, and hospital workers. Groups
of this kind meet perhaps quarterly or bi-monthly, and seek to
promote by lectures and seminars the application of Buddhist
principles within their various domains. It is claimed that 'both the
Education Group and the Health Group have made some impact in
their professions through such activities'.[29] There are also 'heritage
groups' which bring together members who share a common ethnic
or national background. These include, among others, groups for
Indians, South Asians, East Europeans, South Africans, and an
Abibimma group for Africans and Caribbeans. The purpose is to
help new members of distinctive ethnic background to become
integrated into the movement: the groups also maintain their own

[29] *Sōka Gakkai News*, 17, 278 (July 1992), 21.

cultural interests and activities to promote song and dance performances, as opportunity allows. An arts division sustains these last-
mentioned activities on a wider scale for the entire movement.

Sōka Gakkai UK also draws its members into diverse patterns of
service to promote the cause, and relies extensively on the voluntary
contribution of time and effort by members. Opportunity for service
is institutionalized in the Value Creation Group (VCG), whose
members are drawn from the Young Men's divisions, and 'Lilac',
the equivalent agency for Young Women. The VCG undertakes such
tasks as providing the security of centres, keeping the precincts tidy,
and, on bigger occasions, regulating traffic and the movement of
members attending meetings and events. The Lilac teams do similar
work adapted to more conventional women's roles—ushering, caring
for visitors, and ensuring that appropriate offerings are placed before
the *Gohonzon*. Taplow Court itself depends on visiting teams of
volunteers who stay for a week at a time (often members devote part
of their holidays) to act as receptionists, security guards, and to
undertake everything from cleaning and housekeeping to flower-
arrangement. This service, known by its Japanese name, *keibi*, gives
those who undertake it a strong sense of involvement in the
organization, and the chance to participate in collective worship at
the heart of the national movement, where, it is maintained, there
is a higher tempo of activity. To give an instance of the scale of
service for which members volunteer: on the visit of President Ikeda
in 1989, some 125 members of the Men's division performed
transport service, as usual using their own cars to fetch and carry
visitors, and this was, as always, undertaken without recompense
except for the reimbursement of petrol costs. In these various
ways—by subsuming professional and cultural interests under the
rubric of commitment to Buddhism, and by enlisting the goodwill,
skills, time, and energy of adherents, Sōka Gakkai maintains a high
level of personal identification from its members, whose extra-
religious interests and dispositions are assimilated to the movement's
goals, and infused with its values.

Although Sōka Gakkai members undertake the greater part of
their practice at home, meetings are also important, and the normal
programme which a conscientious member is expected to fulfil
involves attendance at and participation in a considerable number of
meetings every month. Group meetings, district meetings, and
chapter meetings are monthly events, but there are also separate

meetings for the different divisions, distinguished by sex and age (Men's division; Women's; Young Men's; Young Women's). There are planning meetings, and meetings to arrange or support special events. A committed member will, therefore, although there is no congregational structure, frequently meet fellow adherents drawn both from his immediate locality (in the group and district meetings) and from a much wider area (in the chapter meetings, and the less frequent headquarters meetings). Thus, although practice is largely private, the votaries of Nichiren Buddhism will generally come to acquire a wide acquaintance over a considerable geographical area. Discussion and study meetings, at group, district, and chapter level, or in the divisions, are the occasions when such inter-personal relationships are forged and sustained. These meetings open with the chanting of the *daimoku* and *gongyō*, the recitation of part of the second and all of the sixteenth chapters of the *Lotus Sutra*, which takes about half an hour. Thereafter they are relatively loosely structured occasions held, usually, at the home of the local leader in the room in which the *butsudan* is housed. Once the chanting has ended, the *Gohonzon* is covered, and the group, which may have chanted seated on chairs or in the squatting position—most members sitting on their heels, Japanese fashion—reassembles, and people sit on chairs or on the floor in a circle.

Those present are invited to introduce themselves by whoever has taken the leading role in organizing the chanting. First names are normal, and each person says a word or two about him- or herself, usually indicating how long they have been practising. All this must be generally known to most others present, but it is a minimal formal procedure. Thereafter, the meeting becomes less structured, although the discussion may have a theme, introduced briefly by the local leader. The theme is not a constraint on other comments and contributions, and members attribute different purposes to the occasions. Some see it as an opportunity to 'open up' and exchange experiences. The short discourses which are offered are an informal species of testimony to the power of the *Gohonzon*, to the value of the practice, and to the support of fellow Buddhists. In particular, they frequently relate the ways in which the individual has overcome states of fear, or, most especially, anger, and quite often they emphasize an acquired ability to transcend judgemental attitudes and to take a positive approach to others. There is virtue, it appears, in being able to be completely open about one's own emotions with people who—but for the shared Buddhist commitment—would have been total strangers, might have found little in common, and might, indeed, have been regarded as uncongenial company. There are some affinities with the attitudes latently present in the testimony meetings of Christian, especially Protestant, organizations. But there are also profound differences: for one, the company is likely to be much less homogeneous in dress and demeanour. Whilst there is satisfaction in the security of meeting with others of like mind, who are especially accepted because of their shared commitment, whatever sense of community prevails is not derived from a specific code of moral prescriptions and interdictions. The Buddhists, while 'confessing' that they have indulged selfish, angry, or ungenerous thoughts, do so in the light of highly abstract exhortations to compassion, positive thinking, and generalized goodwill. This contrasts sharply with the Christian testimony which particularizes about forbidden acts—drinking (perhaps smoking), dishonesty, sexual licence, and backbiting. The Sōka Gakkai members do not endorse such specific moral constraints. Their testimonials are typically concerned with subjective states as described in Nichiren's teachings and not with transgressions of well-specified codes of conduct.

The tone of the Sōka Gakkai meetings is altogether more conversational than exhortatory. Members sometimes express dislike of anyone who 'pontificates' about Buddhist teachings, particularly if they do so for the benefit of any guests who might be present. The occasions may be seen more as a sharing of experience and of opinions than as attempts to define positions or reach decisions. Divergences of view are left unresolved, perhaps even unexplored, but there is no attempt to produce artificial unanimity: indeed, the expression of challenging views, particularly by non-Buddhists, is welcomed by some. Far from being occasions when faith might be disturbed, they are seen as opportunites for self-examination as well as of communication of Buddhist beliefs.

Chapter meetings begin with the reading of an article chosen from the *UK Express*, the movement's monthly, which most members have purchased and brought to the meeting. The chosen article, which often deals with Nichiren's teachings, is read out in sections and commented on by the chapter leader. In this respect, the occasion has some resemblance to *Watchtower* meeting of Jehovah's Witnesses, except that the reading is not organized as a question and answer session. Instead, most of those present make notes whilst the chapter leader expatiates on the content of the article, drawing out its message for modern practice and modern living. After the exposition of the article, the assembly breaks up into small groups for discussion on a theme, not necessarily drawn from the foregoing reading.

Meetings are occasions for study, which is regarded as an important adjunct to faith and practice, but study 'has little in common with academic learning, for although various SGI organizations mount regular courses and monthly lectures on the *Gosho* [Nichiren's treatises and letters to his followers], at its simplest, study consists of reading a line or phrase of the *Gosho* each day in order gradually to assimilate its profound meaning'.[30] Certainly, leaders are well acquainted with parts of the *Gosho*, the *Lotus Sutra*, and even more so perhaps with the writings of Daisaku Ikeda, but 'mere expertise is no more a guarantee of personal happiness in Buddhism than it is in law, medicine, or any other field. As Daisaku Ikeda says, "No matter how much you know about Buddhist doctrines, if your practice is weak, your faith is crippled".'[31] Study is a way of gaining faith and developing conviction, learning to 'see with the eyes of the Buddha . . . usually by first using them to look at the problems which exist within our lives . . . we begin to see a way forward from our sufferings which before did not appear to exist'.[32] Thus is thought to begin a process from self-awareness to enhanced awareness of the wider society. Daisaku Ikeda has said that 'without a thorough knowledge of Nichiren Daishonin's teachings, one's practice can easily become self-centred and one may begin interpreting Buddhism in one's own way'.[33]

Members are encouraged to go on residential courses from time to time. These are held at central locations for a week in the summer, and are occasions for guidance not only in practical issues, but also in the philosophy which underwrites the practice. Courses are held for the different divisions, and members often devote a week of their holidays to attending these events. For those who wish there are examinations on Nichiren's teachings. Alternatively, or perhaps additionally, they may contract to attend courses at the European SGI Centre at Trets in the south of France. These courses are far from being holidays, and are often described as intensive as well as

---

[30] Causton, *Nichiren Shoshu Buddhism*, 265.   [31] Ibid. 265–6.
[32] Ibid. 267.   [33] Ibid.

uplifting. Until the schism of the winter of 1990–1, but more so as an earnest of devotion than as an occasion for study, the ambition of members was to go to Taiseki-ji to see the original *Gohonzon* and to chant before it, and this pilgrimage (sometimes undertaken repeatedly) was seen as the high point in one's spiritual progress.

There are few commemorative occasions or special ceremonial events sponsored within Sōka Gakkai, and, apart from Nichiren's birthday, such as there are do not give rise to specific rituals. But there are occasional promotions which embrace the entire member-ship. The annual general meetings incorporate songs and band performances as well as speeches, testimonies, and 'determinations': the festive atmosphere frequently evoked in the movement is complemented by the choice of location for these meetings—in recent years, the London Palladium. There are also cultural events, concerts, exhibitions, and festivities, particularly the successful May festivals, organized sometimes at national, sometimes at chapter level, when members are encouraged to display their talents in music, dance, drama, and the visual arts. Less regularly, there has been the organization of elaborate stage shows. Such was the production of *Alice*, a musical staged for two (separate) weeks at the Hammersmith Odeon in the mid-1980s. The show was written, produced, staged, and performed entirely by the members, and part of the proceeds was devoted to international charitable organiza-tions. A member comments on such activities: 'Following the principle of *Zui Hō Bini* which advocates that each country should carry out its activities within its own cultural framework, SGI-UK has . . . blossomed in a very individual way.'[34] There is nothing in events of this kind remotely to resemble the solemnity of church assemblies, and the occasions are more celebrations of a free spirit than deliberations on policy or exposition of doctrines, such as might typically occupy the gatherings of other religious bodies.

The movement has, as yet, no permanent premises other than its national centre at Taplow, Berkshire, and its previous premises at Richmond, Surrey: it has yet to plan the type of cultural centres which characterize the Sōka Gakkai organization in Japan. Thus, the linking of the individual member to the movement is through the cells which are organized in expanding areas of responsibility from local group to national leadership. Without congregational

[34] *Sōka Gakkai News*, 17, 278 (July 1992), 21.

activities, the great financial stand-by of Christian churches, the
collection, is not a feature of Soka Gakkai International UK. Since
most activities take place in the homes of members, there is no call
for money for the hire or upkeep of premises. How then is SGI-UK
financed? Certain donations were made on the occasion of *Gojukai*,
the ceremony at which—before the break between SGI and Nichiren
Shōshū—a priest of the sect marked the admission of the new
member by investing him with his own replica of the *Gohonzon*, but
it was emphasized that such moneys were for the head temple, and
to help meet the expenses of the visiting priest.[35] The British
movement also derives income from the guaranteed sale each month
of its own journal, *UK Express*, to which practically every member
subscribes. There are also sales from the shops maintained at
Taplow and Richmond, of articles required for the housing and
embellishment of the *Gohonzon*: (the price of a *butsudan* might run
to well over £1,000, although the average new member will select
one for about £50 including all necessary accessories). In the early
days, there were Japanese subsidies for the British movement, but
it is now claimed that SGI-UK 'takes on full responsibility for the
activities of Kōsen Rufu'.[36]

Over and above these means of financial support, members
understand that, if they wish to do so, they are eligible to make a
contribution to the *kōsen-rufu* fund on a given day every three
months. Although this is not compulsory and the amount is not
specified and the system of giving is essentially private, as in all
religious movements, there is a normative expectation that members
will start to give regularly as the spirit of their faith grows. In the
British Sōka Gakkai at present, between 30 and 40 per cent of
members are not contributing to the *kōsen-rufu* fund, and this has
been so for several years. Leaders assume that those not contributing
are either young or comparatively new in faith.

Buddhism explains that there are two type of offering—'contribution of the
Law' and the 'contribution of treasure'. The former includes offerings such
as the time, energy, and effort we give to our personal practice and to
activities to teach others about the greatness of Nichiren Daishonin's
Buddhism. The latter includes material contributions such as money spent
to buy offerings for our Gohonzon, petrol or fares to get to activities, buying
the UK Express for ourselves and others, and supporting the Kōsen Rufu

fund. . . . the benefit to us is that through making the effort to give we polish our Buddha nature and accumulate the good fortune in our lives to become truly happy.[37]

It is said to be the attitude to giving and not the sum involved which matters, and it is this which determines the benefit which, through the workings of the law of cause and effect, the giver receives in return, and such benefits may be either spiritual or material, or both. The promise of reward for giving is an interesting parallel to the inducements advanced in many Protestant bodies which encourage members to tithe with similar promise of subsequent and enhanced return.

The Practice and its Purposes

The religious practice of the lay adherents of Nichiren Shōshū Buddhism (which, in response to the change of designation being effected, will henceforth be referred to as Sōka Gakkai International) consists of the daily chanting of the *daimoku*, *Nam-myōhō-renge-kyō*, 'to your heart's content', and a morning and evening *gongyō*, the recitation of the two key chapters of the *Lotus Sutra*. These are part of the second chapter, *Hōben*, and the whole of the sixteenth, *Juryō*. In *Hōben*, the 'ten worlds' (or states of consciousness) and the ten 'factors of life' are explained. *Juryō* identifies those who will in future preach the *Lotus Sutra*, and contains, albeit in concealed form, the great secret law of *Nam-myōhō-renge-kyō*. 'These two chapters contain the essence of the entire twenty-eight chapters of the sutra . . . [and] since the Lotus Sutra was acknowledged by Shakyamuni

[37] Ibid. In 1988, it was reported that NSUK's 'net income last year was £233,000, of which half was donated', *The Times* (11 Aug. 1988). The same article reported that NSUK (as it then was) had bought its new headquarters at Taplow Court for £2.6 million and was to spend £2 million more to restore that Tudor mansion. Discussing Taplow and financial matters, Richard Causton wrote, 'The money to purchase Taplow Court came as a direct donation from the Kōsen-rufu fund of Sōka Gakkai International', which had shared with NSUK members in refurbishing the house and its adjacent buildings. Regarding members' contributions, he commented, 'no one in NSUK is asked to pay a subscription. Everyone is aware of the system which lets them contribute—whether they do or don't is entirely up to them. The reason for this is that, in terms of cause and effect, if someone gives grudgingly, it will only bring them a bad effect . . . The subject of contribution is, of course, a delicate subject, but the fact is that under half of NSUK actually contribute to the Kōsen-rufu Fund.' *UK Express*, 252 (June 1992), 9.

Buddha to be his supreme teaching, containing in itself all his
previous teachings, by reciting the hōben and juryō chapters, we are
embracing all the 80,000 or so teachings of Buddhism.'[38] These
chapters are chanted in archaic language, classical Chinese, pronounced according to Japanese phonetics, but comprehension is not
required: 'whilst to understand and remember the meaning of
certain passages from the sutra can be inspirational, it is not essential
in order to gain the full benefit from the practice.'[39] *Gongyō* takes
about thirty minutes. During this ritual, members hold between
their hands a small string of beads like a rosary, sometimes rubbing
them lightly together to enhance their concentration. Normally,
gongyō is performed by members in their own homes, alone or with
other members in the household. That reciting *gongyō* takes an effort
is sometimes acknowledged: 'the innate power of gongyo to elevate
our life condition is amply proved by the negative reaction which
occurs whenever we contemplate doing it! This may take many
different forms such as deciding to go to sleep again or insisting on
having another cup of coffee which we do not really want. This
reaction is indeed the signal of the beginning of the battle for that
day . . . this relatively minor resistance is nothing other than the
devilish force of life girding itself for the real fight to come.'[40] The
purpose of *gongyō* is said to be 'to seize the day' which is then
motivated by emerging buddhahood by 'challenging our negativity—
the negativity we see in ourselves as well as in others'.[41] In addition
to this private practice of *gongyō*, the recitation is also performed
collectively when members hold their meetings.

Chanting the *daimoku*, however, is the vital practice which effects
release for the individual of his Buddha potential. Whilst the *sutra*
chapters purport to explain, or at least to indicate, the significance
of *Nam-myōhō-renge-kyō*, it is chanting the invocation which is held
to affect both the subjective state of consciousness of the believer
and the objective circumstances of the environment in which he
lives. In the basic English-language exposition of the faith, members
are told, 'Whether or not you understand precisely what Nam-
myōhō-renge-kyō means, or how the Three Truths explain the
"mutually inclusive relationship of life and of all phenomena" . . .

---

[38] Dick Causton, 'Daily Practice: Gongyo', in Jim Cowan (ed.), *The Buddhism of
the Sun* (Richmond: Nichiren Shoshu of the United Kingdom, 1982), 76.
[39] Ibid. 78.   [40] Ibid. 77–8.
[41] *UK Express*, 237 (Mar. 1991), 29.

or any other terms or theories explained in this book, you can still
gain great benefit from chanting this single phrase, just as you can
from turning on a light or punching a button on a . . . computer
without understanding the theory supporting them.'[42]

Exemplifying Nichiren's doctrine of the law of cause and effect,
regular chanting is held to create benefits of a material, spiritual, or
altruistic kind, as categorized by Makiguchi (even though he is not
very frequently cited in the movement's literature). Benefits are
divided into two types: conspicuous and inconspicuous. 'The inner
change that one experiences through practice is called *inconspicuous
benefit.*' It may not be evident and it occurs gradually. '*Conspicuous
benefits* [appear] in our environment as tangible improvements:
better relationships, sounder finances . . . the lack of conspicuous
benefit in our lives would be a pointer for something that we need
to change in ourselves.'[43] These benefits are, however, to be seen in
perspective: 'it is only as we develop inconspicuous benefit in our
lives . . . spiritual strengths like wisdom, hope, courage, perseverance, and humour, that we can truly appreciate the values of the
conspicuous benefits that come our way.'[44] Thus it is the inconspicuous benefits which are, in the long run at least, to be regarded
as the more important, and when apparently miraculous material
benefits occur, they 'are not miracles, merely your environment
reacting *directly* to your chanting'.[45] The conspicuous benefits are,
however, not without spiritual importance, since they are proofs of
faith, particularly for neophytes, and this is why members chant for
particular things: 'we are encouraged to set specific goals when we
practice . . . and although they can often be quite self-centred when
we start to chant, they mark an important initial step in proving
to ourselves that the practice works. Once we have gained this
proof, so our practice tends increasingly to turn outwards, towards
practising for the happiness of other people or overcoming our
weaknesses or failings.'[46]

It is postulated that this form of Buddhism provides people with
a chance to control their lives and their environments, and the claim
is made that 'the effect of a great many people practising will be seen
throughout the society: in a lower crime rate, for example, or lower
incidence of drug and alcohol abuse, a lower divorce rate, a stronger
economy and higher standards of living, generally better health, a

---

[42] Causton, *Nichiren Shoshu Buddhism*, 128.   [43] Ibid. 123–4.   [44] Ibid.
[45] Ibid. 125.   [46] Ibid. 248.

greater life expectancy, and so on'.[47] Such claims are not uncommon in Eastern religions, and they might be matched by the assertions of the exponents of Transcendental Meditation, frequently made in the newspaper advertisements which they publish. But Nichiren Buddhists see their social optimism as something unique to themselves. As the British leader has written, '. . . of all the world's major religions, only Nichiren Daishonin's Buddhism foresees the human race developing to a point where it can learn to overcome the many problems which it has created and now confront it, rather than perishing in the flames of some mythical Armageddon'.[48]

In this Buddhist conception of salvation, chanting is important not only for producing material benefits and more spiritual attitudes of mind, but also because it is credited with changing the individual's destiny. The doctrine of karma teaches that individuals in their present life are subject to the effects of causes that they have made in the past. Misfortune, temperament, character dispositions—are all laid to the charge of the causes created in past years or even in earlier incarnations. By chanting *Nam-myōhō-renge-kyō* 'the shackles of one's karma are progressively weakened until they are finally severed completely'.[49] The particular theory alluded to as *esho funi*, the oneness of life and its environment, indicates that not only are our temperaments and fortunes determined by karma, but 'the physical circumstances of our lives, our relationships—even our parents—are determined by past causes we ourselves have made'.[50] Although some aspects of karma are mutable, in the sense that they might be moderated by willpower, only *Nam-myōhō-renge-kyō* provides the possibility of total emancipation from negative karma. Members are told, ' . . . chanting *Nam-myōhō-renge-kyō*, and taking action based on that chanting, is the greatest good cause we can make to change even the worst karma into good fortune'.[51] The *Lotus Sutra* overturns the ideas canvassed in all previous Buddhist teaching, namely that the effect of good causes made in this lifetime will become apparent only in lives hereafter. Every occasion of chanting is held to be an activity creating good fortune which can be drawn upon in the future, and while conspicuous benefits are proof along the way which sustain commitment, it is steady chanting which leads to inconspicuous benefit that 'will lead to every area of your life being filled with the qualities of your true self, which is

---

[47] Ibid. 260.   [48] Ibid. 261.   [49] Ibid. 182.
[50] Ibid.   [51] Ibid. 191.

Buddhahood—wisdom, courage, compassion, purity, and the joy of inexhaustible life force'.[52] This consequence is called 'human revolution', a term which appears to derive not from Nichiren but from Soka Gakkai teaching itself.

As we have already seen, chanting is believed to have its own internal potency, but it is in relation to the object of worship, the *Gohonzon*, that its operation is seen as most effective. It is this which leads the individual to acquire the capacity to observe his life in perspective and to glimpse his Buddha nature at work: 'for example, you begin to find yourself being compassionate in circumstances where you would not have been before . . . you find you have more energy, more life force.'[53] Nichiren instructed his followers not to seek out teachings that suggested that the Buddha was anywhere but within the self, and it was the *Gohonzon* which revealed that. The *Gohonzon* was not a god, nor some form of magic, but was rather 'like a mirror, which seems tarnished and dirty at first, but as you polish it, you see it is reflecting the life of the Buddha which also exists in you'.[54] The *Gohonzon* is to be treasured and protected, and this applies not only to the original mandala enshrined at Taiseki-ji, but also to the authenticated copies which believers themselves have received in the ceremony of *Gojukai* on first affirming their sustained commitment to the faith. Members are advised: 'Treasure and protect the Gohonzon . . . there are two impulses in our lives, the negative and the positive, and we have to maintain control over the negative side by doing *gongyō* twice daily and chanting daimoku. How you treat the Gohonzon is how you treat yourself and how you treat yourself is how you will treat others.' The *Gohonzon* is, then, to be honoured, and then 'quite naturally, the great cluster of blessings will come to you, but if you dishonour or damage it, you are doing the worst thing possible for your life and you are bound to suffer greatly'.[55]

The importance of the *Gohonzon* to believers was for a number of years signalled for new members of the movement in Britain by the ceremony known as *Gojukai*, when a priest of the Nichiren Shōshū sect came from Japan to invest new members with their own individual small-scale copy of the original scroll. Copy though it may have been, the same devotion and protection were demanded for such a replica as was elicited for the original. A member would

[52] Ibid. 194.   [53] *NSUK Bulletin*, 60 (Nov. 1990), no pagination.
[54] Ibid.   [55] Ibid.

enshrine the *Gohonzon* at home in a *butsudan*, an altar including a cabinet, so that the *Gohonzon* would be on view only on occasions when chanting was undertaken. The altar itself would be decorated with evergreen. Considerable importance was attached to the *Gojukai* ceremony, although this might perhaps have been the only occasion when British members would encounter a Nichiren Shōshū priest, except when on pilgrimage (*tozan*) to Taiseki-ji itself. The movement in the United Kingdom had little other concern with the priesthood.

The last of the biennial *Gojukai* ceremonies held in Britain was in November 1990, only weeks before the onset of the schism between Nichiren Shōshū and the Sōka Gakkai. On that occasion, the visiting priest, the Revd Kido Fukuda, told members henceforth to devote themselves to the three treasures: the Buddha, which was Nichiren; the *Gohonzon* of *Nam-myōhō-renge-kyō* of the three Great Secret Laws; and 'the Priesthood, which is the second High Priest, Nikkō Shonin, who alone inherited the Three Great Secret Laws directly from Nichiren Daishonin, the third High Priest, and all successive High Priests who, until the present, have constantly maintained and protected the lineage of Nichiren Daishonin's teachings'.[56] In the ceremony, those receiving a copy of the *Gohonzon* were asked to agree to abandon all other invocations and to embrace *Nam-myōhō-renge-kyō*, and to renounce all other objects of worship.[57] The believer was expected to make 'a special financial contribution, part of which is donated to the head Temple, Taiseki-ji, and part of which helps towards the travelling expenses of the priest . . . one does not purchase the *Gohonzon*, which is actually loaned to us by the High Priest for as long as we are prepared to safeguard [it] and practise to it'.[58] In 1990, the sum required from each member attending *Gojukai* and receiving the *Gohonzon* was £12.

Since the break in relations between Nichiren Shōshū and Sōka Gakkai, no further *Gojukai* ceremonies have been provided for lay believers who remain faithful to Sōka Gakkai International, and no further copies of the *Gohonzon* have been made available to new members, who must now seek to chant to mandalas belonging to those who received them before the recent disruption. The implications of this curtailment of the supply of copies of the object of worship are not yet clear, but the importance attached to the *Gohonzon* as the focus for chanting remains undiminished.

---

[56] Ibid. 1.   [57] *UK Express*, 232 (Oct. 1990), 12.
[58] *UK Express*, 296 (Aug. 1988), 10.

Of the three practices that are enjoined on adherents—chanting and *gongyō*; study; and teaching others—the first takes clear priority for the British members. The movement's organ has addressed the question very frankly, in asking why, if 'Nichiren Daishonin says that the Lotus Sutra is the most important of all sutras . . . don't we study it'?[59] The answer, that the *sutra* must be first seen in proper perspective, we have already encountered. But to this the substantive explanation is added that although the *sutra* revealed Shakyamuni's personal experience of enlightenment, it failed openly to reveal how he had attained it. Further, Shakyamuni had also indicated that in the Latter Day of the Law, the age of *mappō*, the *Lotus Sutra*, like all of his provisional teachings, would lose the power to help people overcome their sufferings. At that time, a great teacher, proclaiming the essence of the Mystic Law, would appear. That teacher revealed himself in the person of Nichiren, the eternal Buddha. In contrast to Shakyamuni's failure to indicate how, in the Latter Day of the Law, enlightenment might be attained, Nichiren offered himself as a practical guide, since, of the three sorts of proof of the validity of a religion—documentary, theoretical, and actual—it is the last of these to which primary importance should be attached. The documentary proof of Nichiren's Buddhism was in the *Lotus Sutra*; the theoretical proof was in Nichiren's own writings, the *Gosho*, but: 'in the final analysis . . . the most importance of these three proofs is actual proof, the actual results that arise when a teaching is put into practice.'[60]

It would be wrong to suppose from this that Sōka Gakkai members eschew study. Courses are organized and examinations are conducted in the understanding of doctrine, and the members of longer standing are certainly capable of reinforcing their advocacy or defence of their faith by copious reference to Nichiren's writings, the *Gosho*, and by reference to the *Lotus Sutra*. Study is not disregarded, but the place accorded to it is subsidiary to the emphasis given to the faith as a thoroughly practical commitment which is entirely congruous, so members maintain, with the everyday affairs of contemporary life.

What then of teaching others? Certainly, this practice is seen as one of the requirements of the faith, and as a way of improving one's own happiness. We have seen the strong calls to proselytize as

[59] *UK Express*, 233 (Nov. 1990), 12.
[60] Nichiren, *Major Writings*, vi. 111; cited *UK Express*, 233 (Nov. 1990), 12.

required by the principle of *shakubuku* enunciated by Jōsei Toda, and although the tone has been somewhat moderated since his time, the expectation is still there. Thus in *Fukyō*, the twentieth chapter of the *Lotus Sutra*, it is averred that the Buddha nature in everyone merits respect: 'Bodhisattva Fukyō's example teaches us that it is the true way of Buddhists to respect other people, regardless of differences of any sort. However, it is one thing to respect other people, and quite another to tolerate erroneous religious beliefs and doctrines without challenge. It is precisely because we respect other people that we must refute the false beliefs and doctrines which draw them further from the truth and plunge them into a state of unhappiness.'[61]

Shakubuku, as the need to teach others, is couched in much less strident terms in the writings of the British Sōka Gakkai than was the case with the movement's early years in Japan. In the 300-page authoritative exposition of Nichiren Shōshū Buddhism by Richard Causton, General Director of the British movement, there is only one reference to *shakubuku*, and that is to gloss the term with a rather more reserved formulation. He wrote: 'showing proof of the benefits of practising this Buddhism, particularly in the form of our own human revolution, in itself constitutes *shakubuku*, when it gradually convinces others of the power of Nam-myōhō-renge-kyō . . . Nichiren Shoshu Buddhism sees *kōsen rufu* [universal proclamation of Buddhism] as coming about by entirely natural, peaceful methods.'[62] Furthermore, 'Nichiren Shōshū Buddhists consequently feel no need to coerce others into practising this Buddhism or to be intolerant of those who practise other religions and philosophies'.[63]

---

[61] *Buddhism and the Nichiren Shoshu Tradition*, 65.

[62] Causton, *Nichiren Shoshu Buddhism*, 257. The same note of moderation was echoed in an article devoted to the subject in the movement's monthly periodical responding to the question of what was meant by *shakubuku*: 'Essentially it is teaching others to practise this Buddhism, but there are many aspects to this. When people know you are a Buddhist they tend to gauge the validity of the practice by seeing how you react to problems—the joyful attitude you have and the dignity with which you live your life. So you can say even a smile in the street could be a form of *shakubuku*. Theoretically speaking, what we follow in the UK is *shōju*, or a gradual introduction of others to Buddhism. *Shakubuku* literally means to refute someone's attachment to heretical teachings—which we don't do here because this country has no past history of heretical Buddhist teachings. The spirit of *shōju* is to teach by example. 'Carolyn Fujii, "Shakubuku", *UK Express*, 254 (Aug. 1991), 16.

[63] Causton, *Nichiren Shoshu Buddhism*, 258. The stance of NSUK towards other religions has been understood in almost diametrically opposed ways by different commentators. Robert S. Ellwood, Jr., *The Eagle and the Rising Sun: Americans and*

It is a general characteristic of religious systems to embrace a body of moral prescriptions; indeed, it might be argued that it is in canvassing a conception of morality that religion distinguishes itself from magic. In many religious traditions, the ultimate and often long-term rewards for religious commitment are depicted as dependent on moral attitudes and performances. In the case of Judaism and Christianity, these moral demands are set forth in codified form specifying required conduct and, in particular, indicating just what is interdicted. Nichiren Shōshū Buddhism is radically different in this respect. Whilst certain general dispositions and orientations are enjoined, they are expected to arise naturally in the believer as his Buddha nature is realized, and they are not cultivated in respose to particular moral exhortations, much less are they ordered by codes that specify the desirability or unacceptability of particular and explicit acts. Indeed, the teachings eschew the type of evaluation and judgement of behaviour which a distinctly moral orientation demands. The attitude comes out clearly in advice given to an enquirer who 'could not respect my district leader'. The official organ commented, 'Our tendency can be judgmental and slanderous . . . because of the law of cause and effect . . . we will [as a result] inevitably sink into unhappiness ourselves, feel discouraged, dissatisfied . . . perhaps desperate . . . The important thing to remember is that whatever the failures of the leader, they are his or her problem. Your problem is the slanderous and judgmental attitude that is causing *you* to suffer.' The doctrine of karma, with its intimations of fatalism, allows the writer to add, '. . . it is your

the New Religions of Japan (Philadelphia: Westminster Press, 1974), 103, wrote, 'The attitude toward Nichiren Shōshū's Judeo-Christian environment has also gone great lengths towards openness. In the early 1950s, Sōkagakkai in Japan published a *shakubuku* manual presenting extremely harsh arguments against Christianity and other religions, and saying that to join Nichiren Shōshū one must destroy all shrines and traces of other faiths in home and heart . . . But it is now said that Nichiren Shōshū is a "philosophy" and one can practice it and still be a good Protestant, Catholic, or Jew. It is said that in a non-Buddhist country such as America, Nichiren Shōshū comes only to embellish other faiths, not to replace them.' In complete contrast, Susumu Shimazono, 'The Expansion of Japan's New Religions into Foreign Cultures', *Japanese Journal of Religious Studies*, 18 2–3 (June–Sept. 1991), 105–32, maintains that Sōka Gakkai differs from other Japanese new religions (such as Seichō-no-Ie, Sekai-Kūseikyō, and PL Kyōdan) in its 'attitude towards the traditional religion dominant in an overseas country'. Whereas these other movements 'allow their members to belong to, for example, the Catholic Church . . . based on the idea that all religions are . . . rooted in the same reality and seek the same thing . . . Sōka Gakkai demands exclusive commitment. Its members must sever their relations with their traditional religion' (p. 123).

karma to be in a group with such a leader, who is simply the external cause of your suffering—your own critical nature. To overcome this, all you need to do is to support the leader, no matter what, and chant for his or her happiness . . . and if we can't do this, we should reflect on our own shortcomings which stop us, and chant to overcome them in ourselves.'[64] Slandering others—that is, thinking negatively about them—is seen as the cause of ill effects for oneself.It is seen not so much as reprehensible (that would be judgemental in itself) but as lacking in enlightened self-interest.

Since every person is potentially a Buddha, the ten worlds (or states of consciousness), the lower conditions of which are hell, hunger, animality, and anger, exist in everyone, and any one of these may be activated from one moment to the next. However,

once we begin to reveal our Buddhahood, we do not have to try to suppress or deny any of our lower states of life, as our Buddhahood quite naturally enables us to reveal the positive aspects of our other nine worlds from Hell to Boddhisattva, and so continually create value for ourselves and others. That is why in Nichiren Shōshū Buddhism there are no commandments, no rules to regulate human conduct. Instead, the emphasis is wholly upon learning more and more about our own Buddhahood, and about how to reveal it and make it dominant in our lives. How you actually live—for example, whether you smoke, drink, or eat meat—is thus entirely up to you.[65]

There is, then, an implicit permissiveness in Nichiren Shōshū Buddhism. Not only are there no objective criteria for judging conduct, but such judgements would themselves be contrary to the spirit of the faith. The specific articles of moral conduct, the 'dos' and 'don'ts', are rejected for what might be seen as a dispensation which is beyond that of the law, and is somewhat analogous to a doctrine of grace, not altogether dissimilar perhaps from what is canvassed for Christians in the third chapter of Galatians.[66] On the

---

[64] *UK Express*, 239 (May 1991), 17.

[65] Causton, *Nichiren Shoshu Buddhism*, 76.

[66] Compare these verses: 'Received ye the Spirit by the works of the law, or by the hearing of faith? . . . He . . . that ministereth to you the Spirit, and worketh miracles among you, doeth he it by the works of the law, or by the hearing of faith? . . . Know ye . . . that they which are of faith, the same are the children of Abraham. . . . as many as are of the works of the law are under the curse; for it is written, Cursed is everyone that continueth not in all things which are written in the book of the law to do them. But that no man is justified by the law in the sight of God, it is evident: for, The just shall live by faith. And the law is not of faith, but the man that

other hand, the emphasis on highly abstract virtues, of which compassion is perhaps paramount, admits, at other levels, a certain hedonism which is, of course, rather the contrary of the ascetic ethic of Christianity. The Sōka Gakkai member is under no constraint to change his life-style by his own exertions. If that life-style is in some way perceived to be unsatisfactory, then chanting is the appropriate exercise. By that means, lower states will be not so much suppressed or denied as transformed, even utilized in realizing something better.

Obviously, in practice, some patterns of behaviour are regarded as less than wholesome, less than satisfactory, if that can be said without becoming judgemental. Smoking and drinking may be in themselves all right, but clearly, from the testimony of members who have wrestled to overcome addiction to alcohol and drugs, there is some point, if not of actual moral censure, then at least of implied moral consensus regarding the undesirability of such conditions. The not infrequent claims, made in published testimonies by members, to have overcome addiction or to have 'got off the booze' make that clear. None the less, the emphasis on the individual and the need for him to take responsibility for his own life suggests that decisions and judgements about such matters are entirely his own affair. There is no community-supported social ethic with respect to concrete issues of this kind. The point emerged clearly from the response of two regional HQ leaders, when asked if they made home visits 'to check up' on people. They denied that that was the purpose. As one put it, 'I generally do home visits when a member has asked me for guidance, so I'm actually visiting them to talk about the practice and their lives. I'm not checking up on their practice, or anything else they might be doing either.' To which a

---

doeth them shall live in them. Christ hath redeemed us from the curse of the law, being made a curse for us . . . Wherefore then serveth the law? It was added because of transgressions, till the seed should come to whom the promise was made, and it was ordained by angels in the hand of a mediator. . . . Is the law then against the promises of God? God forbid; for if there had been a law given which could have given life, verily, righteousness should have been by the law. But the scripture hath concluded all under sin, that the promise by faith of Jesus Christ might be given to them that believe. But before faith came, we were kept under the law, shut up unto the faith which should afterwards be revealed. Wherefore the law was our schoolmaster to bring us unto Christ, that we might be justified by faith. But after the faith is come, we are no longer under a schoolmaster. For ye are all the children of God by faith in Christ Jesus. For as many of you as have been baptized into Christ have put on Christ.' Gal. 3:2, 3, 5, 7, 10–13, 19, 21–7.

second HQ leader added, 'If we visit someone simply because we think they are doing something wrong then we will get the wrong end of the stick and probably make the situation worse.' From the context, it was clear that 'wrong' related essentially to the practice, and in particular to making 'mistakes during *gongyō*' and not to moral matters.[67]

It follows from the foregoing that there is no place for guilt. As Richard Causton has put it, 'One of the truly great things about this practice, is that we do not have to feel guilty about our weaknesses or other aspects of our lives that we feel to be ugly . . . we still have those impulses which Buddhism maintains are a fundamental cause of suffering but, rather than working negatively, they become positive . . . the Buddhism of Nichiren Daishonin is not concerned with the suppression of negative impulses and tendencies . . . but with their total transformation.'[68] The basic psychology of this position is very much the contrary of traditional Christianity. There is no concept of sin, no demand for the repression of particular forms of behaviour, but there is a profound belief in the existence of the inescapable law of cause and effect. It is this understanding that provides the impetus for self-control, which members believe can be achieved through the power of practice. No reliance is therefore placed on guilt as a mechanism to maintain personal control of the self. By implication, if guilt fulfilled specific functions of social control for Western societies and their cultures these are unlikely to be sustained in anything like the same way by this Buddhist faith.

Yet, the recurrently expressed commitment to abstract virtues such as compassion, wisdom, courage, and the like is by no means merely rhetorical. We have seen already the value attached to the claim that Nichiren Shōshū Buddhism is a highly practical religion, proved by empirical evidences that chanting works. These virtues are held to be operative in everyday life, and their increase is part of the progress towards the attainment of buddhahood that is manifested in daily experience. There is an

interdependent relationship between Buddhahood and ordinary life . . . expressed in three important phrases: *bon'nō soku bodai*, literally meaning 'the desires of ordinary life are at the same time enlightenment'; *shōji soku nehan* . . . 'the suffering of life and death are nirvana (or enlightenment)';

---

[67] *UK Express*, 255 (Sept. 1992), 9.
[68] Causton, *Nichiren Shoshu Buddhism*, 92–3.

and *sokushin jōbutsu*, literally meaning 'same body become Buddha' . . . *soku* reinforces the point that Buddhahood is not an ethereal or other-worldly state, but a quality . . . of everyday life. In short, we do not practise this Buddhism to become saints and superhumans, but to become great human beings capable of solving human problems.[69]

The highly individualistic note implicit in these orientations minimizes the possibilities of social control within a system in which they prevail. Every individual is responsible for himself and, based on his understanding of cause and effect, must manage his own karma, and chant to moderate its influences on his life, where they are seen as in some sense unsatisfactory. It might be expected that the consequences of this philosophy would be to create some difficulty in maintaining order and co-ordination within the movement: are goodwill and recourse to chanting for personal benefit enough to maintain internal cohesion and to sustain integrated action? The demand for non-interference with others, for avoiding judgemental attitudes, and for attributing shortcomings to karma might appear to militate in that direction. As the Vice-General Director of the British movement addressed these problems, what emerged was an overriding demand for tolerance. He wrote, 'As HQ chief . . . I'd often find that I'd agree on a course of action with my [subordinate] chapter chiefs, and then some of them would do it well, some not so well, some not at all. But it's no good for me simply to say, "You didn't do well". It's up to me to chant a lot of *daimoku* all the time and to accept that everything everyone does is their best. What they don't manage to do is a result of their karma. And it's my karma if I suffer from [their] not doing it.'[70]

We have already seen that Nichiren Buddhism is a permissive, optimistic, and positively oriented religion, yet all religion has to offer some sort of explanation for the untoward in life, and in particular for sickness and death. Nichiren Shoshu Buddhism responds to these phenomena in conformity with its general dispositions. Thus, complete health is held to depend on the harmonization of all aspects of life achieved through daily practice. Jōsei Toda had declared 'true health' to be possible only when life was based on the practice, while Ikeda has been perhaps more circumspect by acknowledging a role for scientific therapy, saying, 'I hope that as you strengthen your life through chanting, and then on that basis

---

[69] Ibid. 93–4.   [70] *UK Express*, 239 (May 1991), 20.

use the power of science to its fullest extent, you will dauntlessly overcome every obstacle of sickness that occurs.'[71] Yet it is also asserted that if an illness were karmic in origin, only by determined practice would the situation be changed. As with every other apparently negative phenomenon, however, the tables can be turned. Nichiren declared that 'illness may be the merciful workings of Buddha' to awaken a seeking mind, and the British commentator, whilst averring that 'there is no illness that cannot be overcome through faith and practice', adds the again more guarded words of Ikeda that 'we should not judge someone's faith as weak just because he becomes ill . . . Illness can happen to anyone as he eradicates his negative karma and changes his destiny for the better.'[72]

Given the doctrine of reincarnation, the Buddhist view of death is distinctive and undespairing. Death, it is claimed, occurs according to the karmic time-table: 'we need to recognize that someone dies only when the time is right for them',[73] and that is when they have created the maximum value possible for them in this lifetime. The right time is 'determined by their karma'.[74] Death can be viewed positively, since it is 'part of the eternal mission and will create value in the long run, both for those [left] behind in this life and in terms of the right time for the eternal mission [of those who die] to be resumed in their next life'.[75] None the less, members chant to postpone death, for themselves or for those close to them, because 'by practising strongly one can lengthen one's life span and feel a great sense of joy at the time of death'.[76] Perhaps more emphasis is put on the effect of death with regard less to the individual anticipating his own demise than to the effect on relatives: 'if the sudden death of a member . . . does not cause his or her immediate family to stop practising, in time all will actually gain benefit from that event. Once the initial and very natural shock and grief have passed, all will understand more deeply the eternity of life, will strengthen their faith, and so elevate their own life conditions all the more. In other words, they will turn poison into medicine.'[77] The effect of this teaching is to induce members to view the death of close kin with equanimity. Toda even referred to death as 'one of the relatively minor hardships whereby a person can expiate negative

[71] Quoted in *UK Express*, 228 (June 1990), 10.	[72] Ibid.	[73] Ibid.
[74] *UK Express*, 236 (Feb. 1991), 27.	[75] *UK Express*, 228 (June 1990), 11.
[76] *UK Express*, 236 (Feb. 1991), 27.	[77] Ibid.

karma'.[78] Thus, even with respect to this, perhaps the most traumatic among human experiences, the response of these Buddhists is to adopt a positive attitude and to buoy up the consistency of their commitment to an optimistic world-view.

Misfortunes, including illness and death, are thus accommodated and explained, as they must be in any religious philosophy, but the Nichiren Buddhist approach goes further. It does not, after the fashion of Christian Science, deny the existence of evil, but it argues persistently that what is apparently evil can, none the less, be turned to good account and has a role to play in the wider spiritual economy. This orientation is well exemplified with regard to the way in which loss of faith is handled. As the British organ has put it:

Nichiren Shōshū Buddhism teaches that nothing in life is inherently good or bad, and that everything can have both a negative and a positive function. So it is with doubts . . . Doubts can be very useful. They can protect you from rushing into situations that seem attractive but might prove extremely damaging . . . On the other hand doubts can also prevent you from recognizing your own good fortune . . . How can we judge? The simple answer is to chant about your doubts. In this way, you can see clearly whether they come from your Buddha wisdom or whether they are a function of your fear.[79]

Thus, the criterion for testing doubt is the practice: by chanting faithfully, what is expected is clarification of one's mental and emotional processes, and the acquisition of wisdom. It is not only doubts about everyday life decisions that are brought to this bar for testing. It applies no less to religious doubts as well: 'what about fundamental doubts about the practice itself? . . . it is important to realize that such doubts are actually a form of *sanshō shima*, the various obstacles that naturally arise to obstruct our journey to enlightenment.' A Christian might be tempted to see this as analogous to the 'wiles of the devil', and the solution for these hindrances is not very different from what, in its own terms, Christianity might propose. The writer answers his question, 'Doubts are an inescapable part of life, and thus part of the practice . . . doubts about the power of Buddhism . . . can only be answered through constant practice over the course of time. But millions of ordinary men and women have discovered that by sticking to the three practices of *gongyō* and chanting, study, and teaching others,

---

[78] Ibid.   [79] *UK Express*, 237 (Mar. 1991), 11.

quite naturally they gained actual proof of Nichiren Daishonin's teachings and great clarity about their own lives.'[80] However, whereas a Christian enjoined to overcome doubt by prayer would probably have as proof only the transformation of his own inner feelings, the Sōka Gakkai members return to their emphasis on the practicality of their religion, and expect tangible benefits as an evidence that faith is warranted and that doubt can therefore be dispelled.

The experience of doubt and difficulty will normally lead a member to seek reassurance, and such reassurance is systematically available in the guidance of leaders at every level for those less advanced in their understanding of the practice. It may be offered at local meetings, or a member may directly approach his group, district, or, for that matter, any leader privately about his personal problems. What is offered as personal guidance is far from being a reassertion of dogmas, much less a hortatory expression of moralistic injunctions. Leaders 'explain guidance in faith, based on the *Gosho* and . . . try to inspire members to put it into practice, but, in the final analysis, each individual is completely responsible for whether or not he or she does so'.[81] The leader explains the nature of karma which is causing suffering. His ultimate recommendation is always to encourage perseverance in chanting, urging the member to greater commitment and the willingness to open himself up before the mirror of the *Gohonzon* to effect a change of consciousness and a subjective reorientation towards attaining a more positive frame of mind and a greater readiness to accept responsibility for his life and life circumstances.

General guidance in faith, and study and discussion of Nichiren's writings and those of Daisaku Ikeda, form an important practical bond that links members who are at different levels of understanding, and so establishes a chain of experience in faith throughout the organization which is known as the master and disciple relationship (*shitei funi*). As the literal translation of this principle into English implies ('master–disciple, two yet not two') master and disciple are regarded as necessarily spiritually inseparable. Thus, despite the evident philosophical individualism and egalitarianism of Soka Gakkai, a principle of seniority in faith combines with the sense of fellowship, and does so in almost mystical terms. Through the

---

[80] Ibid. 12.   [81] Causton, *Nichiren Shoshu Buddhism*, 276.

principle of oneness of the person and the law (*ninpō ikka*), con-
ceptually, *Nam-myōhō-renge-kyō* or the *Gohonzon* is master; yet,
since Nichiren declared the *Gohonzon* to be the embodiment of his
life, Nichiren is master. Citing Nichiren's writings, Ikeda has said
that 'those who believe in and practise the Lotus Sutra are equal to
Shakyamuni Buddha' and adds that Nichiren's Buddhism is 'to
guide all people in the direction of equality, toward the state where
Buddhas and ordinary living beings are one and equal'.[82] They are
one and equal because, regardless of their level of responsibility,
they all chant *Nam-myōhō-renge-kyō* to the *Gohonzon* to activate their
Buddha nature. At another level, the principle of master–disciple
applies to Toda as Makiguchi's disciple, and to Ikeda as Toda's
disciple: his

absolute trust in his mentor, Jōsei Toda, the second president . . . becomes
the core of our daily activities for human revolution and world peace. With
President Ikeda's inspiration . . . we fulfil our roles in society through our
own efforts and our relationship with the Gohonzon day by day. His words,
his actions, do not represent authority, or power, or mere knowledge of life,
rather, his efforts . . . prove through relating his own experience, that each
individual has potential to be a truly great human being.[83]

This rationalization may not convince critics who regard the extensive
publicity given to Ikeda as a personality cult, but it appears to justify
this attention for (at least the majority of) SGI members.

[82] Ikeda quotes Nichiren, *Major Writings*, iii 49, and is himself quoted in Ricky
Baynes (Vice-General Director of SGI-UK), 'The Oneness of Master and Disciple',
UK Express, 251 (May 1992), 26.   [83] Baynes, 'Oneness', 27.

II

The Size and Shape of SGI-UK

To obtain even the crudest indicators of the size and composition of minority religious movements is by no means always easy. Sects tend to be, if not secretive, then at least wary about divulging information on such matters. Quite apart from such caution, they are often ill organized and do not always know the social parameters of their own organization. The Sōka Gakkai International UK (Nichiren Shōshū UK, as it then was) was a marked exception to these generalizations. Not only were the movement's leaders immediately open and co-operative in their response to the idea of a research project into the movement, but they also provided us with a computer listing of members. With their addresses, we were able to draw a random sample to whom we distributed a postal questionnaire. In addition to the response from our sample, the list also gave us full information of the size and shape of the population which constituted the movement. As in all such organizations, the precise boundaries of membership were not absolutely clear. New people were joining, some who counted as full members were less closely attached than others, and there were, inevitably, some who were in various stages of relinquishing their commitment in anticipation of leaving.

We took as the criterion of fully fledged membership whether the individual had received *Gojukai*—the ceremony in which a member receives (perhaps now, given the rift between the Nichiren Shōshū priesthood and Sōka Gakkai, the past tense might be more appropriate) his or her copy of the *Gohonzon*. Whilst that test was generally appropriate, there were some older members who had come into the movement as dedicated practitioners before the custom of *Gojukai* was instituted in Britain: these persons we readily counted as full members. At the time of our enquiry, the *Gojukai* ceremony was due to be held for new members, but these were not yet included on the listing that was available, and hence were not part of the population from which our sample was drawn. Nor were we faced with the need to consider any sort of alternative criterion for membership, since the schism which brought the priestly performance of *Gojukai* to an end had not yet occurred. The movement, at that time, claimed a membership of about 5,000. We procured a listing with 3,673 names and addresses, since the information about the most recent recipients of the *Gohonzon*, some 849 people, was not yet available.

The sex distribution of the population on the list, as far as sex could be determined (usually from first names, since honorifics were not provided), and that of the *tranche* of new members who received the *Gohonzon* in November 1990, showed some 60 per cent women, 40 per cent men (Table 1). From the address list alone, further information about the movement could be gleaned. In particular, on the basis of surnames, we could hazard a rough guess about the extent to which the membership included people of foreign origin or people married to foreigners—an estimate which could later be checked from the returned questionnaires from our sample. From a first glance, it was evident that there were many foreign names on the list, and that Sōka Gakkai UK had a genuinely international flavour. A further indication of this was to become evident from the results of the questionnaire survey.

The membership lists also provided an immediate picture of the geographical distribution of Nichiren Buddhists throughout the country, since addresses were provided for practically everyone listed. The clear predominance of London and the areas within easy commuting distance of it is at once apparent from the tables, even though a somewhat conservative estimate was made concerning what should be included in that amorphous area 'the Home Counties'. In the event, only the counties of Middlesex, Surrey, Kent, and Essex together with Berkshire and Hertfordshire were included. 'The

TABLE 1. *The sex distribution of members*

Listing at 1 Nov. 1990			Excluding unidentified	November newcomers		Totals end 1990	
Males	1,399	(38.1)	(40.3)	334	(40.1)	1,733	(38.3)
Females	2,070	(56.3)	(59.7)	515	(59.7)	2,585	(57.2)
Unidentified	204	(5.6)				204	(4.5)
		(100.0)	(100.0)		(100.0)		(100.0)

Note: Percentages given in brackets.

TABLE 2. *The geographic distribution of the membership*

	Nov. 1990 listings[a]	Excluding unknown (%)	November entrants	Totals No.	All (%)	Excluding unknown (%)
London	1,778 (48.4)	49.3	310	2,088	46.2	48.4
Home Counties	588 (16.0)	16.3	117	705	15.6	16.3
South	218 (6.0)	6.0	44	262	5.8	6.1
West	247 (6.7)	6.8	79	326	7.2	7.6
Midlands	376 (10.3)	10.4	56	432	9.5	10.0
North	198 (5.4)	5.5	68	266	5.9	6.2
Scotland	103 (2.8)	2.9	20	123	2.7	2.8
Wales	93 (2.5)	2.6	11	104	2.3	2.4
N. Ireland	4 (0.1)	0.1	2	6	0.1	0.1
Isle of Man	3 (0.1)	0.1	—	3	0.1	0.1
Channel Is.	1 (—)	—	—	1	—	—
UNKNOWN	64 (1.7)	—	142	206	4.6	—

[a] Percentages given in brackets.

South' comprised the counties of Sussex, Hampshire, and Dorset; the West included Gloucestershire, Wiltshire, Somerset, Devon, and Cornwall; while the North covered Yorkshire, Lancashire, Durham, Westmorland, Cumberland, and Northumberland. The rest of England was designated as the Midlands. In Table 2, the additions to membership following the November 1990 *Gojukai* ceremony are again given separately from the address-listed members who provided the basis from which our sample of interview respondents were drawn.

The geographical areas are, of course, not comparable in terms of overall population, but even from this rough breakdown the concentration of members is clear. Since, as will become apparent below, recruitment has been largely effected by word of mouth contact among friends and acquaintances, the tendency for the movement to spread within given locations is explicable. Once numbers begin to grow in a given city, the likelihood for any vigorous proselytizing movement is that, through inter-personal networks, further growth will occur there. Apart from London and its satellite territories, the principal concentrations of membership were in Bristol, with 100 members, plus another thirty-two who received the *Gohonzon* in November 1990, after our research had started; in Brighton, with forty-two plus nine; Leeds, thirty-eight plus ten; Oxford, with forty-seven; Southampton, thirty-four plus seven; Glasgow, thirty-five plus four; Portsmouth, twenty-five plus eight; and Bournemouth, with twenty-seven plus three. Taking national regions within the United Kingdom (including members admitted in November 1990) England accounted for 94.6 per cent of the total; Scotland for 2.8 per cent; and Wales for 2.4 per cent (excluding those of unknown address).

Our questionnaire sample was drawn from the 3,609 members for whom we had addresses. We drew a sample of 1,000 members from the address list by computerized random numbers, but from this selection we eliminated all those whom we could identify as Japanese, and substituted a further random selection. This procedure was dictated by the fact that our purpose was to obtain a picture of the United Kingdom residents who had become Nichiren Buddhists, excluding the Japanese, most if not all of whom had certainly become members of Sōka Gakkai in Japan. We were able to distinguish (almost all) Japanese members by their first names. In consequence of the elimination of this group, the actual sample was taken from 3,609 persons less the 302 (8.1 per cent of the pre-November 1990 membership) whom we identified as Japanese. Thus the number from which the sample was drawn was about 3,300 people: this was our research population.

Our total sample gave us 479 addresses in London (47.9 per cent) and 521 in the provinces (52.1 per cent). All of these members were spent a postal questionnaire together with a covering letter from the headquarters of what was then designated Nichiren Shōshū UK, explaining our purpose to the recipients and inviting their co-operation. As usual in this sort of exercise, a small number of letters failed to reach the addressees and were returned by the Post Office. Within a certain time limit, these were replaced by substitutes. In effect, 988 questionnaires reached our sample, but eight of these recipients returned blank forms. Of the 980 questionnaires distributed, 626 usable returns were made, amounting to 63.4 per cent of our sample. Of these, seven respondents declared that they no longer regarded themselves as members, reducing the number of useful returns to 619 or 62.7 per cent of those whom we had sought to contact. It is quite possible that those who did not return questionnaires might have included some who had withdrawn from the movement, but there was no way of discovering this. Overall, for

TABLE 3. *The sample compared to the listed membership* (%)

	Sex		Domicile		Origin	
	Male	Female	London	Elsewhere	Westerners	Others
Population (unidentified excluded)	40.3	59.7	49.3	50.7	87.4	12.6
Effective sample	40.5	59.5	42.4[a]	57.6[a]	90.1	9.9[b]

[a] These are the percentages derived from readable postmarks, which numbered 576 out of 619 returned questionnaires.
[b] This figure is deflated by the deliberate exclusion of Japanese members, who amounted to 8.1 per cent of those listed.

this type of anonymous and confidential survey, the response rate was very satisfactory.

Certain basic information was immediately obtainable from the returned questionnaires, but since we had stressed the anonymity of the enquiry, respondents did not include either their names or addresses on the returns. Since we wished to obtain some idea of the geographic distribution of the respondents, however, we carefully enumerated the postmarks of the return envelopes, and this provided us with an indication from the readable postmarks of the rate of response from, on the one hand, London, and from the provinces, on the other. The basic data relative to sex, place of residence, and country of birth of our respondents is set out in Table 3.

The male/female distribution of the sample relative to the population being surveyed is clearly normal, but, unless our unreadable postmarks were biased towards London, then London is clearly somewhat under-represented by our respondents. There may be other reasons for this, not least the fact that, in London, people—particularly single people, who, as will become evident, are over-represented in the membership of Sōka Gakkai in Britain relative to the general population—appear to be more geographically mobile, less settled, and perhaps, therefore, less disposed, statistically at least, to respond to questionnaire enquiries. The difference in response rate between London members and provincials did not surprise the leaders of SGI-UK. when it was mentioned to them: they volunteered the view that London members were generally later and a little more volatile in response than members elsewhere—something which they attributed to the pace of London life and the extra demands imposed by commuting and such things. The returns from non-Westerners (deflated in number by our deliberate exclusion of the Japanese members) reflect a higher response rate than among the rest of the membership.

What is at once apparent is that, like most if not all other religious organizations in Britain, and like the parent body (Sōka Gakkai) in Japan, the movement in Britain has a higher percentage of women members than of men.[1] This was already evident in the address list of members, and was reflected in our sample. It is also clear that the movement is essentially an urban phenomenon, very much concentrated in the capital and its environs, to the extent of almost two-thirds of the membership.[2] For the rest, it is evident that the members are found much less in industrial areas than in centres of tertiary industry and services. The great majority of members are, expectably, Westerners, even though there is a considerable (if proportionately diminishing) numerical presence of Japanese in the British movement. However, among the Westerners, there appears to be a not inconsiderable proportion of non-British members, which gives the movement a cosmopolitan complexion not commonly found, for example, in the membership of various Christian sects in Britain.

Of the members in the sample, some 618 disclosed their place of birth. Of these, 480 were born in the United Kingdom; eight were born in the Republic of Ireland; and the remainder, some 130 members, were born overseas. Thus 71.2 per cent were born in the United Kingdom, and 28.7 per cent elsewhere (or, if the British Isles be taken as a unit, then 73.4 per cent were born in the British Isles, and some 26.6 per cent elsewhere). Of those born in the United Kingdom, twenty-six respondents specified Scotland as their birthplace, and a further five indicated Northern Ireland. Among those born elsewhere, fifteen were born in the Caribbean, fourteen in the United States, and twelve in Malaysia.[3]

---

[1] A similar sex ratio is reported for France by Louis Hourment, 'Transformer le poison en élixir: L'Alchimie du désir dans un culte néo-bouddhique, la Soka Gakkai française', in Françoise Champion and Danielle Hervieu-Léger (eds.), *De l'émotion en religion: Renouveaux et traditions* (Paris: Centurion, 1990), 77.

[2] There is a similar concentration of French members in Paris, according to Hourment, ibid.

[3] There were, in addition, ten members born in France; eight in Germany; six in each of Australia, Ghana, and South Africa; four in Italy; three in each of the following countries: Canada, India, Hong Kong, Japan, and Kenya; two each in

What also emerged from the sample was that SGI members were almost all first-generation converts. In the entire sample, our returns revealed that only one respondent was born to parents who already belonged to the movement. In this sense, at least, this study of the movement is a unique exercise in the study of religious converts, even though the process of conversion itself follows a different pattern from that which is conventionally envisaged of converts to Christian sects. The picture is, of course, common to new religious movements, and time alone will indicate whether such movements are likely to enjoy the same success in recruiting the second (and subsequent) generations as they have experienced in making their initial converts. One may readily suggest that there are profound differences between religious bodies which are composed entirely of first-generation members, and those which rely for their membership on endogenous recruitment. Our survey revealed that some 10 per cent of the existing SGI members had encountered the movement between 1959 and 1975, the very earliest days of its incursion into Britain. About 55 per cent had joined since 1984—the other third having become members in the intervening years, 1976 to 1983.

We have already noticed the fact that after the very first phase of growth, which occurred before a regular procedure of 'induction' had been instituted, it became the custom to count as members only those who had received the copies of the *Gohonzon* from a Nichiren Shōshū priest in the ceremony known as *Gojukai*. Following the split in the movement, these visits have ceased, and the legitimization of membership may have become more problematic. Eventually, membership will, it must be assumed, be legitimized by criteria other than a ritual conducted by a priest. For the purpose of our research, however, we had already taken a different consideration into account as the effective basis for membership—namely the date at which the respondent reported that he or she had first begun chanting in the prescribed manner. Taking this as the determinant of membership, we found that some 10 per cent of the respondents had begun chanting before 1977 (the two members of longest

China, Malta, New Zealand, the Philippines, and Portugal; one each in Argentina, Austria, Burma, Colombia, Egypt, Finland, Greece, Iran, Iraq, Morocco, Nigeria, Peru, Poland, Rhodesia, Singapore, Switzerland, Thailand, Uganda, Zambia, and Zimbabwe. One additional respondent indicated only 'East Africa', and another, 'South East Asia'.

TABLE 4. *The age distribution of the membership*

Age categories	No.	%	Cumulative %
Younger than 20 years	45	7.3	7.3
20–4	115	18.6	25.9
25–9	149	24.2	50.1
30–4	112	18.1	68.2
35–9	75	12.2	80.4
40–4	49	7.9	88.3
45–9	27	4.4	92.7
50–4	16	2.6	95.3
55–9	18	2.9	98.2
60 or over	11	1.8	100.0

standing had started as early as 1953). This calculation suggests that although it might appear that there had been some slowing down in recruitment in recent years (since only forty-three people began to chant in 1989, and only sixteen by 1 November 1990, when our research began) it has to be remembered that there were 869 newcomers who were listed in November 1990, but who were not included in our sample.

Since we had chosen to regard first chanting as equivalent to an affirmation of religious allegiance, it became important to know at what age people typically assumed this activity, and we asked our respondents that question. It transpired that the mean age for beginning to chant was 31 to 32 years old, the median age was 29 years, and the mode 25 years. Table 4 sets out the distribution for five-yearly intervals. Nichiren Shōshū Buddhism in Britain is a religious affiliation to which people do not become converted at a very early age. Compared to the traditional age of Christian conversion (stereotypically an adolescent phenomenon), Nichiren Buddhists have proved to be relatively mature when they committed themselves. Equally, they do not conform to the pattern established in Britain and America among recruits to new religions such as the Unification Church and Transcendental Meditation, where recruits have been shown to be on average between 22 and 23.[4] At the other

---

[4] Barker reports that 'the average age of those who join the Unification Church was 23'. Eileen Barker, *The Making of a Moonie* (Oxford: Blackwell, 1984), 199. The average age of a group of adherents of Transcendental Meditation was 23.3, and it was calculated that 'they began meditating at an average age of twenty-two'. William Sims Bainbridge and Daniel H. Jackson, 'The Rise and Decline of Transcendental

end, and perhaps expectably, the movement appears not to have attracted many people after they have attained the age of 50. One may suppose that as people attain this age they are likely to be less disposed towards radical religious change. This generation, too, had been less exposed to the range of exotic concepts and rituals which, in recent decades, had become increasingly familiar to the generations born after about 1950.

Nichiren's Buddhism is proclaimed by its adherents as an immediately practical religion with quick proofs of its validity. In this sense, it has an advantage over (most) other religious bodies in being able to invite potential recruits to 'Try it and see if it works'. Since results are expected more or less at once, and since newcomers are invited to chant without knowing anything of the theoretical justification for the practice, people may well be induced to start chanting even on their first encounter with SGI. They may begin with relatively little investment of time or study. We enquired of respondents about the time that elapsed between first meeting Nichiren's Buddhism and the time at which they began to chant. Fully 41 per cent of the members reported that they had started to chant right away on their first encounter with SGI. Twenty-nine per cent had begun chanting within five months of their first contact with the movement, and some 30 per cent had taken longer than five months before making a start on the practice. There was some difference in response between younger and older members. The younger cohorts, that is to say, those born in or after 1956, had needed more time after first meeting the movement before they adopted the practice. For 46 per cent of the older cohorts, that is those born in 1955 or before, there had been no lapse of time between encounter and practice: they had begun at once. But for the younger age category, only 35 per cent could report such an immediate acceptance of the commitment. Another 36 per cent of the younger people had needed more than five months before taking up chanting, as against 27 per cent of the older group.[5]

The differences were evident with respect not only to age but also to length of time in membership. More of those who had been in

Meditation', in Bryan Wilson (ed.), *The Social Impact of New Religious Movements* (New York: Rose of Sharon Press, 1981), 138.

[5] These differences are statistically significant even though Stuart's tau-c is only 0.11 ('Tau' is a measure of association: the higher the tau figure, the more closely are the two variables correlated.)

TABLE 5. *The time interval between encounter and starting to chant* (%)

	None	Less than 5 months	At least 5 months	Total[a]
Those who have chanted for more than 8 years	51	30	19	100 (165)
Those who have chanted for 8 years or less	37	28	35	100 (381)

[a] Actual numbers in brackets.

the movement longer had required no time at all between their first encounter and beginning to chant—51 per cent of those who had been in the movement for more than eight years as against 37 per cent of those who had been members for eight years or less. There may be various explanations for this difference (Table 5). One might speculate that, among the older members, those who had a sudden and swift conversion, with no hesitation, had remained members, whilst those who were uncertain, who needed more time, might have continued to have doubts, and might eventually have dropped out more frequently. An explanation of a different aspect of the issue might suggest that those older people who became converts were prepared, as people possibly of a more settled life-style, to take on the commitment to chant regularly, whilst younger people with less settled habits and more openness to change were reluctant to take on a daily obligation quite so quickly, and were more disposed to temporize until they were more fully acquainted with the movement and its members. It might also be the case that older people who had evinced some interest were more seriously seeking: for younger people the contact may have been less considered, more casual, and perhaps one among a number of explorative encounters with spiritual bodies. Our data do not allow us to endorse any particular explanation of this difference of response, however. Apparently, men had generally needed more time than women to make the decision to chant. Thirty-six per cent of the men had needed at least five months to effect their conversion, against 26 per cent of the women.[6] Even so, interesting as are these data, perhaps the most striking finding does not lie in these differences between age-groups and the sexes, but rather in the fact that so many—fully 40 per cent of those who have become members—needed no time at all before

[6] This difference is also significant, even though Stuart's tau-c is only 0.07.

they took on the quite considerable obligation to engage in a rigorous routine of morning and evening chanting. The offer of this Buddhism is very different in soteriological terms from that of traditional Christianity: there is little of the type of emotional appeal exerted by the idea of the love of an ideal suffering god-man, whose self-sacrifice 'for me' has called forth in many converts a powerful response of gratitude. Nichiren Buddhism urges people to take responsibility; to seek, by chanting, to alter their karma; to take charge of their own lives; and to cultivate the attitudes of mind which it is believed to induce. In many respects, it might appear to be a more difficult message to convey, and yet, if 40 per cent of those who have become adherents experienced more or less instant conversion, this must be evidence of its immediately powerful appeal.

III

Encounter, Attraction, and Conversion

THERE is no one usual pattern by which people first encounter, are then attracted by, and eventually convert to a new religious movement, but there is always a sequence in which exposure occurs, interest is evoked, and commitment elicited. We sought to discover just how dedicated and stable members had travelled this route—what circumstances occasioned their first acquaintance with Nichiren Buddhism; the features of the faith or of the movement which specifically appealed; and whether that same initial attraction was responsible for summoning sustained commitment when the 'interested stranger' became the dedicated member.

Clearly, all new religions which entertain ambitions of growth (and this is common to all such movements, at least in their early phases, and usually long thereafter) must create favourable opportunities for new people to become acquainted with their existing members, and with their spiritual practice and philosophy. Similar as their proselytizing goals may be, however, there is no pattern common to them all. Movements differ in a wide variety of ways, and the typical way in which people first encounter a religion varies from one movement to another. It depends to a considerable extent on the conscious strategy which each organization employs in making itself and its message known as well as on its style and on the intrinsic character of its ideology. There is, of course, likely to be some convergence of strategy, style, and organization. Since all religions function to enhance the sense of personal well-being, wherever proselytizing is adopted as a goal there is always likely to be considerable encouragement of members to spread the word. Religious bodies generally rely for new recruitment to a considerable degree on person-to-person communication and the activation of personal networks, but the extent of that particular dependence varies. A movement sponsoring a relatively impersonal technique of mental therapy, such as Scientology, is likely to put more emphasis on literature and publicity than on personal introductions. Communitarian groups, and to a lesser extent bodies which focus strongly on congregational unity, might be expected to expose potential joiners as much as possible to the benefits of the support of corporate life.[1] Movements with a more individualistic orientation, such as SGI, are likely to rely less on large-scale rallies and collective occasions, such as the revival meetings which characterized Protestant movements in the last century, than on one-to-one relationships and personal introductions. Such was our expectation, and our findings confirmed it.

Only 6 per cent of those in our sample had encountered what was then NSUK through the impersonal agencies of the media—through exhibitions, concerts, the movement's own publicity, or the various media accounts of the organization which had appeared in Britain. Ninety-four per cent met the movement through social interaction. Friends represented the largest category of people who introduced members, amounting to some 42 per cent; 23 per cent were brought into contact with it through their partners or family members. The remainder were first presented with information by acquaintances, work or student colleagues most particularly, but 14 per cent owed the encounter to casual acquaintances.[2] Of all the individuals through whom members in Britain encountered Sōka Gakkai, only 6 per cent were Japanese, a fact which suggests that although many of the early members in Britain were Japanese permanent or temporary immigrants and expatriates working for Japanese companies in Britain, the direct influence of Japanese members had much diminished over time. They were no longer the major proselytizers practising *shakubuku*: the movement, despite a sizeable

---

[1] The point is made relative to a number of movements by Eileen Barker, *New Religious Movements: A Practical Introduction* (London: HMSO, 1989), 27; and more specifically for the Unification Church in Bryan R. Wilson and Karel Dobbelaere, 'Unificationism: A Study of the Moonies in Belgium', *British Journal of Sociology*, 38/2 (1987), 186.

[2] Fourteen per cent introduced by casual acquaintances, and 6 per cent who first met the movement through impersonal agencies, leaves 80 per cent who owed their contact to what have been designated as 'pre-existing extra-movement ties'—a closely comparable figure to the 82 per cent in this category reported for an American sample of members of (what was then called) Nichiren Shōshū of America. David A. Snow and Cynthia Phillips, 'The Lofland–Stark Conversion Model; A Critical Assessment', *Social Problems*, 27/4 (Apr. 1980), 440.

representation of non-British members, had become effectively indigenized.

Despite the frequency of partners, friends, and relatives in effecting introductions, there were some surprising and quite casual encounters which led to conversions. Thus, members described their first encounter with Nichiren Buddhism as occurring in a variety of unexpected circumstances: 'in a night-club'; 'at a dinner party in Copenhagen'; through 'a stranger in a pub'; 'when I was homeless, I met a man in a pub and he let me use his spare room for the night: in the house I encountered what I now know to be the *Gohonzon*'. A psychiatric social therapist recounted, 'My friend's mother met a member at a party and when she told me I was intrigued and wanted to know, as I thought Buddhists did not go to parties'. At least three respondents had become acquainted with the movement through a television programme. One or two had heard chanting and had been attracted by it; another had seen a poster; three had walked into the movement's Richmond shop, one of them because she had 'thought I could buy a Buddha [there] for my daughter's Christmas present'. Others had met the practice whilst travelling—in India; Los Angeles; on a train; by being given a lift. Tutors in craft, ceramics, or drama classes had passed on the word to others. Several had been *shakubuku*-ed by clients of their businesses, one as casually as whilst 'at work, driving my taxi, introduced by a pretty young lady'. Certainly, some locales may have been more propitious environments than others, as the incidence of reference to therapeutic centres suggests in responses such as: 'During a consultation at the East/West macrobiotic centre for my illness at that time'; 'at an informal lecture on macrobiotic diet—during "talk" afterwards'; 'a naturopath I consulted [for] my health problem'; 'through the medical centre for complementary therapies'; 'at a clinic for alternative medicine as a patient'; 'through a tutor at an astrology class'; 'at a lecture on psychic painting, the artists didn't turn up, but three members [of Sōka Gakkai] gave a talk on Nichiren Shōshū; and one respondent reported that 'my doctor said chanting was beneficial and gave me a name to contact (he didn't know Nichiren Shōshū)'.

Night-clubs, craft and drama classes, and alternative medical centres would be less likely places to be introduced to traditional Christian religion in any of its numerous variants. Yet it would be misleading to infer from these reports that Sōka Gakkai is a

TABLE 6. *Who attracted new members?* (%)

	Friends	Partner and family	Other persons
Age 40 or more	37	—	—
Younger than 40	46	—	—
Age 30 or more	—	21	32
Younger than 30	—	30	17

well-integrated part of 'the cultic milieu'.[3] Certainly, some members have dabbled in a variety of spiritual, therapeutic, and alternative philosophies, as the foregoing quotations from their responses indicate, but there are many others, as we shall see below, whose religious experience has not included much if any acquaintance with any of the new religious organizations that have been active in Britain since the early 1960s when the Sōka Gakkai itself began to recruit.

There is a probability that people in different age categories or in different types of marital situation might encounter a new religion more typically in one way rather than in another. The results of our enquiry suggested that more of those under 30 years of age came to know the movement through a partner or family members, some 30 per cent as against only 21 per cent of the older members, and that more of those under 40 encountered SGI through friends—46 per cent as against 37 per cent of those of forty or older. Persons other than friends or family were more important in attracting people to the practice when the convert was 30 years old or older (32 per cent of the older age-group, compared to 17 per cent for the younger cohorts) (Table 6).

Single persons were, of course, more typically introduced to SGI by their friends than by family members (respectively 48 per cent as against 36 per cent). Those who lived as couples, whether married, cohabiting, or gay, were more usually drawn to the movement by persons within their household (often their partners) than were single people (31 per cent compared to 16 per cent). The role of the media did not appear to differ for these two sets of age categories, nor did it differ for the different categories of marital status.

[3] For the concept of 'cultic milieu', see Colin Campbell, 'The Cult, the Cultic Milieu, and Secularization', *A Sociological Yearbook of Religion in Britain*, 5 (1972), 119–36.

The Sources of Attraction

The circumstances in which members first met SGI is only one aspect of the explanation of how it was that they became committed members. Of greater consequence is just what the prospective member found attractive about the new faith that was being canvassed. More than one-third of our respondents said that what had attracted them was *the quality of the membership*. They often specifically mentioned the sincerity of those whom they had met, their honesty, friendliness, happiness, openness to others, and their informality. These respondents were impressed. They were made to feel welcome, and they attributed the qualities they perceived in existing members to the influence of their religious belief and practice. Such importance was attributed to this that their replies to our questions, both on the questionnaire forms and in interviews, are worth citing. Thus, a 35-year-old musician was typical when he briefly stated: 'I was impressed by the people I met and the philosophy behind it.' A free-lance woman journalist confessed: 'I was frightened and insular when I started practising. I was not successful in my work. People [in SGI] were very understanding, caring, and compassionate. It released me. I felt free.'

Others commented at greater length. A 32-year-old opera singer said that the attraction was 'the life condition of the people I met, people full of hope and joy, challenging their life in an honest way, which I hadn't done. This—the people and the philosophy—not the practice, at first. I needed time. I was theoretical. I wanted to read books. I had faith in their faith. Also, there were lots of different nationalities in this group—it looked all-embracing.' A university graduate who had taken a waiter's job maintained: 'The attraction was the people that I met. I was impressed by the man who first mentioned NSUK to me, and then by a friend's girl-friend, who was practising. She was a lively girl and there was something vibrant in her life. Then there was meeting X [the owner of the restaurant where he worked]. It was the strong life force of these people that attracted me, particularly the way [they] looked after the restaurant and their family. They were different from average people.' A community worker with a master's degree said, 'I couldn't understand it at first. It went over my head. It was the people and the way they talked about their lives in a meeting that really impressed me. I was committed to whatever produced that the instant I experienced it.' These aspects—the willingness to talk openly to strangers—impressed a 41-year-old woman secretary whose marriage had broken up; she said, 'Initially [it was] the openness of the people. In meetings [they were] talking about painful and private experiences to strange people openly. This impressed me. They laughed, there was laughter and joy. Every other religion I had explored was very serious.' Thus, whilst some found the philosophical aspects highly abstruse, and others yearned for more of such intellectual under-pinning, what impressed them equally were the style and personality of the members, the openness, and the absence of solemnity.

A 34-year-old violin-maker and restorer found in the welcome he received a boost for his own self-confidence:

The first thing [that attracted me] was the acceptance and trust of the people who were involved. My first feeling . . . was that I was completely accepted as I was. I felt included and it made it very easy, though it was hard to break the ice and say the words [of the chant]. I'd had a lack of confidence since I was a small child. Being accepted as I was meant a great deal to me . . . I don't think I've ever doubted the practice, which may be largely because I trust the people whom I met when starting . . . Without the people I would have doubted it, but it was proof of the people that I met which was important.

Of course, there is nothing particularly to distinguish Sōka Gakkai in the warmth of the welcome to newcomers: most religious bodies go out of their way to greet visitors, and it is precisely the sense of being wanted which is communicated to newcomers which forms part of the appeal of many new religious bodies. Beyond the experience of warmth and the feeling of trust, some members discerned a more distinctive quality in Sōka Gakkai members, even if it sometimes proved difficult to describe. As a shopkeeper in her forties put it, the attraction was 'the positive outlook of the members and their "shining" appearance'. A young woman gold-smith attributed attraction to 'the attitude towards life of the person who introduced me to the practice. The first time I saw her, she was weeding her garden, and although we didn't speak, and she didn't notice me watching her, I could tell that there was something different about her and I wanted to know what it was and whether I could be like that, too.' That theme was echoed time and again by our respondents, in both interviews and questionnaire replies. A 30-year-old woman, a free-lance interpreter, indicated that 'the person who introduced me had an intangible quality that I admired and wished to have also—a kind of freedom which showed in his behaviour'. Nor was this quality one which showed specifically only in members of the opposite sex: a 40-year-old male marine biologist attributed Sōka Gakkai's appeal to 'the quality of life of the workmate who introduced me'. Others were able to express these things as objective qualities: as a 40-year-old male bookseller put it, 'the friendship, honesty and integrity of the members I knew as friends over some years'.

Some who were drawn to the movement attributed this not merely to the quality of the lives of those already members, but to the transformation which they observed in acquaintances or relatives as a result of practising. As a male dental surgeon expressed it: 'The improvement in my brother's quality of life.' A self-employed female puppeteer of 40 ascribed her own attraction to 'the conspicuous positive change in temperament of a friend I had known since childhood'. A 25-year-old secondary school teacher was drawn to the movement by 'the changes I observed in my two brothers who began chanting just over a year before myself. They seemed to become much happier and positive in life.' A woman video producer firmly declared, 'I was not attracted to Nichiren Shōshū as an organization —I was attracted to the practice because of the incredible changes a long-term friend of mine achieved in her life. The organization became more acceptable after *Alice* [the musical show mounted by NSUK at the Hammersmith Odeon].' Another woman, a housewife, was drawn by 'the change in the husband of the couple who introduced me' and added, 'also by the fact that no money was asked for—very important'.

About 20 per cent of our questionnaire respondents recounted that what appealed to them were the direct *practical benefits* which they understood they might expect from regular chanting and from the *Gohonzon*. In particular, they looked for wealth, health, and a variety of material blessings. This group virtually entertained a conviction that chanting worked almost like magic. In particular, those who were experiencing specific problems were often drawn to the movement by the hope or expectation that chanting would, in some way, quickly resolve them. A young woman free-lance journalist averred that she was attracted by 'the prospect of gaining material benefit through practising'. For a male silk-screen painter of 33 the appeal was 'the possibility of curing an incurable illness'.

A single woman clerical officer of 40 said, 'I liked the thought of benefits and really wanted more confidence in myself.' For some the benefits were psychological rather than strictly material. A woman artist of 62 was initially induced to practise by the prospect of 'an easy "magical" method of answering problems in a life burdened with severe mental and material suffering'. A 58-year-old carpenter liked 'the inner strength and peace of mind it gave me at a time when my life was in shreds. It stopped me from destroying myself and gave me the will to fight on and believe in myself.' A retired woman of 63 believed 'in the power of the *daimoku*. I'd had cancer for several years and my life force was very low: at the first meeting I attended we chanted for one hour. At the end it just felt as if the power had been switched on again.' One disillusioned woman, an actress who was single, declared that, whilst she had found the chanting attractive, she had 'believed or hoped the "benefits" sales talk I heard at the time might help me, too. It didn't.' (Understandably, since our sample was drawn from those regarded by the Sōka Gakkai organization as loyal members, there were very few and only incidental responses from those who, having been drawn to the movement, had since had second thoughts and were disillusioned.)

About 16 per cent of respondents indicated that their commitment had been initially elicited by the favourable impression that they had gained of the *characteristics of the organization itself*. Some specifically mentioned the simplicity of the rituals, the aesthetic appeal of the chanting, and the fact that the individual could engage in ritual activity without intermediaries, that they could—as some of them put it—take responsibility for their own lives and their own karma. A young woman solicitor in her thirties liked 'the sound of the chanting and the atmosphere at the meetings. The sense of positivity and something generally strong, caring and "good" from the leaders I met.' The style of leadership in itself often constituted the appeal. Thus, a 44-year-old art teacher was attracted by 'one thing—not having a guru. I don't believe in looking up to heroes . . . I've always been suspicious of rich organizations which subtly suggest that donations are the way of enlightenment. No one has put pressure on us to donate to NSUK—opportunities exist but no pressure . . . Nichiren Shōshū is a practical way of getting enlightenment for everyday life.' A 28-year-old film editor maintained that what appealed to her was, among other things, 'the purity of the organization and the leadership. I liked the way there was no hierarchy as such. Responsibility and positions in the organization were matters of giving rather than taking.' A male administrative officer of just over 50 liked the 'good organization within the movement' and found the British leader 'very inspiring'. Another civil servant, a university graduate aged 22, enjoyed 'the fact that members came across as real people without pretensions, but who were struggling together. We have a principle called *zui hō bini* which means that, apart from accepting the *Gohonzon*, you don't have to change your life-style (although many may do so if they would like to). This means that our leaders aren't haughty or "saintly"; they go to the pub, watch *Neighbours*, etc., in other words they are ordinary— Buddhas are ordinary people.'

Other aspects of the movement had been the principal attraction for some respondents. The moral freedom of members appealed to some, and the fact that in this age—the last age of *mappō*—Nichiren Buddhism taught that moral rules were set aside as individuals took responsibility for themselves, thus endowing the movement with a spirit of toleration and permissiveness unusual in religious bodies, and an undoubted source of satisfaction to some potential members. Various respondents dilated at some length on this subject. A supervisor in the central support system for a regional police force had been attracted because Nichiren Buddhism was 'non-judgemental —free from guilt. The members appeared happy and caring. I liked the idea of taking responsibility for my own life.' The male art teacher liked the attitude to moral matters: 'That was a significant reason when we thought of joining—the idea of there being no sin.' The female film editor made a similar point: 'The great attraction for me was that in Buddhism there were no rules and regulations— no ten commandments . . . the philosophy was very much cause and effect. From this moment on you can change your destiny no matter what you've done in the past.' A 25-year-old, waiting for a place in a polytechnic, declared: 'Everything is accepted. I was upset that you were doomed [by Christianity] if you didn't believe. "God is here to save you" upset me. Nichiren Shōshū says you are to save yourself. No one is to say what is good or wrong . . . it is up to you to make out what is good or wrong.' A woman teacher of 38 was attracted 'by the philosophy—no external rules. I hate being told what to do.' An actress and singer of 42 made the same point; the attraction had been 'the absence of an enforced moral code'. A male analyst programmer 'liked the fact that this religion offered an opportunity to transform my life, whilst not offering any rules or conditions or judgements'. A 25-year-old woman graduate with qualifications in video production liked 'the fact that there are no rules and the people are very positive'.

For some respondents, self-declared homosexuals, the absence of a specific moral code was a particular attraction. A 37-year-old male photographer claimed 'amazing benefits resulting from practising. Their [Sōka Gakkai's] attitude towards personal sexuality—particularly homosexuality—being very positive, i.e. "it is not a sin".' A 31-year-old drag cabaret artiste, a graduate, found it attractive that 'the movement seems to accept me as a practising homosexual. I am not made to feel wrong, bad, guilty, evil, just because of that.' A 29-year-old male theatre lighting operator had chanted to change his sexual karma and 'to feel easy and relaxed with the (homo)sexual part of my being', while a psychiatric male nurse living in a gay relationship said,

finding NS was like being presented with a jacket or coat and finding it fitted perfectly personal philosophies I held already; its acceptance of things that aren't quite the norm, mixed race relationships, same gender relationships. They are genuine and loving. Also you are not told it is bad [not to chant] and you will be punished for not chanting, but more on the lines of 'it is good to chant and you will be rewarded'. So it is much more the carrot and less of the stick approach. A welcome difference from other religions.

Others, not homosexuals, welcomed the endorsement by this faith of everyday life. As a 35-year-old male musician recorded his feelings: 'What attracted me was the lack of rigidity. The girl-friend had been a Buddhist of a different sort—the Friends of the Western Buddhist Order. They believe that [sexual] relationships are not good for you. They remove themselves from the world. I didn't get on with that—the religion was somehow separate from daily life. That was the big difference with NSUK—practice was part of daily life.'

A rather different source of appeal was indicated by others: for them, the prime virtue was in giving the individual access to a life force, and in establishing the individual's unity with the universe. For yet another group of respondents, what they found appealing was the spirit of democracy which they perceived in the organization, the emphasis on egalitarianism among members, which was sometimes alluded to as the emphasis on individual autonomy. The same point was sometimes made negatively and comparatively, when members said that what had appealed to them from the outset was a religion that had no god-figure.

Fourteen per cent of the respondents pointed to the *prospect of personal happiness and self-confidence*, which they saw as a consequence of practising. As the foregoing quotations from respondents illustrate, taking control of one's life was a widely diffused desideratum for members and it was the movement's specific claim that this was what practising would enable them to do. These responses implied the possibility of self-transformation, a radical change of disposition towards the world, and the release of inner resources. Some said, in effect: 'NSUK makes me happy. I enjoy life.'

About 8 per cent of our sample defined the appeal of Nichiren Buddhism as essentially an *intellectual satisfaction* which the teaching of cause and effect provided. The concept of karma supplied meaning and purpose to life; it made sense of the world; it answered questions. The exposition of a convincing theodicy was, for some, what attracted their initial interest.

A small minority ascribed the appeal of the movement to *ethical considerations*. They saw Nichiren Buddhism as contributing to vital ethical concerns, in particular they were impressed by the strong emphasis on work for world peace and social change. As a single young man working for the Department of the Environment told us: 'I found the book by Mr. Causton. It provided answers to a lot of questions . . . and it was agreeing with answers I had worked out for myself . . . basically saying that there is hope for humanity and we can live together in peace and harmony, and there is an actual method for doing that. I liked its down-to-earthness. It seemed so straightforwardly simple. It's all your responsibility. Chanting changes your karma.'

Another group of about the same size made much of the opportunity for *social involvement*, in particular in the cultural events that the movement frequently sponsored. As one 29-year-old free-lance market researcher put it, 'My sister was in the musical *Alice* [in 1986]. She is not a professional actress or singer, however: seeing her and everyone else on stage inspired me to take action and take responsibility for my life.' Those who mentioned events of this kind usually did so in the course of alluding to other features of the movement or its membership which had won their appreciation.

Inevitably, some were attracted for what might be considered extraneous reasons, which, however, led them into a richer experience than they had first envisaged. Such was the case of an airline marketing officer, the husband of a Japanese wife, who was later to become Vice-General Director of the SGI-UK. He was attracted because 'the woman that I desired (loved) was so convinced herself'. Another, a 40-year-old unemployed sales manager, had been impressed by 'reading Tina Turner's book in which she mentions it and how she used the practice to resolve deep-rooted problems in her life'. A 34-year-old woman office worker was drawn by the 'freedom of the practice. I wanted to change my life for the better. Lots of famous people practised and they seemed happy and successful, which is what I wanted.' Others, initially sceptical, were not attracted at all, but in one way or another began practising. So it was with a theatre stage manager, who declared, 'Nothing really attracted me; I was persuaded to "give it a go".' A woman pensioner, who claimed it had cured her of cancer, had 'thought it was a lot of hot air, and [I] began to chant to prove it didn't work'. Whilst another woman social worker had started to chant 'to appease my sister—it worked!'

The various things which initially attracted converts did not vary much among the different social categories within the membership. Those born in and after 1951 were more impressed by the characteristics of the membership and of the organization, whilst those born before that time were more inclined to mention the practical benefits and the intellectual satisfaction afforded by the movement's teachings. But the differences between these two age-groups were small. The younger female members were particularly attracted by the qualities of the membership.[4]

There were also some differences in the way in which people were attracted by the movement when their responses to this question were related to their previous religious background. Those who had no previous religious affiliation or upbringing were overwhelmingly attracted by the quality of the membership. The character of the religious Buddhists they met impressed them. In this, these hitherto unreligious converts contrasted sharply with those who had previously belonged to a Christian church, who were attracted not so much by the dispositions of the members as by the promise of direct benefits from Buddhist practice and by the prospect of gaining in personal confidence and happiness. Those who had a generally Christian

[4] Kendall's tau-b 0.12.

background, usually by virtue of upbringing, but who had not been affiliated to a church, were inclined, much more than were others, when indicating what appealed to them, to refer more specifically to the characteristics of SGI as a religious organization. It might be hazardous to read too much into these differences of orientation when correlated with earlier religious involvement but it might well be the case that, for those who had not experienced association with devoutly committed people, their encounter with Nichiren Buddhists was illuminating not simply because these people were Buddhists, but, at least in some respects, because they were seriously religious. Erstwhile Christians, who were used to the company of committed religionists, were perhaps less readily impressed by the spiritual orientations of their new acquaintances, but found other things—things such as direct benefits which Christianity did not specifically promise, or at least did not always manage to deliver—which convinced them that this new faith was well worth their while.

From Attraction to Commitment

The features of a movement which first commend it to prospective joiners are not necessarily those which continue to command over-riding appeal subsequently. A process of socialization occurs in which new members may gradually acquire a different appreciation of the ideology that they have adopted and the organization to which they have affiliated themselves. This process may be stimulated in a variety of circumstances. Thus, a movement might lure people to join by promises or prospects that cannot be realized, and leaders may consciously, and even deceptively, redirect their newly acquired followers to shift their focuses of attention. A somewhat different pattern would occur where the leaders of a movement saw their task as a process of re-education of acolytes, bringing them to a finer or more subtle appreciation of more elevated goals. (The Christian case, in which the 'strong meat' is deliberately not put before babes in the faith, might exemplify this instance.[5]) A third possibility

---

[5] The analogy of offering milk to babes and strong meat only to those mature in the faith is made by Paul: 'And I, brethren, could not speak unto you as unto spiritual, but as unto carnal, even as unto babes in Christ. I have fed you with milk, and not with meat: for hitherto you were not able to bear it.' 1 Cor. 3:1–2; and in Heb. 5:12:

might occur where converts themselves unconsciously transformed their own conception of the supreme purposes of their faith, a process of transmutation of immediate and perhaps selfish and material goals into more ultimate spiritual fulfilment. In all such cases, the process is one that would indicate a shift from the initial attractions of a new belief system and its sustaining organization, and perhaps even of their relinquishment.

Our acquaintance with Sōka Gakkai indicated that some such shifts might well be evidenced, since the movement so vigorously proclaimed a long-term commitment to the furtherance of world peace. That goal, universally acceptable as it might be, may not perhaps be the strongest initial motivation in inducing people to embrace an exotic religion (since there were other agencies in which world peace was a no less fervently proclaimed goal, and where it was not hedged about by the sort of apparently extraneous and certainly unfamiliar elements which comprised Nichiren Buddhism). The promise of a practical faith, a faith that worked, and of chanting for 'whatever you want' might more readily and immediately capture the imagination of prospective converts. The question was whether such virtually magical promises could sustain long-term commitment, or whether perseverance in the faith was accompanied by a redefinition of its potential. We sought to discover the extent to which, after some persisting commitment to the movement, members understood their goals and its goals—and themselves—differently.

Our evidence suggested that in very considerable measure the things that had initially attracted new members persisted as sources of appeal for them at the time when our research was conducted. There were, however, also some important shifts in the items that respondents chose to earmark as what currently appealed to them about their religion, as Table 7 indicates.

For some 53 per cent of the membership what had attracted them to the movement initially had continued to appeal to them. Yet, it is striking that the percentage is much lower for what had been the leading factor in attracting them as new members, namely the quality of the membership. This item continued to be a significant aspect in the appeal of SGI for only one out of three who had selected

'For when for the time ye ought to be teachers, ye have need that one teach you again which be the first principles of the oracles of God; and are become such as have need of milk, and not of strong meat.'

TABLE 7. *The initial and subsequent attraction of SGI* (%)

Characteristics	Initial attraction	Current attraction	Change	Those whose initial attraction persisted[a]
Quality of members	37	14	−23	35
Practical benefits	19	18	−1	54
Character of organization	16	17	+1	64
Personal happiness and confidence	14	19	+5	68
Intellectual satisfaction	8	11	+3	75
Ethical motivation	3	18	+15	100
Social involvement	3	3	—	47
Total whose initial attraction persisted				53

[a] Indicates the proportion of those initially citing each characteristic as the source of what attracted them who persisted in citing that item as the source of their current attraction.

it as their initial attraction: whereas membership quality had attracted 37 per cent of present members when they joined, only 14 per cent thought that this was still a current attraction for them. This feature declined in importance once an individual who had been originally impressed by it had become a member. Others, who had not designated quality of membership as an initial attraction, rarely identified it as part of the current appeal of the movement. Thus, it can be said that once an individual was a member, the appeal of the movement did not usually depend on the characteristics of members.

Had new members simply come to take the spiritual quality of other members for granted as they became more familiar with them? Had they perhaps become disenchanted, finding people not as different from the generality of mankind as they had first supposed? From our interviews, there was some evidence of that. Thus, a 42-year-old community social worker acknowledged that 'there are some in the organization I would not want to associate with, but you have to battle away to associate with that person, and it may take one or two years before you can get to do things together'. He resigned himself to the idea that 'there is a benefit in participating with so many kinds of people and of seeing the world'. A secretary in her late forties who was also a local city councillor acknowledged that 'some of the members irritate me sometimes. "How did that person become a leader?" I think. You don't like some.' On the other hand, some do remain enamoured of the 'trust and faith' of their co-religionists. A divorced class-room assistant in a special school who had first been attracted by 'the humour of the Buddhists I met—the generosity—the amount of young people, the varied nationalities, people . . . from all walks of life, the ritual and romance of lighting candles, kneeling, incense, chanting' had come to see it all as 'much deeper' but still was drawn by 'the wonderful members I meet'. But most converts, even though initially attracted by the qualities of the members that they had encountered, claimed to have discovered other, more important or more central concerns which commanded their commitment.

The features of the movement which had to some extent replaced the character of members as a source of attraction were, first and foremost, the appeal of the ethical motivation of the movement and its teachings, but there was also an increase in the importance accorded to 'personal happiness and confidence'; 'the characteristics of the organization'; and also to 'practical benefits'. The first two of these items were those that had increased most.

From these responses, it becomes clear that the organization had considerable success in re-socializing its converts. The 'qualities of the membership' and 'practical benefits' are natural and self-explanatory aspects of the appeal of all proselytizing organizations, when they are at all successful. If the attributes of the existing membership were unappealing, it would be unlikely that a new prospective convert would be drawn in unless he found the ideology unusually compelling. Similarly, people are motivated by the prospect, immediate or distant, of the practical benefits to be derived from taking up a particular set of beliefs and practices. It is a rare religion which offers its votaries no benefits or which issues no promises about future prospects. Nichiren Buddhism makes strong claims in this respect, with a bid that is especially strong in offering benefit in this life and in this world and not in a remote hereafter. However, SGI was able to redirect the orientations of those newcomers who stayed in membership and to motivate them to accept the ethical views that it canvassed, even though these had not been the major source of appeal for newcomers. The goals emphasized by the Sōka Gakkai movement were more and more readily espoused by members, who increasingly made them their own. Thus, to contribute to world peace; to promote that goal through the attainment of peace of mind; to accept responsibility for one's own conduct, and for one's own society and its future; to stimulate social change by first recognizing the need for personal change; and to develop respect for others, as a cultivation of altruism, were the salient goals to which members not only assented but which they spontaneously affirmed.

These various motivations were often endorsed simultaneously, and represent an amalgam of several personal, ethical, and altruistic orientations. Thus, for a 62-year-old woman working in the care of the elderly, the prevailing attraction, which replaced her earlier 'magical' ideas, was 'knowing each day that I am in control of all my actions. Knowing I can definitely achieve any goal, having the sure knowledge that we can achieve, through our movement, world peace.' A woman journalist in her twenties, initially attracted by material benefits, was now committed to 'the prospect of fulfilling my potential as a human being by helping others and working for world peace and becoming happy'. The market researcher who had been inspired by her sister's performance in *Alice* had now realized 'that world peace is the most important aspect of the movement and any action that I take contributes towards this goal that NSUK and SGI have'. The silk-screen painter made a similar point: having shifted from his initial concern to cure an illness, he now was drawn to 'Its [SGI's] role in totally transforming society and the world into something we could be proud of, and knowing that we were responsible for the transformation is one of the greatest joys you could have.'

Part of this re-socialization was to give members confidence in the organization, allowing them access to what they sometimes described as 'life force'. The movement's appeal lay in part in its simple rituals, its encouragement of moral freedom, and the stimulation of tolerance. Members appreciated that they belonged to a lay organization, which they saw as democratic and egalitarian, and one which gave wide opportunities to women. One 22-year-old student claimed to have always rejected Buddhism because she had understood that the individual had to be reborn as a man before 'getting anywhere near enlightenment. Learning that this was not so in Nichiren Shōshū was the first thing that made me want to find out more.' Others had developed strong commitment to the movement's leader, Daisaku Ikeda—*Sensei* (Teacher), as he was often called. Thus, a 44-year-old shopkeeper wrote, what had replaced the attraction initially exerted by the membership was now 'President

Ikeda's guidance and leadership, and the constant encouragement from leaders, also the opportunities to be creative in the organization'. A 37-year-old man, a Labour Party councillor, declared, 'what I find so attractive is the approach to the practice that *Sensei* [Ikeda] embodies, but is in all of us'. A male local government personnel officer, who appreciated the profundity of the teachings, also specially commended 'the optimism and positive attitude and energy of the leaders'.

Not all members were so readily attracted by the organization, however: a 29-year-old woman artist, despite benefits, had stopped practising although 'I have not come across any other religion that I could say was better than NSUK . . . the one complaint I have about the organization of NSUK is that they do not get involved with other religious bodies to work together.' A male hairdresser was more critical: 'Nichiren Shōshū is perfect although it is controlled by one organization, Sokka [*sic*] Gakkai, which is anything but perfect, and for which I feel nothing but suspicion. Also, I feel that the personality cult surrounding President Ikeda goes against the teachings of Nichiren and is very suspect.' Yet he acknowledged quite specific benefits from chanting.

What members had also acquired subsequent to joining was the sense that this version of Buddhism, and more specifically chanting, actually worked: it helped them to solve their problems, helped to clarify their minds, and gave them access, they believed, to health, success, and also to wealth. They affirmed that they had gained in a sense of happiness and confidence and a feeling of controlling their own lives, taking responsibility for themselves, and acquiring a sense of being empowered to release their own inner resources. A 52-year-old administrative officer said, 'I am pleased and proud that my practice has made my life more stable and consistent: not so many ups and downs. Also I feel protected. The most attractive feature of the movement is the challenge of the twenty-first century.'

The acquisition of positive attitudes of mind was often mentioned. A male analyst programmer said, 'It offers me the ability to grow as a human being, and to contribute to society as whole, and to continue learning to live positively with a great sense of joy.' This note was echoed by a woman pensioner, 'striving to create world peace and achieving personal growth and happiness, and knowing that when I hit a negative patch I can work through it and win'. A housewife of 40 declared her satisfaction in feeling that she could 'change any negative experience into a positive one'. A 42-year-old general manager, who described himself as gay and working voluntarily for a self-help AIDS-related charity, specified the attraction as 'the discipline which practice teaches you'. And a 41-year-old writer ('at present a cook and dishwasher'), who had been attracted by the positive orientation of the members, now said that the attraction was 'the daily discipline it gives to daily life and the heightened sense of self-awareness and clarity of mind to deal with problems as they surface'. Support and protection were other related themes. A single woman clerical officer declared that what now appealed to her was 'Going to meetings knowing that I can talk about my problems and not be judged. I feel safe. Knowing there's always help if I need it. Knowing that I can change my problems "from poison to medicine" gives me great hopes.' And a single male photographer was committed because he realized 'how much the movement is geared to support individual members' and 'the power to be able to take responsibility for your own life'.

Beyond these various features, members affirmed that one of the main current attractions was the movement's ideology. It provided intellectual satisfaction, giving a sense of meaning and purpose to life, through an understanding of the law of cause and effect, and thus an explanation of the untoward and, of course, a way to circumvent it by diligent chanting. All of these items were characteristics which persisted in strength long after their initial appeal, and remained significant for many of the members who responded to our questionnaire. These aforementioned elements, taken together, represented more than 80 per cent of the motivational strength of the membership.

The ethical motivation had become a strong source of the continuing appeal of the movement, only slightly less frequently claimed than the attraction of 'personal happiness and confidence'. All those who declared that this had been part of the initial attraction NSUK (as it then was) had remained attracted by this aspect. The 15 per cent increase in those affirming the appeal of this facet of Nichiren Buddhism was a net gain, coming especially from people who had initially been drawn to the organization by 'the qualities of the membership' and, in second place, by those who had been won by 'practical benefits'. Of course, the emphasis on ethical concerns, and especially a commitment to non-violence and world peace (not, however, generally expressed as an outright endorsement of pacifism stated as such), is one which receives recurrent reiteration in the movement's English-language publications both from the British headquarters and from Japan. These goals are also kept in front of the international movement by the activities and speeches of Ikeda, and those who remain for long as members become keenly aware of the movement's bid for international and even political influence in support of these vigorously stated aims. These commitments may mean much less to new converts, but they are a very conspicuous part of the movement's objectives, and hence of the self-declared motivations of many long-term members.

'Personal happiness and confidence' was (together with 'ethical motivation', 'practical benefits', and the 'characteristics of the organization') the leading feature currently appealing to most of the members. For two-thirds of them this item was the same as their initial motivation. The numbers declaring it to be the feature most fully sustaining their interest increased, coming from those who, on first becoming acquainted with NSUK, had cited the 'quality of the membership' or 'the practical benefits' as the things that impressed them. The motivation of these members had thus shifted from more material considerations to what might be called psychic (or even spiritual) concerns.

None the less, 'practical benefits' was still an important item. As a secretarial worker declared, because 'I could actually receive proof in my life that it was a valid practice, this was and still is the most attractive part of the teaching for me'. Another woman, now retired, recalled 'the wonderment I felt then [which] is now supported by the profundity of the teachings and their practicality in today's life'. A female solicitor, born in Israel, appreciated the 'practical application of the practice as a tool to create value'. A 25-year-old woman investment banker, a Cambridge economics graduate, who had been initially attracted by the sound and vibrancy of the chanting, by feeling 'plugged into the universe', and by the fact that it was logical and answered questions which Christianity had failed to answer, now felt that her faith was deeper, 'now *I know it works*, so long as I do my practice properly'.

Even so, nearly 50 per cent of those who had been drawn in because of expected practical benefits now indicated that they were oriented also towards immaterial things, such as avowing an ethical orientation, or a concern for personal happiness. Those who pointed to 'the characteristics of the organization' as an attractive feature were about as numerous currently as had been the case when they were originally won over, but this theme had lost about one-third of those whose interest and commitment had originally been summoned by it to the other leading sources of attraction. The appeal of the character of the organization had gained almost exclusively at the expense of the attractiveness of the quality of the membership; their admiration had shifted from personal qualities of sincerity, honesty, friendliness, happiness, informality, and openness of members, which had won their interest at the outset, to the democratic and egalitarian spirit of the organization itself. The 'intellectual dimension' also grew in importance from the interest it had evoked for new members to its place in the current estimation of the members we surveyed. It was a feature that had become more appreciated by those who, initially, had counted the characteristics of the organization and the qualities of the membership as the major drawing points.

The summary result of all this is that nearly 50 per cent of the members were now motivated by psychological and intellectual considerations, and this was double the proportion who had indicated such items as part of what had originally elicited their interest. Social factors still played a not insignificant part in the appeal of belonging, represented by continued admiration for the qualities of members or the organization of the movement, and the social activities that it sponsored—attracting altogether one-third of the membership (initially this had been 56 per cent). And there remained a further 18 per cent who were still motivated by the practical benefits that they might obtain from practising their new religion.

Since more young women members were initially attracted to SGI by what they perceived to be the qualities of the membership, they were the ones who tended to change most in specifying what initially, and then eventually, made the movement attractive to them. External pressures also caused people to look for more acceptable forms of legitimization of their Buddhism, and it was those who encountered negative reactions from those in their close social environment (family and/or friends) who were most prone to change what they regarded as the most attractive features of their religion. People who were criticized by their primary relations or by close friends for changing their religious affiliation, or for becoming religious, could hardly legitimize such a step by reference simply to the quality of the other members. An ethical orientation and the increase of personal confidence and happiness were more acceptable legitimizations. In these cases, external pressure reinforced the encouragement encountered within the movement to espouse more ethical dispositions, and to invoke these as justification for continued commitment.

This process of change can be described as one in which particularistic and personal concerns were transmuted into more universalistic orientations that were much more difficult for others to contest. This section of the membership shifted their defence-mechanisms when faced with external criticism from claiming that they were moving among 'nice people' to the assertion that they were mobilized in pursuit of 'good causes'. Perhaps, in the process, they gained in happiness from this transcendence of purely personal satisfactions, and found enhanced confidence, which, as we have seen, they readily credited to their religious faith. To this correlation, we may add the fact that this change of attraction was most marked among those who were engaged in service activities, and those who had taken on higher responsibilities and positions of authority within the movement.

Karma, Crisis and Conversion

The appeal of a set of religious ideas and practices, of an organization, or of the people devoted to them might be considered as the pull factors in winning the allegiance of votaries. Not everyone who is drawn to a movement actually commits himself, however. Among those who do join, there are often powerful push factors at work as well, even if, for others, there are also deterrents. Some of the push factors are of a very general kind, dispositions or felt needs which might incline potential devotees towards any of a number of religious philosophies or spiritual therapies, should chance circumstance bring them into contact. Other stimuli might be more specific to particular kinds of spiritual relief. What a religious system offered might appear to match the background circumstances and temporal need of the individual concerned, showing a certain 'fit' with previous experience and a direct cogency and application to the issues that had unsettled the potential convert sufficiently to promote in him an openness to a new orientation in life. Among the Nichiren Buddhists, various clusters of push factors, apparently coincidental encounters, and opportunistic concurrence of background, need, and attraction were discernible in the accounts we elicited, significant among them being a sense of destiny, loneliness, life crisis, and acute emergency.

For the Buddhists themselves, such sociological predisposing factors could readily be subsumed under the rubric of karma. The individual was predestined to undergo certain experiences which would prepare him for his encounter with the mystical power of the *daimoku*. Crisis, trauma, broken relationships, illness—all variants of the untoward—were available for retrospective reinterpretation once their role as contributory agencies in opening up for the individual the prospect of realizing buddhahood had been recognized. Given the subsequent encounter with Nichiren's teachings, these various push factors were blessings in disguise, prompting acceptance of a faith which not only relativized past suffering, and which at times transformed it or removed its causes, but which offered a greatly expanded prospect of numerous other benefits far transcending the remedy for whatever incidental problem had pushed the individual towards his new faith.

We asked people about their background circumstances before their encounter with what was then NSUK. Inevitably, for some, that first contact had been casual and they had not felt an immediate and desperate need for spiritual guidance, but others, conspicuously those with problems or anxieties, were open to the offer of a faith to meet just such a need. A casual, yet almost fatalistic, drift into Buddhism was recounted by a 33-year-old musician, who was born in Finland and who had been a university drop-out. He said:

The first encounter was seeing Mr Causton on TV (in the early 1980s perhaps). I did not start practising, but always remembered his sincerity. The second encounter was at a bus stop, when a girl's car broke down in front of me—she told me about Nichiren Shōshū. I did not start practising. The third time was an article in the *Sunday Times* colour supplement in 1985 or 1986. I wrote off for information, and received an introductory magazine, but my fear of 'organized' religion stopped me from starting. The fourth introduction was someone in a night-club told me about it—and I realized that I will meet this practice one way or another, so I might 'just as well' start now—in February, 1988.

Others linked their first contact with immediate benefits. A freelance woman fashion journalist wrote, 'I think that when I first started I was very lonely, and by being a part of NSUK I was kept out and about. I felt that I had a lot of friends and acquaintances.' Most minority religions, in drawing people together who have come to share a common ideology, have the incidental function of providing the individual with company and stable relationships, and SGI-UK, despite its lack of congregational *loci*, is no exception: people have regular opportunities to meet in small or smallish groups, which may provide a warmer and more satisfying social context than would a large and more impersonal congregation. A 29-year-old single male accountancy clerk said, 'Relationships are my stumbling block. Maybe from my youth on, every two years we were living in a different place, always on the move—friends, they disappear. I never kept in contact with anyone. Since practising, I keep contact and enjoy people.' The feeling of being lost was also expressed by a woman opera-singer of 32: 'I was touring with a theatre company and one person was practising. I was impressed with the philosophy. All the things I had always thought were coming together under one roof. I was working as an actress and felt directionless, I didn't know what to do with my life. I was not in a relationship. I felt lost. I was very susceptible to be influenced by my environment . . . I felt powerless.'

Some learned and tried chanting and become convinced before they learned much of the ideology or anything about the organization of SGI. The chanting addressed some persisting need in their lives, and some of them claimed automatic benefit even before knowing anything about the religious rationale for this activity or the principle by which it was to held to operate. So it was with a 35-year-old male musician, who recounted:

I was introduced to Nichiren Buddhism—at least told about it—by a fellow parent at my son's school. She told me she was a Buddhist and I asked a few questions. It rather impressed me. I wasn't looking for it. I was in a rather emotional state at the time—I had split up from my girl-friend, and I was wondering what to do with my life. [The new acquaintance told me] I didn't have to get involved, could practise as much or as little as I wanted. I just started trying it. I did it on my own. For three months, I did it at home on my own, not knowing there was an organization. Very quickly, I got a lot of benefit from it in terms of my emotional state, becoming more positive.

The element of life crisis and the appeal of a means to cope with it were evident in this case, as with others, as well as the idea of inevitability.

A single male accountancy clerk, who had trained as an actor, told us:

Before I was chanting, I was looking for something. I tried 'positive thinking' for six months. I had lived in Bristol before coming to London, living on a friend's floor. I was going nowhere (acting, relationships, drinking). Everything was devoid of joy. I improved myself through positive thinking, drinking stopped. I was more confident and happy. When I was talking to NSUK people . . . the fit was clear. It [positive thinking] was similar to their Buddhism. My friend said, 'What you do is very Buddhist', and I wanted to know about Buddhism.

He went to a meeting after chanting on his own, and continued his account:

When starting practising, I didn't consider it to be a religion. I thought that religion was old-fashioned (singing, ceremony) [but] this practice was functional and real, tangible. It had meaning. I didn't understand what NSUK was at first. NSUK is very practical, purposeful—the benefit, increasing life force. Understanding the theory helps me understand people (I was interested in psychoanalytic stuff)—chanting is physically different, however. I can see it works—improving the picture of myself. Psycho-analysis was my own personal journey into the practice. My life has gradually been pulled to here. There is no coincidence. I practised, I read certain books, I met people. My life was finding Buddhism.

Like the positive thinker, others had looked for solutions to long-term psychic and spiritual problems in other therapies before discovering Nichiren Buddhism. An accountant, who had had a varied career in property maintenance, as a hospital porter, and as a milkman, had such a history:

In 1983, I had a collapse in my life: my company went bankrupt. I had divorced. My children went back to their mother. Why was my life as it was, I kept asking . . . I had a vision to help people and myself. I studied the mind through hypnosis and psychology, 1983–6, qualified as a counsellor, after six months in prison as a bankrupt. I played music for income and studied psychology. In 1986 [I was] practising as a counsellor and hypno-therapist. Basically, I was not satisfied with the training I got. I challenged what I learned: it was not very effective. I did more training in psycho-therapy of various types—family therapy, neuro-linguistic programming. I wrote a self-help programme. I started from the idea that people have the possibility of resolving their own problems. I tried it out, tested the market. It was effective. I had positive feedback. Then I realized one thing was missing: the universe is sound and vibration, fundamentally, everything is vibration. We have to make noise as we change. I met the practice—the noise I was looking for [although] in the first year, I didn't believe one phrase [*Nam-myōhō-renge-kyō*] would resolve all things, but I continued.

Circumstances of chronic or acute crisis were not uncommon in the background of those who accepted the new religion, although this did not apply to everyone. One member, an eye surgeon, recognized that the absence of a crisis in his life was virtually an impediment to his adoption of the practice:

My girl-friend started practising and encouraged me. I was suspicious and hostile . . . Eventually, I did start in 1983. I started to understand that I was not going to be what I wanted to be without chanting. I was a qualified medical doctor and I was not faced with a personal crisis. Since I didn't have [such a crisis] it was difficult to change. I knew . . . during the three years [1983–6] if I didn't practise it wouldn't help me. From knowledge of it to faith was the problem. It was difficult for me to accept that if I wanted to *use* it, I had to *do* it.

Such a considered response without the prompting of unwished-for circumstances was not so frequently reported.

More of those who responded to questions on this subject, whether on questionnaire forms (where there was not so much space for such disquisitions) or in the interviews (where interviewees were free to dwell at length on their life stories), had something more dramatic to tell. A 50-year-old twice-divorced American, who was a largely self-taught musician, declared:

My major domestic problem—I was trying to change my situation of going from one wife to the next. By chanting and NSUK practice, I felt strength. I was looking for something to help me in everyday life. In 1987, I was ready for Nichiren Shōshū. However, I could have used it before. If I had met it and been ready for it I would have stayed with my first wife [who was a Jehovah's Witness]. Within a week [of hearing of Nichiren Shōshū] I started to chant, and I never stopped. I needed something.

The problem of what members almost all referred to as 'relation-ships', by which was principally meant marital or partnership relations, was perhaps the most frequently reported type of crisis. A qualified woman teacher described her situation:

I have three children. Their mother lost custody, and their grandmother brought them up, and I took over as an earth mother. As a family we were very insecure and the children and my husband leaned on me. I wanted to leave my husband and children who depended too much on me. I felt trapped. We were in business [cheap pine antiques]. I had not taught for years. I had no job, no possibilities. I felt trapped again. So I went to church, but it felt alien—a high church, I was from a low church. The church didn't have anything to offer me. I started chanting out of desperation . . . nothing to lose.

Whilst marital disharmony was a frequent theme, others had sought to resolve other problems. Such was the case of a qualified surveyor who had a continuing crisis because he felt he was in the wrong job. He had practised Transcendental Meditation as a way of relieving stress up to the point where he encountered Nichiren's Buddhism: 'I had gone through a lot of stress . . . The stress arose from the fact that I was in the wrong job. I was an estate surveyor . . . for about five years I was dealing with commercial property. I'd chosen the wrong profession. It was changing me and I didn't like it. I didn't feel that I could do well in this work, and it sapped my self-confidence. I was surrounded by teachers who were friends and they all seemed to have much more job fulfilment.' His espousal of Nichiren Buddhism reinforced his decision to take a teacher training course and change his profession. (As will become evident below, SGI members are disproportionately represented in teaching and the caring professions.)

For some there was a whole congeries of interrelated problems. An Austrian hotel receptionist, now separated from her husband, had 'met the practice in 1989. I was living with my husband and was introduced [to chanting] by a French girl who came to rent a room. My life was at a low level. I used to be very fearful . . . I was afraid of talking to people . . . I had guilt feelings about my parents . . . because I didn't relate to them much. I was at a low point in relationships, money, and not wanting to accept myself and not being responsible for my actions.' Another troubled young woman was a French widow who explained: 'I was ill—physically and mentally', following the suicide of her schizophrenic husband. She was immediately affected on hearing the chanting, feeling it to be like the 'end of an exile'. She had 'begun chanting almost at once, not much, about five minutes, after work, but it helped so much. I knew nothing of the background, but it was enough . . . I knew I was going to do it for the rest of my life.' A young male guitar teacher told us:

I was desperate at this time [the time of first meeting NSUK], very unhappy, very alone, and very poor. My psychology was not good. I was very introverted, without purpose and direction. I'd been like it for quite a while—in need of something, if it hadn't been NSUK, it would have been something else. I used to take a lot of drugs—hallucinogens. I'd dropped out of drama school, had an unsuccessful relationship, and poverty breeds unhappiness. My mother sold chanting to me. 'Chant for what you want', she said. I saw it was something that could help: Why not? She'd changed a lot—had a breakdown and I'd seen her brighten up, so I thought, 'Hell, if it works for her, and you don't have to pay a lot of money—why not?' There was extraordinary benefit at once. I was very suspicious and cynical. I put it down to a placebo—as if it was psychosomatically working. I felt good whilst doing it, but even if it . . . sublimated, it suited my purpose. I didn't care—it worked.

Others, who had already toyed with chanting, found that it took a real crisis to bring them to put this philosophy to the test and to take it seriously. A middle-aged singing teacher said:

My middle son started practising five years ago (1986). He took me to meetings, I started chanting but not after the first meeting. I didn't think it was for me. And then, my little world fell apart . . . a long-standing relationship had broken up, and I started to chant because of being so angry. I was afraid of that anger. I chanted to get rid of [it] and that took two or three weeks. Then it was replaced by tremendous grief . . . One day, it reached zenith, reached the bottom while chanting to the blank wall. Then a strange feeling, something inside clicked. I felt light and the grief disappeared . . . A tremendous turning-point. I woke up the next day feeling myself again.

In this case, chanting provided therapy—it was the agency credited with the restoration of equilibrium, the catalyst in coming to terms with changed circumstances which had been an occasion of trauma, the vehicle by which life returned to a sense of normality.

A 42-year-old male community worker, whom we have met before, had recourse to his new faith more seriously when the life of his daughter was at risk:

I was chanting more or less at once, but only faced it with the life-threatening situation at the birth of my daughter. It was a home delivery, but it went badly wrong . . . we had to go to hospital . . . There was a murmer of a Caesarean. Something clicked. I hadn't been doing much chanting just then, and I realized I had to do it. It struck me like a thunderbolt. With hindsight, I came to realize that from the standpoint of

Buddhism and the continuity of life before and after death, and the way relatives are linked through karma, that it was the child's mission to teach her father something important. The experience taught me to take it seriously. I began to learn *gongyō* and go to meetings regularly.

This particular case brings out the relationship which SGI members perceive between untoward events and experiences—what we have labelled as push factors—and the realization of just what Buddhism might do to alter things. For the already nominal Buddhist, such episodes are required not to effect conversion but to reinforce commitment. The trauma or the crisis which comes after the believer has committed himself is no less easily accommodated in the SGI repertoire of explanations than the crisis which prompts a serious first-time conversion. These subsequent crises are equally karmic in origin and have their function in serving to prompt rededication to the practice of those who have in some measure let things slip.

The factors pushing all of these people towards embracing a new system of spiritual therapy differ from one person to another, but all of them accorded a particular relevance to the offer of a new faith. That faith, as some of them acknowledge, and as may be inferred in other cases, might have been something else: indeed, for some, it had been something else—Transcendental Meditation or what was loosely called 'postive thinking'—until a more effective, more convincing, or more intellectually comprehensive religious ideology came along. Given the nature of the traumas which prompted adhesion to this type of Buddhism, it is not surprising that these votaries, whilst continuing to give all credit to their new faith for their personal rehabilitation, should have subsequently come to recognize other themes and motivations to legitimize the continuation of their commitment.

Conversion to Nichiren's Buddhism has some things in common with accounts of conversion to specific Christian persuasions (most emphatic and clear-cut in the case of small sects where commitment tends to be more profound and its onset more climacteric than is the normal experience of believers in mainline churches). Yet SGI conversions are also different in certain respects, and the difference lies in the belief that Nichiren's Buddhism is a practical religion, that chanting works, and can be immediately put to good effect. This pragmatic feature makes SGI a more direct response to every specific crisis, of whatever sort. It claims more immediate and tangible results, and does not depend on a slowly cultivated change of disposition and acquisition of piety. The instantaneity of the effect of chanting, the claim to proof, indicates that conversion to SGI is of a different order from that which Christians expect or experience.

IV

Religious Biographies

RELIGIOUS movements are sometimes represented as being in competition with each other for the attention, time, energy, and perhaps also the resources, of members of the public. The exclusivistic stance of almost all religious organizations (a few eclectic cult movements excepted) promotes the idea that religious bodies are essentially rivals, each claiming the monopoly of truth, and each demanding that believers commit themselves to only one organization. The keen proselytizing policies of many of the less orthodox sects reinforce these impressions. In one sense, these propositions are true, but it is also the case that, for a high, if indeterminate, proportion of the religiously committed members of the general public, there is little if any question of the surrender of their current ideologies and affiliations in favour of others. In a society where only a minority have any sort of religious attachment, it is probably always chiefly among the unattached that new movements expect to make their converts. This appears to have been the experience of SGI.

It is clear from our evidence that, in the main, Nichiren Buddhism in Britain has not been in direct competition for followers with the major Christian churches or with other religious bodies. Fully 76 per cent of our respondents said that they had not belonged to any religious organization before they joined what was then NSUK. Thus, Buddhism did not wean them away from a former allegiance but rather acquired a following which was free of other commitments. Even those who had a religious background of some kind appear to have lapsed or abandoned that faith before finding Nichiren Buddhism. However, just over half the respondents did consider themselves to have been religious persons before they joined NSUK, while 47 per cent said that before becoming Nichiren Buddhists they were not religious.

Of the minority who had previously belonged to a Christian

church, 8 per cent of the entire sample had been Roman Catholics; only 6 per cent had been Church of England, and 3 per cent had been Nonconformists. Two per cent of the total said that they had belonged to a Christian church without specifying of what kind, which in itself might suggest a somewhat relaxed form of affiliation. Our sample included former Jews (2 per cent) and former members of other new religious movements (2 per cent). The remainder of those with religious affiliations were Greek Orthodox, Muslims, or types of Buddhist other than Nichiren Shōshū Buddhism. From this distribution, it would appear that, in general, SGI members were not previously religious seekers exploring the spiritual world. The minority who were in some sort of religious fellowship do not appear to have constituted a category of particularly avid spirituality. On this evidence, it would not appear at least that this new religion represented any sort of proselytizing threat to members of other faiths, despite the notional commitment in Sōka Gakkai generally to *shakubuku*.

Neither the responses by questionnaire nor the information elicited in interviews included any accounts of sudden conversion from an established Christian fellowship. As will be seen below, those who were religiously active in the period immediately before their encounter with Nichiren Buddhism were most typically engaged in one or another form of Eastern religious practice. Of those with some background in the Christian tradition, the story that they told was of a faith seen as inadequate and left behind long before the meeting with Nichiren Buddhism. Curiously, the most detailed accounts came from members born elsewhere than in England. One such instance was of a divorced woman prep school teacher. She said:

I was brought up a Catholic in France, and went through all Catholic rituals up to 18 years. Then I left home and came to England. Ten years ago, I dropped my religion, since I did not feel that Christianity was part of me . . . I didn't want to be Catholic or Christian because I was disillusioned. I did fervently pray on many occasions, but somehow they were not answered. So I was disappointed. In terms of the way I was brought up, it was difficult to let my Catholic upbringing go: guilt and suffering I felt was ingrained in the Catholic faith. I used to believe that one had to suffer to be able to understand joy—otherwise it is against God's wishes, which gives guilt. Buddhism teaches taking 100 per cent responsibility for your life . . . instead of blaming yourself or others. As a Catholic, I was very good at externalizing it; it was either my fault—beating myself—or that of another person, and I became critical of him or her. Christianity externalizes blame onto yourself or others, which makes you angry with yourself or others.

For this young woman, Buddhism was a type of psychic liberation, and even though it imposed the apparently severe requirement that the individual take responsibility for his life, in practice that demand, as we have already noted, is not accompanied by any specific strictures or sanctions.

Another formerly Catholic woman saw things in much the same way. She was a hotel receptionist, 29 at the time of the interview, who had separated from her husband. She recalled how, in Austria, she was

brought up in a strict Roman Catholic way. It never appealed to me—people's attitudes were so false . . . At 16, I lived away from home in a covent [school] for three years, where I was never happy. You couldn't relate to people. There was no support from the sisters. I chant for specific goals, but guilt comes along from my Roman Catholic upbringing—it doesn't fit it. Buddhism is much more flexible and not so stiff. It's a very old teaching, but you can relate to it as if it was written today. In Christianity you don't have much say in it. [It] is like a dead hand . . . Like my mother—she's devoted, she prays, but she's so unhappy, and it spreads out to all members of the family. The essentials may not be wrong, but it needs revitalizing. There is too much authoritarianism. The sisters were just so unhappy—committed to things they didn't want.

Protestants had recollections which they found no less disturbing. A 39-year-old male teacher in a school of vocational therapy recounted that he was:

brought up in Tennessee in a Baptist tradition, not quite evangelical . . . In my last year in high school and first year in College, I was a strong Christian. I did two years in Bible College in 1970–2, but coincidentally I was reading about other religions . . . I became aware of the narrowness of the Baptist faith. I realized I couldn't continue in this college. I said in class that Jesus Christ might be a reincarnation of the Buddha. Nobody wanted to talk about that. I was kicked out of college because I was sleeping with my girl-friend. Then I went to the University of Tennessee—but I didn't enter in religious activities at that time at all, I experimented with drugs.

By the time that he was introduced to Nichiren Buddhism, he had 'done meditation and yoga . . . I had done breathing yoga in University because I was interested in a drug-free technique of

altering consciousness'. Another American, 50 years old, who was
twice divorced and who ran his own band, was once 'a Baptist, then
a Jehovah's Witness. They didn't give me benefit. In Nichiren
Buddhism, I can apply and get benefit. I am in control of my own
life and I find my own qualities. Christianity was a one-day-a-week
religion: as a Baptist, I went to church only on Sunday. Buddhism
is every day.'

A third American, a woman business analyst with a degree in
mathematics, had come to Buddhism via a circuitous route:

I practised Christianity [in] the Reorganized Church of Jesus Christ of
Latter-day Saints, which taught [that there was] no salvation outside the
Church, yet there were some good people outside. My church was very rigid
(drinking rules and such). In 1971, Transcendental Meditation—I was
looking for balance, for a daily rhythm. It helped me feel good—computer
work is very stressful. It was more powerful than praying to God. I did
Transcendental Meditation for a year. I also met Gurdjieff teaching in 1974,
and was part of the Gurdjieff Society from 1974 to 1977. I was against
organized religion—protocol, ceremony. A lady I met in the Gurdjieff group
was starting chanting. She said 'Try it!' When she chanted I felt sick—I was
against trying it. However, I felt the strength. I was searching, but blocked.

As these cases make apparent, the search for a therapeutic faith
was one strong element in drawing some people from the Christian
tradition towards the Buddhism of Sōka Gakkai. In some cases, it
may have been less strictly a spiritual search than the attraction of
a pattern of religious practice that offered distinct therapeutic benefit
for people who had found that their original religious affiliation had
offered them very little of that kind, even when they were seriously
committed. For such people, there had often been other stopping
places on the way. A middle-aged unemployed woman painter
recounted her experience, which embraced personal trauma and
sustained spiritual search:

My sister introduced me [to Nichiren Buddhism]. My [second] marriage
went wrong, and she suggested that I chant. It had a remarkable effect. I
got confidence in myself and . . . optimism. Irish nuns had brought me up.
I got guilt feelings and thought I was condemned when my [second]
marriage broke down. I practised Catholicism until 25 years old. I was
committed. Married, I had problems with birth control. I went to mass out
of fear. Then, I said, 'If I go to hell, I will risk it.' Fundamentally, my spirit
was dead. For three years I didn't practise religion. Then I found Subud.
I needed something. I didn't like what they were doing—'letting go'. I did

it for two and a half years, but people were snappy after meetings—not happy. I left it—but I had this fear on leaving it. At 33 I fell in love with a man, I couldn't understand this passion: to understand it I went into Jungian analysis. I was in the worst period of my life . . . but became pathologically jealous. I became ill, on drugs, and faced severe depression. Then hospitalized for three weeks. One month before this, I had started chanting . . . it brought the real crisis. I was inferior. I lost my identity. Buddhism saved me. I had tried to kill myself.

The association of marital breakdown, subsequent psychological disorder, and then the search for a spiritual interpretation or alleviation of the situation recurred with other members. A very similar sequence of events had occurred to another woman who recounted her past:

My marriage had broken up and I had a baby of eighteen months. I was looking for a religion. I read about Tibetan Buddhism when 19 or 20. My understanding was [of] nirvana remote from life . . . this depressed me. I went to a spiritual church in my twenties. I got involved in spiritualist meditation, invoking a spirit to come into you. In my early twenties, I met someone interested in witchcraft and Egyptian magic. I got interested in that. I also took drugs (marijuana) . . . and a book on Jung—his autobiography —saved me going down the road with drugs. I began to read the books of Jung, and went for eighteen months in psychoanalysis. None [of my previous religions] made me happy. I could get into discussions in my former religions, but I was left empty, not satisfied.

Although Nichiren Buddhism does not present itself directly and primarily as a therapeutic cult, in the way in which Transcendental Meditation or yoga offer themselves, emphasizing much more its specific ideology, none the less, the claim to provide people with confidence and life force works as a remedial agent. Among the practical benefits which SGI claims for its adherents, mental resilience is by no means the least, as these brief biographical accounts attest, and it is perhaps unsurprising that a significant minority of its devotees had found their way to it after experimenting with both psychotherapeutic systems as well as spiritual or quasi-spiritual cults. A 32-year old male dancer had done Transcendental Meditation for two years, but had given it up and 'was looking for deeper understanding of my life'. His brother 'had tried to commit suicide [which] was the catalyst. I also needed spiritual nourishment. I felt I was bored with life. I was interested in Zen, but I never contacted it.' He was introduced to Nichiren Buddhism by a

colleague (a dancer) and started at once, and found it easy: 'I was
ready, prepared, searching.' Transcendental Meditation had also
been the way in to Sōka Gakkai Buddhism for the 33-year-old ex-
surveyor turned teacher whom we have already encountered. As he
dilated on his own pilgrim's progress:

I got into Transcendental Meditation when I was working for a small firm
of surveyors . . . I couldn't settle, and after an awful day, a slip came
through the letter-box which read, 'Are you feeling stressed?' It was all to
do with meditating, so I went along to a lecture . . . and the people were
really nice. Among them I did not feel lonely as one had felt before. It was
a comfort. I gave up Transcendental Meditation after beginning Nichiren
Buddhism . . . I had had a lot of contact with other people in Transcendental
Meditation, and I regenerated a lot of self-confidence during that time when
I felt uneasy at my job as a surveyor.

Another teacher, a man in his early forties at the time of his
acceptance of SGI, had also explored a wider range of therapeutic
spirituality, without, it seems, having had the profound sort of
personal crisis related by some others. After relinquishing his
inherited Welsh Methodism on moving to England, he 'hadn't
joined anything else. I'd tried to do simple meditation. I'd done "the
drug bit" and the "acid bit" in the 1960s. Krishnamurti I'd found,
and still find, interesting . . . he was saying the right things, very
down to earth and unpretentious. He exuded something special, but
I wasn't looking for a guru: "the Maharishi bit" I rejected because
of the guru factor, although the meditation itself may be OK.' This
was a modest spiritual pilgrimage compared to others. The case of
the 26-year-old guitar teacher is not dissimilar:

I had no previous religious experience. Before, I never liked anybody.
People put me off . . . I practised yoga and Tai-Chi, but I didn't see them
as religions. I practised psycho-cybernetics, to put yourself into an Alpha
state. I had had huge benefits at school and I thought chanting was like
that—but with chanting you change fundamentally—psycho-cybernetics
deals only with symptoms. Chanting you never go backwards: other things
deal only with peripheral activity—Buddhism deals with real causes . . . I
really didn't want NSUK. I was looking for a practice, I'd tried yoga, Tai-
Chi. My grandmother [a Scientologist] is impressed by the change in my
life, and she's been told [by the Scientologists] not to have anything to do
with me—but she does. She approved, and you don't have to spend the sort
of money which she spends [on Scientology] to improve your life . . . She
says what I am doing is good. You should support other people in their

practice, and I try to encourage her in Scientology, but Scientologists never get to the end—there are always more courses.

Although a number of members had had some acquaintance with one or another modern therapeutic movement or a version of positive thinking, understandably, far more had had experience of Christianity, even if only by virtue of having been brought up in an (at least nominally) Christian household. Christianity had once been, or might even have remained, an option for those respondents who were consciously seeking spiritual guidance. We therefore asked both those whom we interviewed and the respondents to the questionnaire about the way in which they perceived the differences between Christianity and their present faith. Not all of them professed to know very much about Christianity, but others, of course, had had first-hand experience. One 29-year-old graduate declared:

[I] had not been satisfied with Christianity as it had been presented to me. In Christianity there is enlightenment through suffering. [It] did not encourage taking responsibility in one's life. In Christianity, there is the last judgement, you can't escape—and criticism and guilt go with it . . . there are the ten commandments, and rules and authority. Faith implies a God, an authority figure outside of oneself. In Nichiren Shōshū, authority is always yourself . . . the three practices are guide-lines for enlightenment, not rules which carry punishment because they are rules.

A married woman nurse entertained essentially similar conceptions of Christianity as a rule-bound religion. She said, 'I had a cousin confirmed in church last week—I went along to support her. There was something they said that made me realize that in Buddhism you are your own boss—no one says anything if you drink too much. In church, they read out you shouldn't do this and shouldn't do that . . . they are relying on something outside themselves to sort out their lives. The church has moral attitudes: in Buddhism you take responsibility for yourself.'

Two features of Christianity were identified again and again by respondents as points at variance with their conception of reality, and as items which showed Christianity in an inferior light: they were the required belief in an external deity as an object of worship, and the inculcation of guilt through moral rules. One woman, a teacher in prisons, saw the difference in the fact that Buddhism had 'no external object of worship' (her emphasis being on the fact of externality). 'Guilt' she continued, 'is typical of Christianity. In Buddhism you don't have it . . . you may be responsible, yes, but to carry round guilt is not constructive. I am still struggling with it since I was brought up as a Christian.' This respondent and the Catholics, the comments of two of whom were cited above, made the inculcation in childhood of a sense of guilt the strongest reason for their subsequent disenchantment with Christianity. Of course, their Christian upbringing was now seen retrospectively after the discovery of a very different religion, the theodicy of which eliminated the idea of guilt as such, and taught the importance of self-respect. The reappraisal of Christianity and, in particular, the deprecation of the notion of guilt might have been a reinterpretation of experience learned since taking up Nichiren Buddhism. Certainly it was a frequently echoed theme. [1]

The woman who was an unemployed painter stressed more the other focus of criticism: she maintained that because, in Christianity, 'God is outside us, so we are inferior. We have to please him, to plead to him, and then he is kind to us. You are a child: God is parent, and as long as you are good children it's OK. Buddhism puts it *in* you, you yourself are responsible.' The eye surgeon had

turned away from Christianity. There was war in Northern Ireland, violence was public, general, and random. I was struck by the inability of religious teachings to address it. In Christianity, to be effective you need to believe in a God or a Christ, which implies relativity between the human and the almighty: they are unequal. In Buddhism, all people can manifest Buddhahood—you don't have to go through a higher person to achieve it. It is a humanistic religion, better than a theistic religion.

For others, a powerful claim of Nichiren Buddhism was never far from their advocacy of their religion, namely that it was a practical religion, a religion which could be tested and proved by the concrete and psychic benefits which sustained commitment to it produced.

[1] The image of Christianity as a religion of guilt is, of course, a perception not peculiar to Sōka Gakkai members. Guilt has been seen as a significant and typical characteristic of occidental culture in earlier centuries. See Jean Delumeau, who wrote, 'To the oriental religion of "tranquility", exemplified in Hinduism and Buddhism, is opposed more than ever the religion of "anxiety" typical of the Occident . . . No civilization has ever given such weight—and at such a price—to culpability and shame as did the Occident from the thirteenth century to the eighteenth.' Jean Delumeau, *Le Péché et la peur: La Culpabilisation en Occident: XIIIe–XVIIIe siècle* (Paris: Fayard, 1983), 9–10 (authors' translation). See J. G. Arapura, *Religion as Anxiety and Tranquility* (The Hague: Mouton, 1975).

In this it was seen to differ from Christianity, which, for this population of young and early middle-aged people, often appeared remote from the everyday realities of contemporary life and society. The community social worker with two university degrees expressed a typical opinion: 'I don't regard myself as a religious person: "religiosity" [implies] someone wrapped in "holier than thou" ideas. I can't understand that. I'm married. I've children, bills to pay—and none of that [Christianity] relates to it. But I see myself as living my life in a more expansive way, based on clear teachings [of Buddhism], a doctrine that stands up in theory and practice. It's part of everyday life.' The young guitar teacher made similar points:

There is a need for Christian experience, but it's not a useful practice, it doesn't seem to work. Christians don't seem happy or fulfilled . . . You can't equate God and Buddhahood—they just have to realize inner compassion. Christians make compassion into pity. They talk of suffering a lot . . . they flagellate themselves and don't see suffering as a way of growing, the pain of having to open your life, revolution of character. Suffering from practice is always healthy, a source of value which lessens the suffering. The Christian attitude is just endless suffering—you are sinful and bad, and it's up to God to forgive us. Christianity might be seen as a precursor or a provisional Buddhism. I know for a fact that chanting is more useful than going to church.

Although we stimulated the comparison of Buddhism with Christianity by asking direct questions about members' perceptions of the two, there was little doubt that for many of them the contrast between these two faiths was something already well recognized, and may indeed have formed the substance of what many had felt the need to draw out during the local group, district, or chapter meetings. Even though a large proportion had had relatively little direct experience of sustained involvement with a Christian church, others had, and could draw both on that and on the general perception of the majority faith of British society as commonly and publicly represented. Any minority religion has to be understood by its votaries in some relation to the religious norm, and, in this case, that invited comparison both with the general secularity of British society, and with the major Christian churches and their teachings. Minorities need to justify themselves, and their constituents acquire a heightened sense of the major differences of doctrine and orientation.

As we have seen, almost half of the members did not consider that they had experienced a religious past. Of the remainder, more than half said that they had in some degree a Christian background, amounting to some 28 per cent of the total sample. The majority of these, constituting 19 per cent of the sample, had belonged to a Christian church of one sort or another. The rest, just a quarter of all our respondents, defined themselves as having been religious without, however, having had a specific religious attachment to any type of Christian church. Among these, some 8 per cent of the entire sample indicated that before joining SGI they had been searching for meaning, or, as some put it, searching for truth. Six per cent simply suggested that they had maintained a certain interest in religion, whilst 4 per cent declared that they had believed in a life force and in a sense of intrinsic order which they perceived as religious. Taking all these claims together, one out of four members had in the past, been at least notionally open to a religious interpretation of life, even if they had not committed themselves to any sort of religious affiliation. Of course, it is possible to read the answers of some 25 per cent as saying that since they were now NSUK members, so they might well be considered to have been searching for meaning and truth before their encounter with the movement. That is perhaps to over-rationalize the situation, and the evidence suggests that, apart from the 28 per cent who claimed to have had a religious background (of whom some 24 per cent of the entire sample had belonged to one or another religious organization, or more than one), the remainder were most probably neutral or indifferent towards religion. Clearly, it may be said *ex post facto* that they were all open to religion, in the sense that they had been converted to Sōka Gakkai Buddhism, but on their own assessment, half of them had not engaged in any sort of religious practice or belief in their pre-SGI days. Thus, whilst some of our respondents acknowledged that they had been seekers searching for religious meaning, at least half of them had not been in that position, thus lending support to the contention that seekership is by no means a necessary precondition for conversion.[2]

We can obtain some idea, in respect of sex and age, of just which members constituted the 47 per cent who, on their own definition, were not religious before joining SGI. Since more women than men claimed to have had a Christian background, the men comprised the

---

[2] This is the contention, in refutation of the Lofland–Stark model of conversion, made by Snow and Phillips, 'The Lofland–Stark Conversion Model', 438.

greater part of the previously unreligious. Housewives tended to have belonged to a religious body more so than was the case with working women, who, if they claimed to be at all religious, were more likely to claim no more than to have had a generally Christian background. Above all, however, it was the young people[3] who said that they did not belong: 60 per cent of those who were 30 years old or younger, as against 29 per cent of those who were 45 years old or older—that is those born before the end of the Second World War.

Previous Encounters with Other Forms of Buddhism

Nichiren Buddhism is a distinctive form of Mahayana Buddhism, as we have already noted, and in certain important respects it negates central features of the Buddhism of the Hinayana tradition. It appeared possible, however, that some members might have undergone some previous informal and unintended socialization before the encounter with NSUK, in the sense that they were already acquainted with some of the cardinal principles of Buddhist thought or practice, and had already some idea of the scheme of salvation of that general tradition. We asked members about the experience of Buddhism prior to being introduced to Nichiren Shōshū Buddhism. A surprisingly significant proportion, some 38 per cent, indicated that they had encountered Buddhism of one variety or another before joining NSUK. Twelve per cent had some acquaintance with multiple forms of Buddhism, of which Zen and Tibetan Buddhism were the most frequently mentioned. Four per cent had had contacts only with Tibetan Buddhism, and some 12 per cent only with Zen. The remaining 10 per cent mostly referred simply to Buddhism in general, without specifying the type, but a minority referred to Hinayana Buddhism or were acquainted with the British movement the Friends of the Western Buddhist Order.

Understandably, perhaps, those who had previously been acquainted with other forms of Buddhism were not particularly those who had defined themselves as being unreligious. Nor were they those members who had previously belonged to a Christian church. The people who had had some experience of Buddhism tended to be

[3] Stuart's tau-c: 0.13.

those who claimed no more than a general Christian background, and who held themselves to have been 'open to religion', that is, those who had defined themselves as religiously oriented but who had no religious affiliation. These associations were evident in both the older and the younger sections of our sample (as divided between those born in or before 1950, relative to those born in 1951 or after). Educational background also had an impact in this regard. University students had a greater likelihood of having encountered Buddhism, and this was particularly the case with those who were studying for higher degrees—that is, those who continued their studies after the age of 22. Again, this association held for both the older and younger sections of the membership. Consequently, it may be said that, whatever their age category, previous religious orientation and involvement, and educational background, 'predispose' people for contacts with this Buddhism. The encounter with Buddhism is also reflected in the occupational structure of the membership. More of those who belonged to the caring professions—nurses, doctors, teachers, for example—and those whose work was in the graphic or performing arts, had had previous experience of Buddhism than had others in the movement. Since Buddhism of any kind remains an exotic religion for the British, and one which is known largely through literature and in presentations that generally emphasize the intellectual aspects of this faith, it is not surprising that it should be those whose studies or work entailed intellectual, aesthetic, and in some respects psychological concerns who had become acquainted with it in one form or another.

To what extent an earlier or a deeper acquaintance with other varieties of Buddhism promoted commitment to NSUK is not easily assessed, nor is it possible to appraise the depth of such knowledge in the various instances. Two somewhat divergent responses emerged from interviews. A male teacher of occupational therapy entertained some misgivings, committed as he was to the movement. He said:

I retain a sceptical attitude. I know more of the history of Buddhism, and I see how Nichiren fits in. He is profound but at the same time a maverick. He talks about compassion and wisdom—Shakyamuni Buddha takes another view. 'Who was this man?' I ask myself. I also read former Mahayana texts. He [Nichiren] is openly critical of them. He says that he is superior to their teaching. 'Is this arrogance or not?' I ask myself. But more and more I can identify with the guidance and writings of Ikeda, past presidents, and other

:rs. A past leader says, 'When doing *gongyō*, a common
.ime without beginning, and a Buddha (embodied in the
facing one another.' Indeed, it is a central feeling when doing
.ing proves it—it is an intuitive feeling about my life, about the
y entity has no beginning and no end.

    acquaintance with Buddhism raises doubts, lack of
.on for the metaphysical and philosophical side of the
  did not make matters easier for a male musician who had
.ced and been less than enchanted by the doctrines and
.s of the Friends of the Western Buddhism Order. He
.ed that although he acknowledged the simplicity of the
.ctice [of Nichiren Buddhism] he had doubts about the teachings:
they were

so unbelievably complex. Reincarnation I find difficult. Nichiren says you
must be concerned for the next life, but I find that hard—I'm concerned
with this one. The mystical side is the main difficulty, but my knowledge
is limited . . . Nichiren is so steeped in the Buddhist and Eastern tradition—
a study aspect. I can have faith in it, but more, not as an absolute belief,
but as a suspension of judgement. The only way that I can find out is doing
the practice and proving it within my life now. I take it all on board, but
if you questioned me deeply, I wouldn't be able to answer convincingly.

Acquaintance with Other Eastern Religions

New religious movements have often been said to operate in a cultic
milieu. That is to say that those who join such organizations are
frequently people who are acquainted with a variety of such religions,
and who move relatively easily from one to another, or who have
'dabbled' in different exotic philosophies. The upsurge of new
movements in Western countries in the 1960s certainly promoted a
measure of experimentation in spiritual and religious activities,
particularly among younger people. Many new movements were
prepared to take up opportunities to present themselves alongside
others which might in some sense be their rivals in competing for
the attention of a clientele, and did so at such occasions as the annual
festivals of spirit, mind, and body held in London. Nichiren Shōshū
had not participated in such occasions, and the tendency of this
particular form of Buddhism was much more exclusivistic than was
the case with a wide variety of human potential, therapeutic, and

New Age organizations that were prominent in the cultic milieu. Nichiren himself had excoriated rival Buddhist teachings, and the principle of *shakubuku* rests on the assumption that other beliefs are a form of poison. Despite this orientation, however, in certain respects Nichiren Buddhism had some general characteristics in common with some other new movements, and it was a matter of some interest to see to what extent those who had joined NSUK had any acquaintance with other Eastern religions. We have come across a number of specific instances already in the quotations from members' accounts of their spiritual biographies, but it is important to explore the statistical significance of such encounters with exotic belief systems.

Sixty-one per cent of our respondents declared that they had had no experience of other Eastern religions, while 20 per cent had encountered one or another of them, and 11 per cent had had some acquaintance with one of the other new religious movements. Of those who had some experience of Eastern religions, 11 per cent of the total sample claimed acquaintance with more than one such body, whilst 4 per cent specifically named Hinduism; 2 per cent mentioned Taoism, and 1 per cent named Islam. Those who had encountered Eastern religions tended, not surprisingly, to be those with a university education.

Of those who had some involvement with new religions, 3 per cent of the entire sample referred to a multiplicity of movements. The one most frequently mentioned was Transcendental Meditation (of the Maharishi) by 2 per cent, followed by yoga, Hare Krishna, Sufism, and the Divine Light Mission, which, taken together, were named by 4 per cent of the sample. Some members had experience of other movements: Subud; I'Ching; Sai Baba; Krishnamurti; Rama Krishna Vedanta; the Unification Church; Gurdjieffism; and the Baha'i Faith were each mentioned once; while Bhagwan Rajneeshism was mentioned twice. The incidence of acquaintance with these movements is perhaps higher than might be expected for the general population, but is none the less not exeptionally high. Many of the members had expressed their openness to spiritual experience, and many of these various new movements were active, conspicuous, and eager for people to join. Given that it was evident, by virtue of their subsequent willingness to explore Nichiren Shōshū, that these people were receptive to new religious experimentation, the incidence of their previous experiences is perhaps not to be seen as surprising.

TABLE 8. *Those who had encountered an Eastern religion (including Buddhism) before converting to NSUK* (%)

Previous religious orientation	No	Yes	Total[a]
Belonged to a Christian church	69	31	100 (97)
Was not religious	60	40	100 (293)
Had a religious background and/or was a seeker	35	65	100 (224)

[a] Actual numbers in brackets.

Taking as one category those members who have encountered either other forms of Buddhism and/or another Eastern religion before their conversion to Nichiren's Buddhism, we may discover whether our findings about the encounter with another type of Buddhism are confirmed (Table 8). What emerges is that it is particularly those who, whilst having had a religious background, did not belong to any religious organization, and those who were searching for a religious orientation, who had encountered Eastern religions and new movements. In this category, more men than women had had such experiences. The findings are also related to the level of education. It was those who had pursued university studies who had become acquainted with some form of Eastern religion. The case is the same with those who declared themselves not to have been previously religious. The impact of education holds, as we have already seen for Buddhism, for younger as well as for older members.

An Interest in Things Japanese?

Sōka Gakkai is not only a religious movement of Japanese origin, it remains markedly Japanese in its philosophy, in the style of its practice, and in the location of its central organization. Despite the schism between the Nichiren Shōshū priesthood and the lay Sōka Gakkai organization, Japan is also the location of its sacred sanctuary, which was its place of pilgrimage. The very designation of the movement—as Nichiren Shōshū, at the time when all our respondents joined it, and subsequently as Sōka Gakkai—was, and remains, Japanese. Members use many Japanese concepts as part of their religious vocabulary, and the Japanese-language expressions for these. Above all, the invocation used in chanting is in Japanese, and *gongyō* is recited according to Japanese phonetics. There has been no attempt to Anglicize either. All of this gives the movement its distinctly Japanese flavour, and this is not at all diminished by the encouragement that is given to national groups to express themes drawn from their national cultural traditions in the various festivals and artistic performances that the movement so vigorously promotes, and in which virtually all members find a part to play.

It was, therefore, a pertinent question to ask to what extent the membership were drawn towards a Japanese religion because they were already interested in one or another aspect of Japanese culture. It was conceivable that the movement might have a special attraction for those who knew something about Japan and who were already admirers of the Japanese people, culture, or way of life. We were aware, of course, that at least a few members had become such by virtue of having been converted by an already committed Japanese spouse (usually a wife), but these instances accounted for only a tiny minority of the British membership. Our question was a more general one, seeking to discover the incidence of any one of a range of interests in things Japanese which might have been the path to a Japanese variant of Buddhism.

In response to our question, 55 per cent declared that things Japanese had held no appeal for them before their conversion to NSUK. Of those who had entertained some interest, most of them, 38 per cent of respondents, had had an aesthetic interest, while only 7 per cent had been interested in non-aesthetic aspects of Japanese culture. The non-aesthetic interest focused particularly on Japanese cuisine, although there was some mention of Japanese business methods. Some had been attracted by Japanese mentality, life-style, and history. But the dominant concerns of those who acknowledged a previous interest in things Japanese had been in the aesthetic—in painting, sculpture and calligraphy, and in the performing arts, music, dance, theatre, and films. They indicated less concern with literature and the martial arts. Some suggested that their previous interests had also extended to aspects of material culture such as ceramics, architecture, fashion, costume, interior design, and gardens. Although these interests were randomly spread across the membership, a somewhat higher incidence of interest in specific subjects was evident among those who were professionally trained in particular areas. Thus, those occupied or trained in the performing arts or the graphic arts had developed aesthetic interests in the Japanese manifestations of those same activities.

We have no means of knowing with any degree of certainty whether the incidence of interest in Japanese culture and life-style was greater among would-be SGI members than among the population at large but, from general observation, it seems unlikely that the British public would match the 45 per cent of the Nichiren Buddhists. Even Japanese films, which might be thought to have a wider following than Japanese dance, music, theatre, or paintings, appear to have remained a distinctly minority taste in Britain, and have hardly had a following of almost half the population. On the face of the evidence, one might surmise that concern for things Japanese might indicate a greater openness to Japanese religion. The effect might be further enhanced by the emphasis which Sōka Gakkai has placed on cultural expression and its encouragement of the performing and graphic arts which, whilst not exclusively Japanese, has given wider opportunity for members to become acquainted with those aspects of Japanese culture.

Nichiren Buddhism was not perceived by members to be a specifically Japanese religion. If taxed, most members would probably have put less emphasis on its inherited Japanese tradition and style than on its universal aspirations as a religion for all mankind in the coming age of *kōsen-rufu*. Yet, for some, it was already too Japanese. One woman interviewee said, 'Nichiren Buddhism is Japanese Buddhism. How will it be translated to an English way of life? It is becoming international. I find Nichiren Shōshū has Japanese glamour to it and cultural values. Some I like—attention to detail, commitment to family. Others, I dislike . . . They don't seem to regard the individual too much. Individuality has no real place. I find this Japanese ethos difficult. It is a different culture . . . I feel it is not Buddhism.' A 32-year-old male dancer found himself 'suspicious of the [male and female] divisions. I thought it was sexist, coming from Japanese Sōka Gakkai. We have to grow and establish our own identity. There is too much Japanese cultural influence.'

Some of the features of SGI that occasioned criticism from members were sometimes identified as Japanese. There were additional reservations about the separate male and female divisions, which were seen as distinctly oriental. The policy of putting into distinctive uniforms the corps of young men and women who engaged in service activities was attributed to Japanese influence. Nor was the Japanese concept of master–disciple relationship a cultural trait that all British participants found easy to accept, and some of our respondents were less than enthusiastic about the esteem which this principle conferred on their president, Daisaku Ikeda.

These were certainly minority opinions, and the movement in Britain, as elsewhere in Western countries, has done much to adapt its style of operation to British culture. Throughout the world SGI devotes time and resources to the promotion of festivals of music and dance, and sometimes of drama and gymnastics, and these occasions take on, and indeed celebrate, local cultural styles and colour. The British movement has found for itself a historical and once aristocratic country estate as the location of its headquarters, and its leader is a British national, whilst in the United States and France the leaders, although of Japanese origin, have taken out the citizenship of their adopted countries.[4] If SGI has not yet become fully indigenized in Western societies, it might be recalled that the movement has as yet a short history of no more than thirty years' operation in these cultures, which is not to be compared with the centuries which the religions of the Middle East have had to become thoroughly acculturated to the diverse locales to which they were disseminated.

---

[4] In answer to a member who asked how SGI could be truly international when so many of those with responsibility in the organization were Japanese (adding that even the Public Relations Department was very Japanese in 'almost creating a personality cult' of Mr Ikeda) the NSUK General Director said, *inter alia*, 'SGI . . . links organization in 115 countries, each of which conducts its activities for human revolution and *kōsen-rufu* independently, in accordance with the laws, customs and culture of each country . . . Buddhism teaches us to tolerate differences we see in others . . . the same should apply in a collective sense in terms of relations between nations and races. For example, the way we, as NSUK, are able to influence and change British society for the better must inevitably follow the priorities in which our unhappy "collective karma" is revealed to us . . . Hence, we have no right to make judgements on what is right and wrong for the Japanese. We should concern ourselves, instead with what needs changing in ourselves and in our own country. It is in our own country that we have to work for *kōsen-rufu*, not Japan . . . It is inevitable . . . that Japanese-initiated public relations . . . follow the culture and customs of Japan. What the questioner views, from a Western veiwpoint, as a personality cult, is in fact a manifestation of Japanese culture generally.' Richard Causton, *UK Express*, 249 (March 1992), 32–3.

V

The Members, their Families, and their Friends

In an increasingly individualistic society, new religions generally win converts singly rather than as whole families. Whilst long-settled sectarian bodies are most typically composed of families and some-times of extended kinship networks, as intermarriage and endogamy have led to a cumulative process of internal recruitment, new movements and movements devoted to vigorous proselytizing have a much higher proportion of individuals who have no kinsfolk in the movement. The new religious movements active in Britain since the 1960s have all recruited principally by converting one person at a time, and quite frequently the relatives of these members have not followed them into the new fellowship. Sometimes they have disapproved and actively opposed the adoption of a new religious persuasion by a family member, and it has been a commonplace, particularly in movements like the Unification Church and the Krishna Consciousness movement, for parents to have vigorously opposed the conversion of their offspring.[1] Nichiren Shōshū is a very different organization from either of these, most conspicuously in not drawing its members into separated communities, and its recruitment has been generally among people who, at the time of their conversion, were older than has typically been the case for Moonies or Hare Krishna people. None the less, the adoption of a religion with beliefs and, more conspicuously, practices so alien from indigenous Christianity or Judaism might well be expected to occasion disquiet from unconvinced family and friends.

The prospect of engendering opposition is perhaps heightened in

[1] For discussion of various aspects of parental opposition to conversion of their young people in these and other new religious movements, see David G. Bromley and James T. Richardson (eds.), *The Brainwashing/Deprogramming Controversy: Sociological, Psychological, Legal, and Historical Perspectives* (Lewiston, NY: Edwin Mellen Press, 1983). For an overview of the problem and the ways in which it might be addressed, see Barker, *New Religious Movements*.

the case of SGI because of the home-centred character of the movement. As we have noted, the movement is not congregationally organized, and not only individual worship but also the movement's meetings take place in believers' homes, as part of their domestic life. Communication among members about movement activities requires much telephoning and, in consequence, the family members of a convert are likely to find themselves not infrequently reminded of the 'deviant' religious adherence of their kinsman. Since the central practice is chanting—and chanting is what members mean when they speak, not so much of someone as being 'religious' or 'converted', but of their 'practising'—commitment to Nichiren Buddhism becomes a very demonstrable activity within sight and, particularly, within sound of others in the immediate household. The believer's practice can scarcely be concealed, or even kept quiet. If there is opposition, religious performance is likely to stimulate it, and performance is specifically what the believer is committed to undertaking.

The question posed is the extent to which SGI members experienced support for their involvement from their family and friends. Clearly, where family members also practise, whether by conversion or because the family was founded on the basis of already shared religious convictions, the individual member has all the advantage of home support, but, as we have indicated, this is very much the exception in new movements, and where there are religious differences, opposition is always likely. We sought first to discover the actual incidence of involvement in practice by the families of members, and since so many members were recruited singly, we also looked beyond the family to friends to see what measure of support the member might receive from that quarter. We have also attempted to assess the extent of negative reactions by family members or friends, and to discover in what circumstances members have had such experiences.

Of the members in our survey, 54 per cent did not have any family members in the movement. Of the 26 per cent who had relatives in the movement these were generally their partners (wife, husband, girl-friend or boy-friend), but in some of these cases there were also other close kinsfolk. Fifteen per cent had only close family members also practising—usually one or sometimes both parents, and one or more siblings. A further 5 per cent had in-laws or other relatives in the movement. Although 33 per cent of respondents had children of

18 years or older, in only one in four cases were those children also members of SGI, and in such cases, only in one out of four of these families—amounting to about 3 per cent of the total sample—were all of the children members. From these figures it is apparent that the practice of Nichiren Buddhism had not yet become a solidary family faith for many people in Britain. It was not yet manifesting a clear capacity to bring in the second generation, although this might change when more children have been brought up in the faith from birth, which was, at this date, rare for children who had reached adulthood.

Somewhat more women (18 per cent) than men (9 per cent) had members of their family in the movement. Of those living as couples, whether married or cohabiting, 60 per cent of the men had a partner who was also in SGI. In contrast, only 34 per cent of the working women had a partner in the movement. The percentage was 53 for housewives. It follows, that of men who were members, there were nearly two out of three cases where the partner was also in membership. However, in the cases where a woman member was working (and consequently might be assumed to be more independent of her husband than were housewives) only one out of three had a partner who was in SGI. Working women constituted the category the members of which possessed fewest co-religionists among their partners, family, or relatives: some 49 per cent. This figure compares with 29 per cent of the men, and 18 per cent of the housewives. We may infer that working women demonstrated more independence in their religious preferences than did housewives or men, and that, in contrast, men were more likely than women to follow their partners in religious preference. That this has been a recognizable pattern in the Sōka Gakkai movement overall was already apparent from the frequency with which Japanese wives were able to persuade their foreign husbands (most conspicuously, American servicemen stationed in Japan) to take up their religion— a phenomenon that has been credited as the probable basis for the expansion of the movement in the United States in the years following the American occupation of Japan in the post-war period.[2]

---

[2] See Ellwood, *The Eagle and the Rising Sun*, 96.

The Retention of Old, and the Acquisition of New Friendships

In those religious movements which might be described as 'totalist' or communitarian, it is not uncommon for members to abandon all their former friends and to count as friends only their fellow religionists. Such is the case with various Christian sects which fall short of being communitarian but which tend to withdraw from the affairs of the world, as is the case with the Exclusive Brethren and the Christadelphians.[3] This tendency is pronounced among some new movements, including the Unification Church and the Krishna Consciousness people. Sōka Gakkai is, however, far from being a totalist movement in this sense, and although it is committed, ultimately, to an exclusivist position, there is also an open spirit and a considerable manifestation of tolerance, at least among the British membership. There is certainly no suggestion that joining the movement necessitates relinquishment of past associations, even in the way which has sometimes been alleged of the practices in Scientology, some of the members of which have been advised to abandon relatives and friends who are defined as 'suppressive persons'. Our concern was to discover just to what extent these Buddhists—all of them, be it remembered, converts and thus likely to have non-Buddhist friends—now retained old friendships with outsiders, and to what extent involvement in SGI had led them to draw their friendships from among their co-religionists.

Of all our respondents, 4 per cent reported that they did not have any close friends at all. Of those who had such friends, 13 per cent (of the whole sample) said that none of those friends were members of (what then was still called) NSUK. That in itself is an indication that it is possible to practise Nichiren Buddhism without needing to engage oneself in very close association with like-minded others. The faith could be pursued without needing to establish close friendly links: after all, it was not a congregational organization and, although there were groups meetings and many opportunities for social activities, including shared occasions for chanting, and numerous occasions on which members might perform service for

---

[3] On the Exclusive Brethren, see B. R. Wilson, 'The Exclusive Brethren: A Case Study in the Evolution of a Sectarian Ideology', in Bryan R. Wilson (ed.), *Patterns of Sectarianism* (London: Heinemann, 1967), 244–86; for a recent study of the Christadelphians, see Charles H. Lippy, *The Christadelphians in North America* (Lewiston, NY: Edwin Mellen Press, 1989).

the organization, none the less, the believer could operate perfectly well without committing himself to close association with his fellow Buddhists.

About 36 per cent of the sample said that only a minority of their friends were members, and a similar proportion (32 per cent) said that about half of their close friends were in membership. Over all, then, it was only a minority—some 19 per cent—who stated that the majority of their close friends were members, and of these 19 per cent only one out of six averred that *all* their close friends were in NSUK. Nor was there any variation relative to the age of those who claimed that the majority of their friends were in the movement: for all age-groups the figure remained at more or less 19 per cent. However, there was a tendency for the younger members (70 per cent of them) to report that they had only a minority or a half of their close friends in the movement. This was a far higher percentage than was reported by the older members, of whom only 50 per cent made this claim. Furthermore, these older members more frequently declared that there were no members among their friends: this was asserted by 30 per cent of this age-group, as against 10 per cent among the younger generations. These findings are a consequence of the age composition of this young movement. Whereas each five-year age-grouping of those between 25 years old and 44 amounted to some 20 per cent of the total membership (i.e. 71.7 per cent in total), the entire age-group of those over 45 represented only a little more than 20 per cent of the membership, this percentage being distributed over a forty-year span of those aged from 45 to 84. For this older age-group there was, inevitably, less opportunity to make friends of a similar age within the membership, first because the age-group was itself so much smaller, and secondly because friendships across significant differences of age are less easily made and are relatively uncommon.

As might be expected of any organization, however, the longer people had been members of SGI, the more likely it was that their close friends were drawn from the membership, as Table 9 illustrates (albeit not exclusively so). Only a quarter of those with no close friends or only a minority of close friends among fellow members were themselves members of long standing (that is of seven or more years' membership). Of those who claimed that all their close friends were SGI adherents, more than 50 per cent were from this long-standing category.

TABLE 9. *Duration of membership and incidence of friendships (%)*

	Years in SGI-UK		
	0–2	3–6	7+
1. No close friends of any kind	41	27	32
2. None of close friends are members	44	32	24
3. Minority of close friends are members	44	30	26
4. About half of close friends are members	30	39	31
5. Most of close friends are members	31	24	45
6. All close friends are members	21	26	53
Consequently we may distinguish three groups:			
(1) + (2) + (3)	44	30	26
(4) + (5)	30	34	36
(6)	21	26	53

Note: For those without any close friends in SGI-UK, the mode is 0–2 years in membership.

Although members did not withdraw from intercourse with the wider society, in their work, study, and leisure there was a tendency for their religious affiliation to provide an increasing proportion of intimates for those who had remained in membership over a longer period of time. Such friendships might reinforce religious commitment, but equally, enduring commitment to the movement and its ideology might lead to more extensive social intercourse with other members. Yet such findings are clearly no more than evidence of a natural tendency for shared faith to encourage increased association, and were in no sense a consequence of any policy to direct members to choose their circle of friends exclusively from within the movement.

Social Differences and Common Religion

Despite such evidences of spontaneous increase of association among members over time, it is clear from these data overall that Nichiren Buddhism is primarily a commitment to a set of beliefs and practices, rather than to a collectivity of believers. Much as the organization does for members, members not infrequently made it plain that they perceived a distinction between the teachings and practice on the one hand, and the organization of NSUK (SGI) on the other; that the practice was the prime concern, and that this was something which the individual believer could conduct on his own and for himself. Of course, Nichiren Buddhists have a common cause and engage in numerous group activities which bring together adherents who share common interests which are outside the religion, but which are amenable to the infusion of Buddhist values. These interests, as we have seen, may be professional, cultural, educational, or—as in the case of the Afro-Caribbean participants—a shared ethnic identity. Even more important, the movement promotes small discussion meetings in which personal problems and experiences are considered in the light of Nichiren's teachings. Such meetings furnish individuals with a significant measure of group support, at least with respect to the exploration and resolution of their problems. Yet this is of a different character from the strong congregational or collective emphasis such as is found variously in most Christian minority sects, and may not always lead to a strong sense of identity with others in the movement.[4]

Some members volunteered to us frank reservations about the life-style of other members, not all of whom had they found congenial or even socially compatible, and for some this had created difficulties in sustaining their commitment—to the movement, if not to the practice. A Japanese confidant reported of a middle-aged woman employed in the civil service that

she often finds it difficult to mix with other members because many members come from non-conventional families, and their manners, language, and jokes, etc., are often untolerable [*sic*] for the members who come from conventional families. Since the meetings are often conducted in such ways, she hesitated to attend or invite her guests to the meetings. I know how this is a problem in Japan, too, as my parents feel the same way. But in England this is a much . . . greater problem, I think.

Similar ambivalence was evinced by a male teacher in a school of occupational therapy: 'other group members and their life-styles are

---

[4] Hourment, 'Transformer le poison en élixir', 94, writes of group meetings among French members, 'group discussion [is] the only place where members of different divisions (men, women, young men, and young women) assemble as a small group. They know each other well. Contrary to the lessons on the *Gosho*, where the "class" is relatively passive, discussion meetings . . . stimulate exchanges. The leader starts discussion, sometimes giving clarifying doctrinal points and taking care that people stay within the expected . . . tone and content . . . "You must not forget that you are in the presence of Buddha. You must not refrain from speaking about your problems, without however pouring them out".' He comments further that 'the style of the interventions is not uptight; the climate of conviviality, marked by humour, reflects the fact that many of the participants have friendly relations with one another'.

unattractive [but] they are also practising. Still others, though, are
good role models.' An art school teacher, somewhat critical of the
organization as such, said, 'I am there to chant and use organization
to introduce others to chanting. There are all sorts of people who go
[to meetings] and some you mix with, some not.' An eye surgeon
saw the association with others as transcending whatever political
differences there might be: 'left–right conflict, we find it every-
where, and it is influencing everything. [In Nichiren Buddhism] you
can move through all that. You have to practise with other people,
so it has political implications and it gets you away from the
traditional left–right conflict.'

Others also saw the diversity of social types as a fundamental
advantage: a third-time married woman teacher said, 'I liked the
variety of people: it was a complete cross-section. I meet people from
all walks of life that I wouldn't if I didn't practise . . . it was fun.'
A community social worker, holding a position of responsibility in
the movement, sought to interpret the inter-personal differences and
difficulties:

it has been hard to accept that particular members of NSUK seem hell-bent
on disrupting it in a chaotic or critical way, and no value comes from it.
People who say they'll do something but never do . . . You need to tolerate
such destructive persons. Buddhism sees society like mud in the bottom of
a pond . . . yet out of it comes a beautiful plant— a Lotus flower. Looking
at the roots of NSUK, you can find grotty things down there. There are
conflicts, uncertainties in NSUK, but there's a transformation that's always
going on—there is a sufficiently strong foundation for this not to be
disturbing.

Despite the misgivings which members articulate, there remains
a strong commitment to the practice and at least to individual action
and responsibility. Members generally perceive the need for association with one another, even if they do not all or always expect to
make personal friendships from among those whom they encounter
in the discussion meetings. Latently, there may even be a lingering
sense of difficulty in reconciling the commitment to cultivate values
whilst at the same time being counselled to avoid being judgemental
about others and their conduct. The idea that others' behaviour and
dispositions are part of their (as yet not escaped, if not actually
inescapable) karma imposes a demand for toleration. Yet toleration
of widely discrepant life orientations may not always be easy for

those who have a substantive conception of the values that they believe they are endorsing and creating.

Clearly, Nichiren Buddhists are often friends, but they are not drawn into a community in which all involved are expected to share completely each others' interests or to manifest special inter-personal affection in the manner sometimes found in exclusivistic and collectively oriented sects. It is evident from the friendships which members reported that membership of SGI does nothing, either by policy or ethos, to discourage the continuance of former friendships with non-Buddhists, or to hinder the formation of new ones. Despite the injunction to promote *kōsen-rufu* by spreading the faith—a matter which members certainly declare themselves to take very seriously—and despite the celebrated commitment to undertake *shakubuku*, SGI members sustain a wide range of amicable relationships with outsiders. Their reserve regarding the practice of *shakubuku* perhaps facilitates the maintenance of those relationships.

When we enquired about attitudes to the doctrine of *shakubuku*, most members maintained the same spirit of cautious reserve that we have noted in the work of the leader of the British movement. The tendency was to reinterpret this obligation in terms in keeping with traditional British reticence, rather than to adopt the aggressive evangelistic posture which characterized the early days of Sōka Gakkai in Japan. The community social worker who was a Men's division headquarters leader represented the most forceful commitment:

How to defeat the ego without going out towards others? To have a position of responsibility in NSUK, you have to do *shakubuku* . . . There's a relation I've established with a few others I've been teaching: it indicates that there's a correct time for someone to come forward. You may be giving out to others to deal with something in yourself. They may not practise, but others may come forward. It is necessary for us to do it . . . it is taking up a challenge to defeat the ego and master oneself to an increasing degree. Try to find those whose time is right to practise. The cause is in their lives—we are not trying to ram anything down anyone's throat.

Whilst not 'pushing' was a recurrent theme in the responses to our question on *shakubuku*, some had learned only with time to overcome the spontaneous enthusiasm which they had felt as new converts. The 32-year-old male dancer recalled that 'At first, in enthusiasm, I tried to convert everyone—wanting them to have the magic, too. However, this leads to being pushed away. Now [I speak] to individuals who come into my circle—those perceived to be suffering in their life.' An accountant who was also a purchasing manager dilated on the same concerns, 'When I started, I made a nuisance of myself. I was full of it. I told everyone. Now I chant to meet people who want to practise. It now happens naturally.' A number emphasized the need to target people who were good prospects. As a male musician said, 'I single someone out who has problems.' A debt controller working for British Telecom said, 'If someone is suffering, I want them to see my practice is strong, and then they are attracted', and the female opera singer also specified people who were suffering, saying, 'I just tell people. I don't push, except if it's a really good friend whom I know well enough, and who suffers, then I suggest what to do: "Try it!" and I try to chant for the suffering.' Some articulated the ideas that *shakubuku* had to be done out of compassion, and not as a duty: as a young woman who had trained as a teacher put it, 'If I do it out of duty, I don't succeed', while the dancer made the point that '*Shakubuku* is for the good of individuals, not for the growth of the organization.'

Other members were inclined to see *shakubuku* as a requirement (to put the matter in Christian terms) to 'let your light shine before men', taking the cautious note of the headquarters leader rather further. A 33-year-old teacher said, 'My responsibility is to prove the power of Buddhism in daily life so that people want to ask about it.' A young French widow held that by example she had accomplished much *shakubuku*, at least in a passive way: 'I've *shakubuku*-ed quite a lot of people because they see the way I live. The girl I live with saw the change—saw me getting stronger. Now she has started [chanting] and I have done nothing. It's difficult when you bring people to a meeting . . . it's up to them, their decision.' The same thought was echoed by a young woman accounts clerk, 'I don't do *shakubuku* except in letting people see the change in me, how I contribute every day . . . and that's proof. People need proof. I can say I'm a Buddhist, but if they see a change they ask, "What has she got that I don't have?" and that way I *shakubuku*.' That active proselytizing was difficult was affirmed by a 35-year-old musician: 'I'm not very good at *shakubuku* . . . I'm somewhat recalcitrant. I don't blurt out to others [that I'm a Buddhist] but everyone who knows me knows I chant, but I'm not very pushy about it. I think people will find it if they're looking for it.' Likewise a 34-year-old male violin-maker said, 'I find *shakubuku* very difficult personally . . . the idea of imposing on someone else. I find it hard to go out of my way to try to convince others to try it . . . more people than not find it difficult.'

That so many members retain friends who remain outside the movement suggests that endeavours to convert them have either never been attempted or have been tried, have failed, have been abandoned, and that all this has happened without hard feelings. Just as there are no interdictions against involvement in external social activities, so there is no attempt to constrain members in respect of their personal relationships, even though the movement seeks to infuse a wide range of social concerns with its own distinctive ethos.

Members' Primary Relationships

To have in one's primary group friends and kinsfolk who are also members of SGI might be regarded as of great importance for the level of involvement of members of the movement. To that effect, we examined the primary groups of members to see to what extent they were composed entirely, partially, or not at all, of SGI members. About one-third of members had primary groups that were highly heterogeneous, with all or almost all of these close kin and friends outside the movement, and a further 20 per cent were also predominantly composed of outsiders. About one-third lived in primary groups where most or all of the people involved were members of SGI. Of those living as couples (being married or cohabiting) more women than men lived in a heterogeneous situation, while more men than women lived in a homogeneous situation. There appeared to be no further differentiation by reference to other social variables. If we take those living as couples (whether married or cohabiting) and those who were single but who had a girl-friend or boy-friend, we see that a narrow majority of couples had a partner in the movement, whilst by far the greater number of those who were still single had primary attachments to people who were not in the movement.

We asked members more specifically about the religious disposi- tions of their partners—that is, their spouses, boy-friends, or girl- friends—and we related this to their home circumstances, whether they were living singly or as one of a couple. By a small margin, the majority of those living as couples had partners who were members of SGI-UK. But the vast majority of the partners of those living singly were not in the movement.

Thus, only about half the members were likely to have active support in their immediate home environments for their particular religious practice. This does not necessarily imply active opposition, of course, but it does indicate that Nichiren Buddhists must, in considerable part, draw on their own resources rather more than might be expected to be the case for the adherents of perhaps most other religious affiliations. No doubt similar findings might emerge for some other new movements, particularly for those which emphasize a strongly individualistic orientation such as the human potential movements, the so-called 'self-religions'. It might also be the case that this phenomenon was pronounced at this stage of its development, because SGI was, and remains, a very young movement in Britain, and thus was still recruiting mainly separate individuals. There has as yet been little time for generational succession in religious commitment to develop, although there has been time for matrimonial bonds to be formed between some people in the movement.

The Experience of Opposition

Given the considerable heterogeneity of religious commitment in the family context of many members, it seemed probable that some of them might have been subject to some measure of opposition or discrimination from non-members, and we asked our sample about their experiences in this regard. Of all the members, 45 per cent had never encountered negative reactions to their religion, whilst, by a small margin, this had been the experience of the majority, some 55 per cent. Most of the negative reactions had occurred in their own family (some 36 per cent). Some had had this response from their in-laws (5 per cent) and some from other relatives (6 per cent). A considerable number, some 23 per cent, had also experienced negative reactions from their friends. In some cases, such reactions were cumulative, coming from more than one source; in other cases, they were confined to either the family or friends. Few had experienced such criticism from outside the primary group, but this had occurred in some instances—5 per cent reported this of work colleagues; 2 per cent from neighbours; 1 per cent from employers, and a further 1 per cent from teachers. Negative comments from these categories of people were hardly ever the sole source of criticism, but were rather additional to the reactions of friends and/ or family members.

We sought to distinguish the bases of the negative reactions to Nichiren Buddhism, in so far as our respondents could specify these. Some people, it was reported, reacted negatively towards this movement because they objected to religion *tout court*: these accounted for 8 per cent of the cases. A further 8 per cent of the objections were to the extent of the time that Nichiren Buddhist practice required. The overwhelming majority of negative reactions —some 22 per cent— were directed to the beliefs, practices, chanting, and regalia of SGI-UK. Virtually any new religious movement is likely to attract opposition, and that hostility is likely to be most pointed, most intense, and most conspicuous among the close kinsfolk of the converted. Whilst Nichiren Buddhism entails little severance of social bonds, as we have noted, and certainly does not seek to detach individuals from their families by persuading them to take up a communal life or to commit themselves to itinerancy in the way found among the Moonies, the Krishna Consciousness movement, the Family of Love, or the Jesus Army, none the less, those who become Nichiren Buddhists do have their distinctive commitments. In particular, they are supposed to do *gongyō* twice a day and to chant the invocation for a period every morning and evening, and, at the discretion of the individual worshipper, chanting might continue for as long as an hour or two, and is usually not less than twenty minutes. When converts live with kinsfolk who are unconvinced, chanting can undoubtedly create family problems, and this was apparently the burden of at least some part—perhaps a considerable part—of the negative responses incurred by SGI members.

In one instance, the wife of a Labour Party councillor, who was herself not a member, objected to his chanting for three hours a day, particularly when she wanted to watch television. In another case, it was the overall commitment of time which alienated the wife of a management consultant, whilst his mother would not tolerate his chanting in her house, and his father worried that he was going through a mid-life crisis. The wife of a director of a language school disliked his Buddhist friends and resented his involvement in SGI activities: he also met the disapproval of his mother, who was a strong Christian. An unemployed business manager in radio communications found that Buddhism was blamed for the suicide of a close Buddhist friend. The son of a committed female member said the practice 'caused alienation in the family. He does not live at home.' The male teacher in the school of occupational therapy reported,

My wife is/was opposed to my practice. We have separated. She suggested Nichiren Shōshū [initially] and I tried it. We are separated but very close. Practice brings up weaknesses—my relations with my wife . . . One hour a day . . . she resented the time taken for it. I was not helping with the children or the dishes. I tried to do it [practice] when it was in my own time and not on shared time. However, she still resented it. It was difficult, twice a day—I felt guilty if I didn't do it.

An unemployed male sales manager of 41 had seen the negative reaction of his wife to Nichiren Buddhism 'leading to the break up of home and relationships [and] to some close friends drifting apart and/or the dissolution of friendship'. Perhaps the most encompassing of all hostility was the action of a husband seeking the custody of the child of his community worker wife: he fought the custody battle on 'the grounds of my being involved in a "sinister cult"'.

The actual teachings of Nichiren are less likely to occasion objection, whilst the ethical concerns of the SGI, and in partiuclar its emphasis on work for world peace and on the preservation of the environment, as represented by the teachings of the unity of man and nature, and the positive emphasis on freedom and the enhancement of life opportunities, might find general endorsement from a wide spectrum of religious and secular opinion. Nor are the movement's cultural activities likely as such to evoke criticism, even though some might cavil at such promotions as going beyond what they conceive to be appropriate activities for a religious body. But the actual practice, undertaken in bedrooms by single individuals within family homes where there is no appreciation of the movement as such, appear to have been a considerable source of irritation for some of the kinsfolk of SGI adherents.

We have already suggested, in an earlier chapter, that negative reactions of friends and family may not have been without consequences for the aspects of SGI to which members were now attracted. Adherents who were criticized by their primary relations for becoming religious or for changing their religion were pressed for more acceptable legitimizations of their conversion to the movement than the idea that the quality of its membership was superior to that of the generality of people. The quality of the existing membership was the feature overwhelmingly chosen by members as the prime initial attraction to them of the organization. We infer that the criticism of non-members, and most significantly of close kinsfolk, was an influence causing members to invoke quite different considerations with respect to what now, at the time of the survey, sustained the appeal of SGI. We did not find that any particular social factor influenced just which individuals experienced negative reactions: nor did such factors provide any indication of just which type of negative reactions might arise. It was, indeed, virtually always the case that the objection to an adherent's conversion came from a primary relative. That is not surprising, since these were the people most affected by the assumption of such an allegiance and by the activities and practices which it entailed.

VI

The Social Structure of SGI-UK

MINORITY movements tend to manifest distinctive characteristics. They recruit differentially from the various sections of the general population, and, in so far as like attracts like (a hypothesis which had considerable immediate plausibility in these cases), it was reasonable to expect that the general demographic characteristics of the membership of SGI would be at marked variance with the population at large. To this end, our sample was compared with national statistics.

The age profile of the movement's membership proved to be at marked variance with that of the United Kingdom as a whole. Compared to the estimates for the population (calculated for 1989), the category of those aged 39 years or younger in the movement was significantly over-represented. From Table 10, it is evident that some 56 per cent of members were born between 1946 and 1960, and thus, at the time of the survey, they were between 30 and 44 years of age. It can thus be seen that whilst the movement was composed of a relatively young membership, when compared to the public at large, none the less it differed markedly from those new religions which, in Germany, have often been given the generic name *Jugundreligionen*, the general membership of which reflected the fact that recruitment to those bodies tended to take place when people were in their early twenties or even younger. SGI members were typically recruited at a later age,[1] yet it is quite clear that the appeal of Nichiren Buddhism was not to the elderly, who tend to be set in their ways, but to people who were at an age at which change and adaptation were still contemplated, and for whom life's horizons were still expanding.

Of course, if the movement were to retain a considerable proportion of its present members, and short of a compensatory increase

---

[1] See p. 45, above.

TABLE 10. *The age structure of SGI compared to that of the United Kingdom population*

Age	Birth year	Nos.	%		UK %
70+	1920 or before	9	1.5	} 2.4	15.8
65–9	1921–5	6	0.9		
60–4	1926–30	15	2.4		
55–9	1931–5	25	4.1		
50–4	1936–40	25	4.1	} 37.0	37.4
45–9	1941–5	58	9.3		
40–4	1946–50	106	17.1		
39 or LESS	1951–5	117	18.9		
	1956–60	123	19.9		
	1961–5	98	15.8	} 60.4	46.8
	1966–70	29	4.7		
	1971 or later	7	1.1		
Missing value		1	0.2	0.2	

Note: Mode 1956–60 or 31 to 35 years; median 1951–5 or 36 to 40 years: i.e. 37 years; mean 38 years (38.1).

in the recruitment of young people, the prospect would be for the age structure of SGI-UK to change, with an increase in the proportion of older members. On present trends in recruitment, however, the likelihood is that growth will persist, and that the movement will continue to appeal to a constituency of young (but not the very youngest) adults, and so might retain approximately its present age distribution.

Marital Status

Minority religions that are of long standing generally consist of whole families, and it is not unusual for there to be extensive networks of kinsfolk within such a movement, even when they are geographically dispersed. In contrast, new religions of exotic provenance have generally tended to recruit single individuals, many of whom have no relatives who share their conversion to the new persuasion. The extent to which a movement is comprised of stable families must be assumed to have considerable importance for its durability, as well as for the transmission of ideas and values from

TABLE 11. *The marital status of members compared to the population of the United Kingdom (%)*

	SGI sample	Gt. Britain
Married	31.9	51
Living as married	11.4	n/a
Divorced and separated	17.4	4
Widowed	2.8	7
Single	34.5	38
Other (homosexual/lesbian)	2.0	n/a

one generation to the next, which is more easily done if those generations are parents and their own children. Thus, it is a matter of importance, not only to the sociologist who seeks to explain, and perhaps predict, the development of a particular organization by uncovering the pattern of marital and familial involvement which obtains, but also to the leaders and administrators of the movements themselves. Of course, a movement which recruits a population which has a disproportionate number of younger age-groups is likely to have a lower incidence of married members than one which is more typically distributed with respect to age, but it is evident from Table 11 that, even allowing for this particular circumstance, SGI has a much larger proportion than normal of single people in its ranks when the divorced, separated, and cohabiting members were taken together with the single. Clearly, cohabitation might lead to unions no less stable than those of the officially married, but the absence of the marriage bond might be said to represent an additional hazard to durability. The modal group among our respondents was single, and they outnumbered the married. Compared to the country as a whole, there was a higher percentage of divorced people in SGI, but the percentage of the married and of the widowed was lower.

How Members Made their Living

Even on cursory acquaintance with SGI, the outsider becomes aware that, in occupational and educational terms, the membership of the movement presents a distinctive and untypical cross-section of the public at large. This is not so much a matter of members being

TABLE 12. *Employment and self-employment of SGI members (%)*

Employed	47.0
Self-employed	31.8
Retired or pensioned	3.0
Housewives	5.0
In full-time education	5.8
Unemployed/on social security	6.4
Missing value	1.0

concentrated at a particular level of occupational status, but rather a consequence of the high concentration of members at various status levels in a number of distinct areas of occupational activity. Our concern in seeking an occupational profile of SGI was less to assess, in what have perhaps now become rather old-fashioned sociological terms, the social class of the membership, than to get a picture of the more general social involvement of those who belonged. In consequence, we were interested as much in types of occupation, and not specifically, and certainly not exclusively, in social status as such. This consideration was reinforced by the observation that SGI members appeared to have cultural and social affiliations that were unlikely to fit into the conventional categories of social classes. The initial finding of importance from our survey was the relatively high proportion of members who described themselves as self-employed.

As Table 12 reveals, almost one-third of the members declared themselves to be self-employed, 31.8 per cent compared with some 11.5 per cent of the civilian labour force in 1989.[2] In contrast, the 6.4 per cent who described themselves as unemployed or in receipt of social security benefit exactly matches the percentage for the country as assessed by OECD concepts in 1989.[3] If we compared the national figures with those members of SGI who were in the civilian labour force, the contrast is even more pronounced. Excluding housewives, retired people, and full-time students allows us to calculate what percentage the self-employed and unemployed constituted of those members who were part of the civilian labour force. The self-employed comprised 37.3 per cent of the actively employed members, and the unemployed comprised almost 7.2 per cent. In comparison with the proportion of students in full-time

[2] *Social Trends 21* (London: HMSO, 1991), 67, 71.   [3] Ibid 75.

education, as a percentage of the national civilian labour force, which stood at 2 per cent in 1989, the proportion of SGI members in full-time education as a proportion of those in the labour force was 5.8 per cent.[4]

What is then apparent is that SGI members represented an unusually high proportion of what might be termed independent people—people who were engaged in full-time education, or people who had, as they themselves would like to put it, taken responsibility for their own lives, in this instance by embarking on self-employed careers. Nichiren Buddhism apparently exercised significant appeal for people who were not bound into the structured systems of work within modern society, for people who had launched themselves on the basis of their own skills and enterprise, some of whom may also have been employers of others. The emphasis in the teaching that 'practice'—the regular chanting of the *daimoku* and *gongyō*—inspires self-confidence, teaches the individual to face up to reality, and encourages him to take charge of himself and his own affairs is a philosophy that may readily be seen as accommodating self-employed people, or of encouraging people to take the challenge of self-employment. We need assert no more than that there is, in Weberian terms, an elective affinity between the ideology and the career patterns pursued by a sizeable section of the membership. The idea that one might, by practice, alter one's karma, in effect eliminate bad luck and control the untoward, is a reassuring proposition for people who have struck out on their own. Given that the membership is also disproportionately young, this sort of encouragement is perhaps most appropriate for those who had made such decisions relatively recently and were still forging their own destiny.

A number of members reported that in their chanting they had set themselves the specific goal of a self-employed career in work in which they could retain or acquire personal independence. One 22-year-old male administrative officer 'chanted for success as a musician' among other things, and maintained that he had, in consequence, 'had some good fortune as a musician'. A woman of 32, born in New Zealand, declared her profession to be 'musician, singer, percussionist, printer . . . I do anything to get by'. She had chanted 'to achieve financial independence as a musician' and had 'been

[4] *General Household Survey*, ed. Eileen Goddard (London: HMSO, 1990), 14.

self-employed for two years now—a struggle, but still here'. A 33-year-old silk-screen painter was hoping 'to make a world-wide declaration and set something unprecedented in history in motion, similar to *Band Aid* but with greater and bigger . . . impact, through music, media, etc.'. Whilst his goal had not yet been realized, 'the declaration hasn't been made yet, but I've become more creative, a comic is taking shape. I've performed on stage, know I can sing, know I can write songs, and the pathway is gradually opening up. It's not an easy goal.'

Such idealism is associated with the desire for self-determination in many instances. Thus, a woman play therapist reported that 'in 1985, I left work to study with only an idea of what I wanted—to work with "children and drama', . . . with the courses I studied, I always followed my heart, i.e., did what I wanted to do, and got the job at the place [to which] I had originally gone as a student. It almost felt as if I was being "honed" for the right job—it uses every bit of my past experience, and I'm constantly learning new things, every day'. A 62-year-old woman had set herself the goal 'to be independent', and subsequently, could declare, 'I found work—no qualifications—age 60'. A 38-year-old writer and producer of video scripts had chanted for 'a successful change of career', and was able to report, 'I was offered a job in Monaco by a man I had met in a bar four years earlier. I didn't even remember him. He had kept my number and simply called me with an offer which I accepted and has provided my main income for the past eighteen months.' A woman describing herself as an 'active parent' said, 'I recently found the courage to embark on a musical career, and as soon as I made my decision, the right singing teacher and piano teacher came into my life and are prepared to help me, which is really astonishing to me, partly because I am of an age where most people have finished their studies (I am 36) and partly because I am starting to realize my potential.'

That the unemployed, as calculated on the figures provided in *Social Trends*, should also exceed, albeit only marginally, the figures for the nation as a whole may not be unassociated with the tendency of the movement to attract those whose working lives or working prospects are relatively unstructured by stable and long-term attachments to particular firms or industries. From our data, it also appeared that some of the unemployed members were people who were looking for openings for self-employed ways of making a living rather than by becoming employees.

The attraction of embarking on a self-employed career, even at the risk of unemployment, may be very considerable for people who are being encouraged to face challenge and whose religion inspires them to take control of their lives. The individual remains much more at liberty and acquires a much more vivid sense of living up to the precepts of his faith, believing that his prospects and his prosperity are in his own hands. For people who opt for self-employment, Nichiren Buddhism offers not only encouragement but also the promise of support from the practice. In such jobs, and the same holds in some measure for various professional and semi-professional roles in which there is a strong fiduciary element and a wide area for individual discretion, chanting may serve as a confirmation of one's dedication and an affirmation of one's determination to succeed.

Not only had many members taken up self-employed careers, but others, who had not, looked forward to doing so. One single young man dilated on his aspirations:

I went from school to college for a year in computer and business studies, and worked six months as a programmer, but I wanted to do conservation work. I applied to College and went to a tree nursery and a farm as a labourer, in preparation. I did [i.e. studied] rural resources and their management. I worked as an electrician's mate for a bit to pay off debts. Then I did a Permaculture course—two weeks in Scotland, and then work for the Department of the Environment for two months, and then went into the planning section of the Department of the Environment for fifteen months. But I will be moving soon—it won't be a job, but it will be work. Once I have design experience, I can become a free-lance designer. Till then, I hope to join a training course to train trainers to train others, operating as a 'design hit-squad'. I shan't be working for anyone—it will be a co-operative . . . My girl friend and I, when we've got our lives sorted out—will be off to travel the world, when our careers are sorted out. We'd like to go from one Permaculture site to the next—Australia, and New Zealand is a goal for me.

Sectarian movements in the Christian tradition sometimes also appear to encourage a certain independence of life-style among their members, and some of them appear to have a higher than average proportion of the self-employed among their membership, although hard data are lacking. Certainly, some Jehovah's Witnesses have chosen to take up work in which they can be their own bosses, even at the cost of loss of income, in order to be free to undertake proselytizing activities. One may, however, detect in this a rather different motivation from that which appears to be consistent with the orientations of Nichiren Buddhists. The Witnesses deliberately sacrificed job opportunities for the sake of their religious commitment, and often accepted lower incomes or part-time employment, in preference to full-time, in order to devote time to house-to-house canvassing. The Sōka Gakkai members tend rather to see self-employment as an arena in which to experience the benefits of their religion, which is expected to open new opportunities for success rather than to close them. Again, the Exclusive Brethren show a marked tendency to develop their own small businesses: self-employment is a strongly cultivated ideal among them. The grounds for this orientation lie in the desire to reduce to a minimum all contact with the outside world. As self-employed people, Brethren can escape trade unionism, employ only their own fellow religionists, and determine more of their own lives than would otherwise be the case. Since they do not work on Saturdays, and engage in corporate worship early every morning, the practice of their religion demands that they control their own circumstances as fully as possible. Their motivations in encouraging self-employment differ from those of Nichiren Buddhists. The latter are outgoing into the world and seek to succeed there: self-employment is not a retreat into a sequestered enclave so much as the choice of one's own ground on which to seek and display worldly success in experiencing happiness and attaining self-control of one's life and its circumstances.

Our respondents were asked to state their professions or occupations—the work for which they were trained—and also to indicate the actual work in which they were engaged. Obviously, to a considerable extent, the responses to these two questions were likely to be the same, but because of the high incidence of self-employment, and also because such a high proportion of the sample had trained in artistic professions, in which job security was far from guaranteed, the comparison was potentially worth pursuing. There seemed to be little possibility of assigning occupations to the census categories of social classes, and a cultural rather than a structural breakdown proved to be both more feasible and more clearly indicative of just who, in occupational terms, the SGI members were.

What is immediately apparent from Table 13 is the rather small percentage of members who were engaged in manufacturing or

TABLE 13. *The professions and the actual jobs of SGI members (missing values excluded) (%)*

	Profession	Job
1. *Caring professions* (social work; medical; dentists; pharmacists; medical auxiliaries; fringe therapists; teachers; professors; beauticians; trainers; lecturers; nannies)	18.9	18.0
2. *Administration and office staff* (secretarial; administration; computer analysts; finance; banking; accountancy; librarians; booksellers; salesmen; company directors and secretaries; civil servants; managers, programmers)	27.2	27.3
3. *Performing arts* (musicians, actors; ancillary workers)	13.6	11.9
4. *Public relations* (media, PR, advertising, market research; marketing; journalists; broadcasting; writers; tourist couriers)	6.5	6.3
5. *Graphic arts* (graphic arts; crafts (potters, weavers, antiques; décor; design); fashion trade; garden design; landscaping)	10.8	8.7
6. *Industrial and service workers* (engineers, surveyors, drivers, postmen, gardeners; catering; hotel work; mining; retail trades; fishing; storemen; painters; cleaners; manufacture; factory workers)	10.4	11.9
7. *None* (students; housewives)	12.7	16.0

industrial work. Certainly, there were some who were engaged in engineering, and others in factory work, and one or two in extractive industries and unskilled manual work, but they were a minority, since even in this category those engaged in service activities, such as hotel work and catering, constituted a significant element. The listing of employment in *Social Trends* is too gross to make comparison possible, but it is evident that the caring professions, and more especially the performing arts and the graphic arts, were over-represented among the Buddhists.

The high incidence of members in these occupations is not accidental. Nichiren Buddhism teaches the importance of service to others, encourages a strong humanistic concern and emphasizes the supreme importance of human life. Its general ethic is a ready-made underpinning for those engaged in medical or social work. Whilst, at least in the Japanese context, Nichiren's teachings have sometimes been held up as in themselves a valuable medicine, for the Buddhists in

Britain what appears to be of relevance is the orientation to service and life enhancement which functions to reinforce the caring professions, rather than any intrinsic therapeutic power in the actual teachings.

Christianity has had a chequered record of response to the arts, particularly the performing arts, having sought in centuries past to interdict acting and to control, if not to monopolize, musical performance. In its more radical Protestant expression, a negative attitude towards artistic performance has frequently prevailed, and in some movements that inherited hostility is still preserved. Performing artists and even, in some circumstances, graphic artists have not been comfortably accommodated in the traditional Christian denominations. Nichiren Buddhism has had no such reserve about artistic endeavour, and, from its origins as an educational philosophy based on Nichiren's teachings, Sōka Gakkai has canvassed a keen concern to promote both education and the arts as agencies that 'create value' and enhance human life. The ideology is not only congruous with, but actively encourages, employment in the artistic professions. To this is added the demand that individuals realize their capabilities in taking up with confidence the challenges of everyday life. It is easy to see why people engaged in the arts find in this teaching a supportive sytem of ideas. Nor is this support solely ideational. SGI, in common with its parent organization in Japan, is itself the sponsor of artistic ventures and occasions. Concerts, theatrical productions, art exhibitions, photographic displays—all are encompassed in the movement's regular programme of activities. There are ample opportunities for performers and artists of all kinds to stage their productions under the movement's auspices, and to contribute to the occasional special events which the movement promotes for the general public. Thus, in practical as well as in theoretical respects, and with respect to its tolerance of unconventional life-styles, this religion encourages and supports creative talent in a way which makes it uniquely hospitable to the artistic community, and it cannot be surprising that among its membership there should be such a high proportion of people in these occupations.

The Educational Level of Members

Although SGI membership encompasses people of very diverse educational attainment, what might be inferred from the

TABLE 14. *Age of members on completion of full-time education (%)*

Less than 16 years	12.8
16 years (now the lower legal limit)	17.9
17–18 years	20.8
19–22 years	23.3
23 years or more	18.9
(Still a student	6.3)

occupational distribution among them is confirmed by the proportion of members with high educational accomplishments. There are no comparable statistics for the nation as a whole, but the percentage of the sample who had continued in education until after the age of 18 speaks for itself (Table 14). Those who completed education below the age of 16 were generally those advanced in years, in whose schooldays the age of compulsory education was lower, or were from overseas. Of those who had continued beyond the age of 23 many had been engaged in professional training at this age, but some had pursued university studies beyond first degree level. Those in the largest bracket, who had continued in education to some age between 19 and 22, included, besides university students, those who had attended teachers' training colleges and various professional institutions.

In answer to a different question, just over 30 per cent declared that they had received only basic education; just over 40 per cent had gone on beyond secondary level; whilst almost 24 per cent had attended university–thus illustrating an involvement in higher education considerably greater than that of the general population. Asked to indicate any special training that they had undertaken, some 18 per cent mentioned training in the media, the arts, recreational skills, or music, and almost 7 per cent had had such special training in the caring professions (including a small number in fringe therapies). Thus, it appears that overall the SGI members were considerably better educated than was the public at large. According to the *General Household Survey for 1990*, 38 per cent of people aged between 16 and 69 (excluding those who were currently in full-time education) had no qualifications, and only 8 per cent had a degree or an equivalent qualification. Whilst the membership of SGI-UK have an age distribution weighted towards the younger and middle-aged, and these age-groups have greater proportions of well-qualified people than have older age-groups, none the less it is clear that there is a much higher proportion of highly qualified people among the Buddhists even when age differences are discounted. Although our data do not allow strict comparability, the fact that some 42 per cent of our respondents had been educated to the age of 19 or later suggests, even within the lower age-groups, a proportion much higher than in the nation at large of people with university degrees or equivalent special or professional training.

That those taking up Nichiren's Buddhism should be such a well-educated section of the population is scarcely surprising. To be properly understood, the teachings demand literate intelligence, a willingness to study, and lack of fear in the face of unfamiliar concepts and languages. Only one of our respondents was an in-born member, with the advantage of familiarity with distinctive SGI terms and expectations from early life. For the rest, acquiring the terminology, the procedures, and the ethos of this religion of Japanese provenance entailed not only a willingness to come to terms with a set of totally unfamiliar ideas, but also a readiness to undergo something of a learning process for which they lacked all previous grounding. Not all of them, even those well-educated, found the chanting easy, particularly the speed at which *gongyō* was uttered, with its many unfamiliar sounds. As a 44-year-old art teacher put it: 'I started chanting slowly . . . There are people who chant instantly, but it didn't come like that to me. I was happy with the sounds of the words, but found it difficult to pronounce quickly. I find the whole liturgy difficult to do as rapidly as they want.' A young French widow has also had problems: 'Practising, yes, is very difficult. The first time I chanted with others fifteen minutes, it felt like torture. I wanted it to stop. All the time you are breaking through your limits. You have to do it every day even if you don't want to.'

Religious minorities differ markedly in the general educational level of their adherents, and also in what they assume about the education of new converts. In some instances, the message is made simple and repetitive as, for example, in the proselytizing techniques of both the Mormons and Jehovah's Witnesses. The Witnesses discourage members from pursuing any form of higher education, and the Exclusive Brethren prohibit all forms of higher education for their young people apart from learning practical trade skills. Other sects, notably the Seventh-day Adventists and, in recent decades, the Christadelphians, have adopted a more positive approach towards education, especially in the sciences, if less emphatically so in arts subjects. The new religions spreading in Western countries in the past thirty years or so, particularly those of exotic provenance, appear to have appealed especially to the better educated, some of them because they have deliberately paid special attention to the universities. Whilst Sokā Gakkai has not focused particularly on the university population in Britain, it has, none the less, attracted many well-educated people into its ranks. It has also maintained a positive attitude towards education, since learning is seen as complementary to its teachings rather than, as with a number of the Christian sects that we have already mentioned, as being antipathetic to them.

VII

The Values of the Value Creators

SŌKA GAKKAI, as we have seen, means Value Creation Society. Its members are dedicated to the creation of value. It was, therefore, pertinent to seek to discover the actual values to which SGI members subscribed, and to find out to what extent there was value consensus among them. Given the emphasis within the movement on toleration and the cultivation of non-judgemental orientations, the extent of convergence and divergence was of particular interest. Beyond this, the availability of data from the European Values Study offered the opportunity of a comparison of the values of SGI members and those of their fellow citizens of Great Britain, and thus we were able to attempt an appraisal of the degree to which the values they espoused differed from or coincided with those of the public at large. Most religious minorities embrace value orientations considerably at variance with those of the wider host society, and generally that divergence in part legitimizes their separate identity and is part of their *raison d'être*: we were interested to assess to what extent that was true for this Buddhist movement. Of course, it cannot be assumed that any differences which might be revealed are necessarily and automatically attributable to religious allegiance. It could be the case that converts, or at least some converts, selected themselves for conversion because they were already committed to particular value-orientations, and we have already seen some indications of that in respondents who declared that they took to Nichiren Buddhism as presented by SGI because its philosophy fitted exactly their own, or because it brought together various of their own ideas 'under one roof'.

Leaving this question of the source of values aside, we may first describe the extent to which the attitudes of SGI members converged or diverged from those of the European Values Study sample with respect to the importance which they attached to such major concerns as: work; the family; friends and acquaintances; leisure

TABLE 15. *The value attached to major areas of social activity*

	SGI	UK	UK-AS[a]
Family	1.18	1.14	1.34
Religion	1.25	2.50	2.43
Work	1.42	1.81	1.65
Friends and acquaintances	1.42	1.59	1.62
Leisure time	1.69	1.73	1.70
Politics	2.36	2.72	2.70

Note: Values given on a scale of 1 = most important; 2 = quite important; 3= not very important; 4 = not at all important.

[a] United Kingdom Adapted Sample to match the age structure of the membership of SGI-UK.

time; politics; and religion, respectively. Our respondents were given four categories of answer from which to choose: (1) very important, (2) quite important, (3) not very important, and (4) not at all important. However, to provide a comparison of greater validity, we constructed a sample of the general UK population adapted to match the age structure of the membership of SGI, since the movement had a higher proportion of younger people than had the general population. In Table 15 we refer to this adapted sample of the UK population as 'UK-AS'.

It is clear from the table that, for both SGI members and for the population of the UK of matched age distribution, the family was regarded as the most important concern, but the SGI members attached a little more importance to it than did the general population of the same age structure (1.18 as against 1.34). As might be expected, given the general secularity of Britain, religion was regarded as of more importance by SGI members than it was by the sample of the public at large. Again, the Buddhists attributed more importance to work than did the control group. Although there was not a great difference between the members and the general public, the members saw friends and acquaintances as of more importance. There was scarcely any difference between the two samples with regard to the importance they ascribed to leisure time. Whilst politics was seen as the least important item in this listing, even here the SGI adherents accorded it greater significance than did the general public. Thus, every one of these areas of social experience, except leisure time, was accorded more importance by the SGI members than by non-members of the same age distribution. The members attached almost the same significance to religion as they did to the family, with a score for religion almost twice that of the general population sample. That result is perhaps not very surprising, since the SGI was sampled as a self-defined religious group, and members were aware that the research was concerned with their religious adherence. None the less, the result makes it apparent, should there have been any doubt, that Nichiren Shōshū Buddhism was seen by its votaries as a religion, and that they constituted a religiously committed public.

Work was seen as of greater importance by the Buddhists than by the general population, although the difference diminished somewhat when they were compared to the age-adjusted sample; but age does not explain the whole of this divergence of attitudes. That the general population might be less oriented to work than the younger populations both of members and of the sample adjusted to match their age structure is understandable, since the general population would include many more people at the later stages of their working lives or in retirement. What, however, might account for the enhanced importance of work for SGI members? There is no particularly explicit work ethic in Nichiren's thinking, but there is a strong emphasis on self-determination, and the disproportionate representation of the self-employed (and the would-be self-employed) among the membership might imply positive orientations towards work.

Yet, if work matters very much to the Buddhists, they accord no less importance to leisure time than the general population, and they are significantly more positive in the importance they attribute to friends and acquaintances. All of this conveys the idea of a certain zest for living, and that certainly would be one of the explicit benefits they would expect to experience from practising their rituals. It is clear that friends matter more to them than they do to most other people. This might in part arise from the fact of their minority status, of being a religiously deviant minority, the members of which draw support from each other for their practice. As was made evident by some of those interviewed, the friendships they had made in SGI had been important to them, and the continuing admiration for other Buddhists on the part of many of those who had been attracted by the 'vibrancy' of their new co-religionists suggests that they were inclined to approve of their new acquaintances perhaps to a higher degree than is general among those outside such movements.

Perhaps unusually for a religious organization, the members attributed more importance to politics than did the sample of the public. Whilst politics is for them of less importance than religion, SGI adherents differ from many Christian sects which hold themselves entirely aloof from politics and attribute no worth to political activities at all. Members are aware that their own movement sponsors a political party in Japan—the Kōmeitō, which has its own distinctive political approach, as its name, the Clean Government Party, indicates. The British members are serviced by literature which makes much of the political activities on the world stage of the President of Sōka Gakkai International, Daisaku Ikeda, who regularly travels to meet, or is visited by, political leaders of many different countries, and who has outspoken views on such issues as peace and preservation of the environment. Whilst SGI members as such are not explicitly committed to party politics in Britain, and there is no suggestion, even informally, of anything but a sustained neutrality towards parties, the higher value attached to politics than that which characterizes the general public no doubt reflects the metapolitical philosophy expressed by the movement's international leadership.

Both the Buddhist sample and the sample of the British population valued the family more than any of the other institutions on which they were invited to respond. How did these two publics react to the idea that, in the near future, more emphasis might be laid on family life? Both groups welcomed the idea: it was endorsed by 89 per cent of the United Kingdom public, and by 74 per cent of the SGI members. Conversely, only 2 or 3 per cent thought that greater emphasis on family life would be a bad thing.

Sexual and Moral Attitudes

A further question probed this orientation more deeply. In the background was the traditional position of the Christian West, which had confined sexual activity to marriage, but no less significant, in the climate of the 1990s, the fact that the younger generation had largely challenged sexual restraints and taboos. Given these conflicting currents of contemporary opinion, we sought to discover how the non-Christian SGI membership compared with the public at large. We sought reactions to the following statement:

If someone said that individuals should have the chance to enjoy complete sexual freedom without being restricted, would you tend to agree or disagree? (See Table 16.)

TABLE 16. *Should there be complete, unrestricted sexual freedom?*

	SGI	UK	UK-AS[a]
Tend to agree	25	29	32
Tend to disagree	24	60	57
Neither, it depends	49	9	10
No answer	2	2	1

[a] United Kingdom Adapted Sample to match the age structure of the membership of SGI-UK.

Whilst those agreeing with this proposition were about the same in the two populations, there was a significant difference in the numbers disagreeing, 24 per cent of the SGI members compared to 60 per cent of the general population. The population at large supported more unequivocally the conventional traditional moral demand for restraint than did the Buddhists. And this is not explained by the difference in the age structure of the two samples, since when the British population sample is adjusted to match the SGI membership in age, the percentage disagreeing with the statement changes very little (at 57 per cent). Of those who, with respect to whether they agreed, said 'it depends', the answers of the Buddhists were more nuanced, but it must be remembered that, since they were responding to this question on a written questionnaire, they had the opportunity to write in their reservations, whereas the European Values Study was conducted orally, and there was no opportunity for respondents to enlarge on the qualifications appertaining to the answer, 'Neither, it depends'. Among the 49 per cent of the SGI members who gave this qualified response, some commented further:

No one should attempt to impose sexual restrictions by law other than those acts which impose on others' freedom. But that does not mean that sexual freedom is a good thing.

Depends on what you mean by sexual freedom.

As long as one doesn't hurt people or involve children.

Depends on the other involved parties.

It depends on their age and understanding of the pitfalls.

Most people have no real understanding of cause and effect.

In a similar way, some of the SGI members who expressed agreement with the statement added some qualifications:

Although restrictions should be set from within with regard to respect for others and not from an external body.

One should be self-disciplined in this area.

With the proviso that one's freedom respected others' basic freedoms and didn't make another suffer.

Between consenting adults.

They are responsible for their own causes.

As long as people do not hurt each other.

Assumes that people are mature and responsible.

Providing it's not causing pain by 'abusing' or 'taking', i.e. a person unable to properly give consent, a very young child or someone dominated or coerced into something.

Must be *consenting* and *adult*. Any parties concerned must take full responsibility for their actions.

Many of these responses show evidence of the application of Nichiren Buddhist principles to this proposition, in particular in reference to the need to take responsibility of one's actions, and the allusions to cause and effect. The general orientation of their responses also reflected the expectation that in the present age, known as the last age of *mappō*, the time is no longer appropriate for the imposition of external forms of social control, that objective moral rules must give place to patterns of action that reflect the individual's enhanced capacity to determine his own behaviour. Thus, whilst there is a strong likelihood that Nichiren followers will presume that there is to be moral freedom, they are also conscious of the countervailing need for each individual to evolve his own self-imposed patterns of control in the awareness of the karmic consequences of irresponsible acts.

The questionnaire also carried items which asked respondents to indicate whether they thought it proper for religious bodies to speak out on such matters as abortion, extra-marital affairs, euthanasia, and homosexuality (among other issues which included disarmament; Third World problems; employment; racial discrimination; ecology and the environment; and governmental policy). Before comparing the responses of the Buddhists with the general population, some of the comments of respondents on these subjects are worthy of report:

The subjects listed are personal and individiual decisions. Religion in most cases does not supply the individual with the means to make well-founded decisions—Nichiren Shōshū does. But to speak out as an organization would be to say that this organization as a whole stands for or against this or that which in effect the individual does . . . I guess No is my unsatisfactory answer.

Yes and No. Some religion does not believe in abortion. It depends whether the quality of life and the dignity of life [*sic*]. Through chanting we can bring forth wisdom to do the best for the unborn. Depends on circumstances.

Yes, the problems the world faces are as a direct result of people's action. Without *correct* guidance these problems proliferate.

Yes. It entirely depends on whose side they are. If they are against the issues they are not fit to speak out.

Speak out but not dictate.

Everyone has the right to speak.

No, but religion is bound to overlap with politics.

Depends what you mean by speak out.

I do not believe a religious body should provide final answers.

As individuals—yes.

Not to speak out via the media: however, as a member [of SGI] I appreciate the guidance that is offered by senior members on this subject.

Reflecting a strong conviction that the Church, etc., should speak out on matters of the day, not merely supporting the Establishment.

Providing the view is pro-active towards the people's needs, and ultimately provides a focus for people to improve the quality of their own life.

Yes, on guide-lines.

They should speak in (not out) to members.

I find this question very difficult to answer.—However, I should feel confident if President Ikeda, or other senior Buddhist leaders, were to speak out on any subject.

I think these are all issues which the members of religious bodies should be able to have views on and speak about. The religious body should exist for its *members* and individuals will inevitably have different views on all of these topics. Respect for differing views and attitudes is essential. I don't think that religious bodies should tell individuals what to think about issues but should be able to encourage everyone to examine the issues carefully in relation to the religious teachings and examples (i.e. the *Gosho*). I don't agree that religious bodies should tell individuals what to think or do or bar anyone from practising a religion because they hold a personal view.

The Values of the Value Creators

I think it is important for individuals within a religious organization to take part in the debate on these issues, though perhaps in a crisis situation we might speak out as a body.

Yes, provided that individual is entitled to their [*sic*] own opinion and not expected to bow to the opinion of the organization.

Which religion?

TABLE 17. *Affirmative answers to the question: 'is it proper for religious bodies to speak out on issues related to the family?'*

	SGI	UK	UK-AS[a]
Homosexuality	35	57	51
Extra-marital affairs	35	52	54
Abortion	48	56	58
Euthanasia	55	58	64

[a] United Kingdom Adapted Sample to match the age structure of the membership of SGI-UK.

About 50 per cent of the general population appeared to think it proper for religious bodies to speak out on homosexuality and extra-marital affairs, compared to only about one-third of the members of SGI. The difference on abortion and euthanasia was much less conspicuous, whilst on all issues not relating to personal morality the Buddhists gave affirmative answers more readily than did the general population. The differences in the foregoing table are instructive. The question is about the right of religion to speak out, but clearly respondents had some idea in mind regarding the direction in which religious bodies were likely to speak out. The Sōka Gakkai is a movement with a strong commitment to life enhancement. Indeed, Daisaku Ikeda's first excursion as the joint author of a dialogue (with Arnold Toynbee) bore the title *Choose Life*. The movement is avowedly opposed to the taking of life, and it may be readily assumed that, in responding to this question, the members took it that to 'speak out' was to be understood as to speak against, in this case against abortion and euthanasia. It seems probable that most members also assumed that to speak out was to speak against in the case of homosexuality and extra-marital affairs, but here they are less content to accord religion this right. These personal moral matters were seen by the majority of SGI members as issues within the domain of the individual's own arena of choice, and since their own religion takes no explicit stand against such conduct, they were less willing that other religions should speak out on these matters, which to them are matters of personal responsibility rather than matters of public concern—or such appears to be the case, at least for the majority.

As the sample of UK respondents adapted to match the age structure of the SGI membership illustrates, the differences between the members and the general public on these subjects is not explained by the particular age distribution of the members, since the unadapted and adapted samples of the public show little difference, whilst the comparative SGI figures are strikingly at variance with both. The smallest differences occur with respect to euthanasia and abortion. It is apparent that the SGI members have a distinctively different stance on these issues from the population at large, and even from others of their age-groups.

From these responses, a particular facet of Nichiren philosophy emerges strongly—namely the rejection of the right or role of religion to prescribe moral precepts. As long as individuals act in ways that are considered responsible, this is seen to suffice as moral guidance. The idea of religion as an agency of instruction in the matter of specific rules of comportment is implicitly denied. This privatization of morality, the rejection of all specific moral constraints, and the implicit commitment to democratic choice in moral matters stand in sharp contrast to traditional ideas of religion as a socializing and educative agency, schooling people in appropriate comport-ment, setting objective standards of socially acceptable behavioural codes, and indicating the contours of a 'divine command' moral order. The assumption is that the acquisition of a sense of respons-ibility, attitudes of compassion, and belief in a somewhat undefined capacity for wisdom, courage, and resilience will be enough to ensure the required measure of social cohesion and value consensus not only for human survival, but also to usher in something approximating a golden age—the *kōsen–rufu* of the twenty-first century.

Last among these family-related issues, respondents were asked, 'How satisfied or dissatisfied are you with your home life?' People were given the opportunity to rate their measure of satisfaction on a scale from 1 (dissatisfied) to 10 (satisfied). In the United Kingdom in general, those who responded to this item registered a high degree of satisfaction: the mean being 8.29. For SGI members, the score was less, at 7.48. Nor was the difference a consequence of differences in age distribution between the two populations, since even when the United Kingdom sample was matched for age, the score there was 8.2. The highest score for SGI members was for those who were widowed, at 8.6, and the lowest was for single people, at 6.8. Since single people constituted a large proportion of the membership (more than one-third), their relative dissatisfaction brought down the general figure. The married and those 'living as married' had satisfaction scores of 7.9 and 7.6 respectively. Regrouping the entire membership, putting together those who lived as couples (whether married, non-married, gay, lesbian, etc.), the score achieved was 7.8; whilst the total of those living separately (as single people, divorced, or widowed persons) achieved a score of 6.9.

Political and Economic Values

In the foregoing dicussion of the family and the attitudes towards related issues, we alluded to wider political matters, and in Table 18 we set out the responses on all the issues on which respondents were invited to say whether religious bodies should 'speak out'. We record the percentages of affirmative responses. On all issues that were concerned with bio-ethics and sexual ethics, the issues

TABLE 18. *Affirmative answers to the question: 'is it proper for religious bodies to speak out on' the various issues listed?*

Issues	SGI	UK	UK-AS[a]	Difference between SGI and UK-AS
Third World problems	81	76	82	−1
Racial discrimination	81	66	70	+11
Ecology and environment	84	61	67	+17
Euthanasia	55	58	64	−9
Disarmament	83	56	63	+20
Abortion	48	56	58	−10
Extra-marital affairs	35	52	54	−19
Unemployment	60	48	50	+10
Homosexuality	35	57	51	−16
Government policy	44	35	39	+5

[a] United Kingdom Adapted Sample to match the age structure of the membership of SGI-UK.

that might be labelled matters of personal morality, the Buddhist respondents were less inclined to favour religious bodies speaking out; but on other, more political issues, they were more favourable to comment from religious bodies. We have already noted the strongly 'pro-life' orientation of the official Nichiren and SGI ideology which may incline members to take a different attitude to euthanasia and abortion from that evident among the similar age-groups of the general population. But against this must be set the consideration that SGI strongly demands that the individual should take full responsibility for his own life, and that no organization should tell him what to do. Their inclination is to favour much less than the general population censorious attitudes towards homosexuality and extra-marital affairs. But on the more general political issues, the SGI members are at least as disposed as the general public to call for outspoken religious responses, and in most areas—conspicuously, racial discrimination, ecology, unemployment, and, above all, disarmament—they make a stronger demand. In this, they echo faithfully the preoccupations of the leadership of their movement, and endorse the general policies of Sōka Gakkai International on all these subjects.

There is, however, a distinction to be made between the meta-political concerns and the more immediate national political issues such as government policy and unemployment. Here, the respondents generally, but the general public more pronouncedly than the Buddhists, appeared to endorse the need for a firm line between religion and politics, and between Church and State. On the evidence of these replies, it appears that the general public more readily accepts that religion might appropriately speak out on issues, as the Dutch say, 'far from the bed', but are more ambivalent on the remaining topics. The SGI members discriminate much more markedly, reflecting their tolerance on personal morality, the rules of which are not laid down by their religion, and global metapolitical concerns, about which they may be better informed than the public at large, and about which they are certainly more sensitized, since these subjects are the focus of much comment in the literature produced by the British movement and also by their parent organization in Japan.

Following the European Values Study, we asked a question directly related to unemployment:

Why are there people in this country who live in need? Here are some possible reasons. Which one do you consider to be the most important? And which one is the second most important? (See Table 19.)

TABLE 19. *Why are there people in need?* (%)

	UK	UK-AS[a]	SGI
Because they are unlucky	16.8	17.0	7.1
Because of laziness and lack of willpower	24.4	22.3	8.3
Because of injustice in society	28.0	30.0	26.1
It's an inevitable part of modern progress	23.6	24.1	7.1
Karma: the law of cause and effect	—	—	38.9
Others	3.1	3.6	4.7
No answer	3.9	2.8	7.8

[a] United Kingdom Adapted Sample to match the age structure of the membership of SGI-UK.

By giving a weight coefficient of 2 to the most important reason, and a 1 to the reason chosen as second most important, we were able to calculate the importance given in general to these various causes by the SGI members in comparison with the United Kingdom population. (We have again adapted that sample to match the age structure of the SGI, but, as the figures indicate, in this instance, age differences in the general public were of relatively slight consequence.) Four reasons were offered, and SGI respondents had the opportunity to write in a further, fifth cause. As can be seen from Table 19, the members took advantage of that possibility.

The Nichiren respondents stressed karma and the law of cause and effect as the explanation for the fact that there were people living in Britain who were in need. Present effects were the consequence of past actions, and those living in need today were clearly the victims of the causes that they had created in the past, and particularly in earlier incarnations. Some of the written-in responses offered variants on this them, with phrases such as: 'a lack of understanding of life: the cosmic order, the law'; or 'they don't conform to NSUK teaching'; or 'they haven't met NSUK: they lack the strength to change, which may come through practice, it is powerlessness on their part'; or 'it comes from economic greed, from selfishness, from bad causes'. Other causes that were suggested in response to this issue were a lack of love by parents, the uncaring attitude of the authorities; and structural alienation.

The second choice of the SGI members was *injustice in society*, which is a more or less Marxist explanation for need, but this option was the most preferred explanation of the general public. Personal *laziness and lack of willpower*, which amount to a quality of the individual, and need as a *latent function of progress* ranked second both in the population at large and among the members, but among the members, these explanations are offered at a much lower percentage. Pure chance, or *bad luck*, is the least favoured option of both groups, but is mentioned less than twice as frequently by the Buddhists—with their ideological commitment to explanation in terms of causes—than by the general public.

Some 39 per cent of the SGI population appeared to find in their religious philosophy the most convincing explanation for what happens in society. If we add to that the Marxist-type explanation, which cites injustice, we may say that two-thirds of this group favoured explanations which they could relate to the absence of Buddhist influence either on individuals or on society (or both). Nor should we ignore those who indicated 'laziness and lack of will-power' as a cause, since some respondents linked this directly to the absence of enlightened understanding. When that connection was made, this reason also became a facet of Nichiren-type reasoning: lack of willpower and laziness were themselves associated with the fact that people did not practise Nichiren's Buddhism. According to Nichiren philosophy, changes in society are a consequence of individual actions and effort. If the individual acquires the strength to discipline his own greed, to practise in order to neutralize the bad karma that he has earlier caused for himself, and to create good karma by current other-regarding and life-enhancing acts, so good social consequences will follow, including, it must be presumed, a fairer society in which need will be diminished or eliminated.

The principal difference between the general population and the Nichiren Shōshū members lay in what might be taken as an explanation in terms of 'latent functions', namely that there are people in need because this is an inevitable side-effect of progress. One in four of the general sample subscribed to this view, whereas only one in fourteen of the SGI members gave it credence. The reluctance of the Buddhists to endorse this proposition is, of course, entirely consonant with their overall philosophy, which rejects any sort of zero-sum approach to human happiness and well-being. The expectation is that value creation can be limitless, that there is a real prospect of sufficiency, perhaps even abundance, for everyone, and that this can be realized if only people will adopt their Buddhist religious practice. For these devotees, there should be no dark side to human progress and evolution. Bad karma inherited from the past can be overcome by diligent chanting, and future prosperity and well-being can be assured by adopting wholesome and positive attitudes of mind now. Those attitudes will be cultivated by contemplating the *Gohonzon* during the periods of chanting the invocation to the *sutra*, and by the performance of regular *gongyō*. Injustice in society can be indicated as a cause of need, but that injustice may also be attributed to the fact that as yet not enough individuals have become committed to taking responsibility for themselves, and so have permitted deficient or corrupt institutions to persist which otherwise might have been eliminated.

For further comparison of the political orientation of SGI members relative to the general public, respondents were asked to locate their political dispositions on a graduated scale numbered from 1 (the left) to 10 (the right). There was very little evident reluctance to respond to this question, and fully 95 per cent of those who returned the questionnaire dealt with it. The result was to show SGI members very average in their political dispositions, and further, to show that they differed only slightly from the general population. For all three groups, the median and the mode were 5, but the three groups differed in the mean, with 4.8 for SGI members and 5.5 for the general population (and 5.4 for the age-adjusted sample). Thus, such differences as existed between SGI and the general public were not attributable to differences in age distribution. The general public shows itself to be of the centre, whilst the SGI members revealed themselves as more inclined towards a centre-left position: 0.7 to the left of centre. This result supports the preceding table. In itself, of course, SGI is a non-political, politically entirely neutral organization, but the expressed concerns of the membership with such matters as environmental and ecological issues and the peace movement are perhaps expectably more likely to attract people whose general inclinations are more to the left than to the right. Beyond this, it is clear that Nichiren Buddhists in Britain constitute a distinctive minority who certainly do not see themselves as part of the country's settled establishment, and hence are likely to regard themselves as part of a broadly dissenting tradition, even if this has never found expression in direct political terms. Given this circumstance, a somewhat left of centre position for membership is unsurprising.

How Public Institutions are Regarded

Thus far, we have discussed the family and the polity, the former of which is rated as the most important institution by SGI members, and the latter of which is seen as the least important, just as they are by the people of the United Kingdom generally. Another approach to the same issues, closely linked to concerns that follow, is taken up by the question of confidence in public organizations, to which we now turn.

Respondents were given a list of the major public organizations in Britain, which included the churches, the armed forces, the educational system, the legal system, the press, the trade unions, the police, parliament, the civil service, major companies, and the social security system, and of two international agencies in which

TABLE 20. *Confidence in public organizations*

	UK	UK-AS[a]	SGI	Difference between UK and SGI
Armed forces	1.90	1.96	2.85	−0.95
Police	2.00	2.08	2.54	−0.54
Social security system	2.36	2.77	2.97	−0.61
Nato	2.38	2.40	2.59	−0.21
Legal system	2.39	2.43	2.64	−0.25
Education	2.40	2.44	2.70	−0.30
The churches	2.41	2.50	3.20	−0.79
Civil service	2.53	2.60	2.84	−0.31
Major companies	2.54	2.53	2.89	−0.35
Parliament	2.54	2.59	2.75	−0.21
European Community	2.54	2.56	2.08	+0.46
Trade unions	2.92	2.94	2.91	+0.01
The press	3.12	3.18	3.09	+0.03
General confidence	2.39	2.54	2.78	−0.39

Note: Highest confidence level = 1; lowest = 4.

[a] United Kingdom Adapted Sample to match the age structure of the membership of SGI-UK.

Britain is involved, the European Community and Nato. Respondents were asked how much confidence they had in these organizations on a scale ranging from 'a great deal' (which scored 1), through 'quite a lot' (which scored 2), 'not very much' (score 3), to 'no confidence at all' (score 4). On the basis of the scores that were recorded, we computed a mean. In Table 20 we have ordered these organizations according to the confidence reposed in them by the United Kingdom population (and that population matched for age with the SGI sample), indicating the extent of the difference in attitude towards that rating from the scores recorded by the Buddhists.

There are different ways of looking at this table. First of all, the general public had greater confidence in these organizations than had SGI members: a score of 2.39 as against 2.78. In general terms, the public tended towards the response of 'quite a lot of confidence', while, over all, the Nichiren people were inclined to say 'not very much confidence'. In general, they manifested much less confidence in public bodies, and especially in the armed forces, the churches, the social security system, and the police—a difference between almost 1 point and 0.5 of a point. (Nor were the differences to be explained by the different age distributions of the two populations, as our figures show, except perhaps in the case of the social security system, in which the level of confidence of the age-adapted sample for the country as a whole was closer to that of SGI than it was to the higher level of confidence registered by the United Kingdom as a whole).

The two groups exhibited more or less the same measure of trust towards the trade unions and the press, or, more accurately stated, they manifested the same degree of distrust in registering 'not very much confidence' in these organizations. For the general public, the organization which was third least able to summon confidence was the European Community, with a score (2.54) which lies between 'not very much' and 'quite a lot', a position also occupied by the major companies and parliament. In each of the last two, the Nichiren Buddhists manifested even less confidence, but they took a more positive view of the European Community, in which they claimed to have quite a lot of confidence and this is, indeed, the one organization about which they were significantly less sceptical than was the public at large.

If we may take the mean of both populations respectively as a departure point, somewhat different comparisons emerge. For the general public, the greatest measure of trust lay in the armed forces and the police (1.90 and 2.00), but other institutions—the social security system, Nato, the legal system, education, and the churches —all attained the average measure of confidence (2.36 to 2.42). Scores below average were achieved by the civil service, major companies, parliament, and the European Community (2.53 and 2.54), while the least confidence was accorded to the trade unions and the press. In the SGI population, education, parliament, the civil service, and the armed forces all got the average score of confidence (between 2.70 and 2.85), while the police, Nato, and the legal system achieved scores higher than average (2.54 to 2.64). Apart from the European Community, which got the highest score of confidence from the Buddhists, all the rest—the major companies, the trade unions, the social security system, and the press—fell markedly below average (2.89 to 3.09) and least confidence was accorded to the churches, which received the low score of 3.20.

Whilst the findings overall indicate a considerable degree of scepticism about the major organizations in both populations, the SGI members had signficantly less trust in them than had the general public in almost every instance. The confidence of the Buddhists in the European Community reflects the emphasis in Sōka Gakkai on international goodwill. The movement seeks to proclaim its message internationally, makes vigorous efforts to promote international cultural events, and, as we have noted, strongly endores the goal of world peace. All of these concerns induce a certain commitment to international agencies. Had the survey included the United Nations as a public organization, it is highly likely that it would have outshone in the confidence it inspired among the Buddhists, all of these other agencies, since Soka Gakkai International became one of the recognized non-governmental organizations at the United Nations some years ago.

That the SGI members should register so little confidence in the churches is equally expectable. The votaries of this movement were not generally committed churchgoers before becoming Buddhists, and those who were so disposed may well have become disenchanted with the churches before joining the Nichiren movement. Might the considerably lower manifestation of trust in the social security system reflect unfortunate encounters experienced by members of a group with a strong disposition to pursue sometimes hazardous forms of self-employment? The limited trust in major companies may also relate to the belief in self-reliance and enterprise among a membership with high rates of self-employment, or it may be affected by the extent to which such companies are perceived as lacking in a sense of responsibility towards the environment.

That the appreciation of the legal system and the police should be lower among members than among the general public may reflect the rejection by the Buddhist movement of belief in an external and constraining agency which seeks to impose the values of an objective morality rather than encouraging personal integrity and responsibility. That they should also record a much lower degree of enthusiasm for the armed services may again be related to the stance of their organization in respect of world peace. The movement is avowedly opposed to war, and this orientation may dictate a general scepticism about the value of the armed forces, and perhaps indeed the need for them. In this light, that Nato should stimulate more confidence than most other organizations, and above the average amount of confidence registered by the members, may be attributable to its image as an agency of international co-operation, which might weigh more profoundly than its role as an organization of military defence.

Overall, the scores of the Buddhists indicate a modest measure of alienation from contemporary social institutions somewhat in excess of that of the general population, and a lack of confidence either in the values embraced by these organizations or in their capacity to achieve them. SGI members are, on average, better educated than the public at large, and this may encourage a more critical posture towards agencies and institutions which, for many people, are apathetically taken for granted as they are. Undoubtedly, the public campaigns of SGI, the promotion of activities, exhibitions, and publicity in response to Third World problems, in support of world peace, ecological conservation, and general cultural goals, must have resulted in a measure of 'consciousness-raising' which leads members to challenge the record and the values of national and international agencies.

Work, Authority, and Change

As we have already seen, SGI members attach a high degree of importance to work, exceeding that of the general public. Such a disposition might, among traditional Protestants, indicate a persistence of the work ethic, and it is not inconceivable, even if it is not explicitly articulated in the movement's ideology, that something approaching that ethic, or ideas and orientations leading to similar effects, might obtain within the community of adherents to Nichiren. Alternatively, commitment to work might indicate a materialistic outlook on life, and with regard to this possibility there is a means of examining a possible connection by the use of the Englehart twelve-item battery which was employed in the European Values Study, and of comparing SGI attitudes with those of the wider public.[1] As Englehart conceived it, a materialistic outlook was associated with an emphasis on the need to maintain a high level of economic growth; the need to fight rising prices and crime; the maintenance of order in the nation; and a demand that the country should have strong defence forces. People who opted for these priorities, so it was hypothesized, were those who put high value on economic and physical security.

In contrast, those who are designated as post-materialists are said to stress the need to protect freedom of speech; favour giving people a greater voice in how things are decided, at work, in their communities, and in the decisions of government. They favour a friendlier, less impersonal society, and a society in which ideas count for more than money. Of course, in actuality, people may have mixed and ambivalent attitudes when faced with choices in these matters, but certain broad findings are worth noting. The Englehart twelve-item battery made possible the production of a ten-point scale

TABLE 21. *The materialism scale: the United Kingdom and SGI compared* (%)

	UK	UK-AS[a]	SGI
Pure materialists (scores 1–3)	25	21	2
Mixed materialists (scores 4–5)	28	28	3
Mixed post-materialists (scores 6–7)	29	30	20
Pure post-materialists (scores 8–10)	18	21	75

[a] United Kingdom Adapted Sample to match the age structure of the membership of SGI-UK.

[1] R. Englehart, *Culture Shift in Advanced Industrial Society* (Princeton, NJ: Princeton University Press, 1990), 131–5.

for the European Values Study, and we were able to compare the SGI population with that of the United Kingdom (Table 21).

It is evident from these results that, even though SGI members accord a high value to work, none the less they are overwhelmingly disposed to be what this scale designates as post-materialists. They attach more importance to belonging, self-expression, and intellectual and aesthetic satisfaction than to physical and economic security. The Buddhist results are only very slightly influenced by the age structure of the membership, as our adapted sample illustrates: 75 per cent of the SGI members score as pure post-materialists, against 21 per cent of the general population matched for age. Within SGI, the younger members do show a stronger disposition to this orientation than the older members: even so, the overall picture is transparently clear—on these criteria of differentiation, the Buddhists differ markedly in tendency from the corresponding age-groups within the general population.

A different device for discovering the values of our sample was also derived from the European Values Study, which had already subjected a random sample of the general public to the same test. The samples were asked to evaluate possible changes that might occur in the future by labelling them as simply 'good', 'bad', or

TABLE 22. *Which prospects of change are regarded as good or bad?*

		UK	UK-AS[a]	SGI
If the following eventualites were to occur, would you regard it as a good thing, or a bad thing, or would you not mind?				
Less emphasis on money and material possessions	Good	63	65	86
	Bad	10	9	2
Decrease in importance of work in our lives	Good	31	34	28
	Bad	49	46	43
Greater emphasis on the development of the individual	Good	78	80	96
	Bad	5	4	1
Greater respect for authority	Good	73	72	28
	Bad	9	10	29
A simple and more natural life-style	Good	81	80	75
	Bad	4	4	2

[a] United Kingdom Adapted Sample to match the age structure of the membership of SGI-UK.

'would not mind' (Table 22). On this test, the Buddhists exceed the general public in favouring the development of the individual, and, by an even larger margin, if not quite so overwhelmingly, in their enthusiasm for a society which places less weight on money and material possessions. In these matters, and in the desirability of a simple and more natural life-style, they reveal very little internal division, and their dispositions are in broad conformity with those expressed by the general public; in the matter of individual develop-ment and a lesser emphasis on material possessions, a higher percentage of the sample endorses these values. The two issues on which the Buddhists differ among themselves most profoundly are on the question of whether it would be a good thing were work to be of less importance in people's lives, and on the desirability of greater respect for authority. Like the general public, the Buddhists by a small but significant majority endorse the view that it would be a bad thing were work to diminish in its importance in our lives. Together with the rejection of money and material possessions, this result suggests that work is identified less as a source of monetary reward than as a positive value in its own right for at least a considerable number of members. Work is perhaps still seen as a source of meaning and purpose in life, as a major focus around which the individual shapes his own sense of identity. This orientation may be strongly reinforced by the extent to which SGI members are disposed to look for self-employed work, and their relatively dispro-portionate concentration in various artistic and caring professions. These interpretations go beyond the direct evidence, but we may venture them as distinct probabilities.

The single most striking result of this aspect of the survey is the polarization of the Buddhists who, in almost equal proportions, divide on whether a greater emphasis on respect for authority would be a good thing or a bad thing, with fully two-thirds of their number being undecided or indifferent on the matter. In this, too, the Buddhists show greatest divergence from the sample of the United Kingdom population. In part, this response may reflect the strong Buddhist emphasis on taking responsibility for one's own life. Yet it is also clear that, much as some members stressed the egalitarianism of Sōka Gakkai, and saw it as an unhierarchic organization, the movement does, none the less, enjoy vigorous and resolute leader-ship, at international level and within each individual country. From their responses to this survey, it appears that this leadership, and

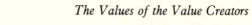

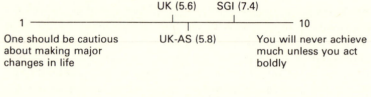

UK (5.6)   SGI (7.4)

1 ———————————————————————— 10

| One should be cautious about making major changes in life | UK-AS (5.8) | You will never achieve much unless you act boldly |

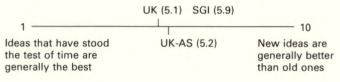

UK (5.1)   SGI (5.9)

1 ———————————————————————— 10

| Ideas that have stood the test of time are generally the best | UK-AS (5.2) | New ideas are generally better than old ones |

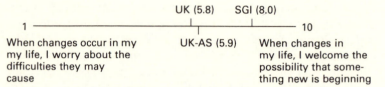

UK (5.8)   SGI (8.0)

1 ———————————————————————— 10

| When changes occur in my my life, I worry about the difficulties they may cause | UK-AS (5.9) | When changes in my life, I welcome the possibility that something new is beginning |

Notes: Respondents could score from 1 to 10 on scales offering divergent attitudes to change.

UK-AS denotes United Kingdom Adapted Sample to match the age structure of the membership of SGI-UK.

Fig. 1. Attitudes to change

the strong emphasis on the role of leaders as agents who provide 'guidance', is not seen, at least not seen by some members, as authority in the normal sense. In some respects, Nichiren philosophy admits, where it does not actually encourage, a certain strain of libertarianism—individuals must make their own decisions, and in this sense, normal authority structures in society might be put at a discount. There is a strong demand that members be non-judgemental and unmoralistic, and this may feed the idea that, in times past, part of society's problems may have lain in a too readily accorded respect for established authority which those wielding authority had not always merited.

It was possible for us to adapt for SGI members another of the questions designed to make apparent the value commitments of those surveyed in the European Values Study, and this was the way in which change was regarded. How, in their attitudes towards change, would the membership compare with the general population?

Respondents could score from 1 to 10 on scales which offered divergent attitudes. For each population, we calculated the mean (see Fig. 1). Clearly, SGI members were less conservative and more disposed towards change than was the case with the United Kingdom population. They wanted to take opportunities as they arose, and to explore possibilites. To ensure that this difference from the general public was not a consequence of the fact that the members had a lower average age than the population at large, we again adjusted the UK sample to match the age structure of SGI, and we see that it clearly is not. The Nichiren Buddhists, however, since all of them were converts to their new faith, have already made one extremely important decision in which they had chosen to change their way of life and to accept a comprehensive ideology which, if not new in itself, was new to them. Beyond this, the willingness to take up a challenge, to strike out, and to approach life without fear are all things emphasized in the literature which they read, and are the burden of many of the testimonials that are published in the *UK Express*, the organ of the British movement. Nichiren philosophy teaches that to have good results you have to create good causes, and that present opportunities are the consequences either of having laid down such causes in the past or of diligent chanting. Nichiren's followers are committed to promoting change. They use chanting to effect changes in their lives, using the *Gohonzon* as a mirror in which to see themselves reflected and through which to effect changes, in a process that might be likened to a type of sacred self-induced psychological analysis. The goal is self-improvement, which of necessity implies undergoing a process of personal change, and a further consequence of such changes in many individuals, so it is believed, is that the world itself might be changed.

Whilst there is an emphasis on the capacity for personal change, there is also a strong assertion that, by adopting a Buddhist perspective, the inherent quality of the individual is not so much changed as *realized*. The Buddhists recognize that they differ considerably one from another, and take pride in their capacity to tolerate these differences. At the same time, they emphasize the importance of the unity of their movement, claiming that unity does not imply uniformity. Thus the guide-lines which they adopt in appraising their own behaviour are expressed in terms of the courage to take up challenges, taking responsibility, being compassionate,

TABLE 23. *Ideas of good and evil*

	UK	UK-AS[a]	SGI
Here are two statements which people sometimes make when discussing good and evil. Which one comes closest to your own point of view?			
A There are absolutely clear guide-lines about what is good and evil. These always apply to everyone, whatever the circumstances.	38	34	14
B There can never be absolutely clear guidelines about what is good and evil. What is evil depends entirely on circumstances at the time.	58	64	54
C Disagree with both A and B	2	2	28

[a] United Kingdom Adapted Sample to match the age structure of the membership of SGI-UK.

and transforming into something better the various lower states of consciousness described in their Buddhist psychology. They espouse certain general, rather abstract principles of conduct, but eschew, as we have seen, fixed rules which many of them see as rigid, as stultifying personality, and as a hindrance to that vital concern to be in control of one's life. Thus, it is not absolute guide-lines by which they measure their performance, as becomes apparent in the comparative responses to another test drawn from the European Values Study. The question was posed as in Table 23.

Situational Ethics or General Principles?

The majority of the Nichiren members, like the majority of the public, adopt a situational ethic, in which circumstances, motives, goals, and intentions are taken into account in appraising good and evil. Our adjusted sample shows that a United Kingdom population with a similar age structure would adopt this attitude to an even greater extent. But far fewer SGI members endorsed objective guide-lines for good and evil, again marking them off as distinctly different from many who adopt minority religious orientations (particularly within Christianity). A proportion of more than one in four felt unable to endorse either an objectivist or a situationalist position. This greater degree of discrimination may reflect the general higher level of education among this group in comparison with the general population, which might readily be supposed to lead to greater difficulty in endorsing what are necessarily rather gross dichotomous categories. Some of them made that position explicit in the comments which they spontaneously wrote on the questionnaire form:

Clear guide-lines, but circumstances are important.

Prefer to think of value creation or not.

I think it hard to answer this question without defining what is evil, and what is good. And to hold the view within the context that no one is wholly good or wholly evil, but we all have potential for both. Also great evil can sometimes be turned around to create great good. And both are an essential part of life. I would define basic evil as a lack of respect/true understanding of ourselves and other people, basic good as a deep respect for ourselves and others. Within this context (A) is applicable.

One respondent added to the statement listed as (B) on the questionnaire form the words 'and the result or effect on the circumstances of people'. Others commented:

I disagreed and agree with different things in both and now I'm confused. There is good and evil inherent in all, but I think we are responsible for our situations that we find ourselves in, and therefore responsible for the actions we take in each situation. Good or evil actions—we have to face the inevitable from either, and I would rather face good effects.

There is good and evil in every human being, but it depends on their fundamental attitudes and beliefs as to what state they manifest (which is more answer (B) than answer (A) .

My view: some evil and good is clearly defined (murder, rape, etc.). But some good and evil depends on circumstances.

Each individual knows in his heart what is right and what is wrong, good and evil.

The idea of Good and Evil originates purely in the minds of people according to their particular beliefs.

Evil is part of everyone as is Buddhahood, either can appear in any moment. I would like to refer you to Richard Causton's book *Nichiren Shoshu Buddhism*: in it he explains the ten worlds. This is the real answer to your question.

Crap! To respect the dignity of life is correct, to slander life is incorrect. But you must chant to get the wisdom to know what this means and how to apply it.

Good and evil are clearly defined. One's responses only vary and only depend upon (a) one's self; (b) circumstances.

Though (B) is nearly right, but who can judge good and evil?

The variety of opinions relative to the nature of good and evil reflect the subjectivism encouraged by a faith which promotes personal judgement on such issues, and which eschews concrete interdictions. Unlike many Christian minority faiths, SGI has not sought to establish its probity by prohibitions or proscriptions on the way in which members comport themselves or choose to spend their time. Leisure, for example, is a free area of choice, and there is no suggestion that association with the world or the general public is in any sense likely either to pollute or to infect the Buddhists, or to lower their ethical standards. Indeed, those high ideals of courage, wisdom, and compassion which they profess are to be realized perhaps as much in the wider society as within their own community. There is no suggestion that the liberty of members with regard to the use of their leisure time is in the slightest degree impaired by their religious predilections, and there is no attempt to constrain them in respect of how they choose their recreations.

Leisure Time and Good Causes

As their responses showed, and as our interviews abundantly confirmed, leisure time was very important to SGI members as time that might be devoted to friends or family, and to engage in recreational activities. Some 94 per cent of SGI members declared themselves to be involved in recreational pursuits. From the list presented to them, and the additions that they made to it, we were able to distinguish different types of recreational activity–social, solitary, physical, and technological.

The significance of these categories is that they provide an indication of the extent to which the followers of this minority religion hold themselves aloof from the normal activities of the public at large. It is not by any means uncommon for the adherents of what are colloquially designated as sects to eschew activities that are considered in some sense to be either worldly or frivolous, or a distraction from the urgent need to maintain religious probity and/ or to communicate religious ideas to others. Many of these movements make concessions only in the sphere of necessary economic and educational activities, and draw a firm line with respect to permitted and proscribed recreational pursuits. No one with even a cursory acquaintance with Sōka Gakkai International would expect to find any interdiction of normal recreational activity, but what the responses to our questionnaire illustrate is that neither is there any informal inclination to relinquish normal leisure uses, even though maintaining the serious practice of their faith is a demanding and time-consuming undertaking. There is neither a religio-moral expectation that members should abandon hobbies or interests, nor, apparently, does commitment to religious practice squeeze out such avocations. Indeed, as the social programme of the movement makes apparent, a wide variety of leisure-time interests are actively encouraged, and occasions are created in which both professional and amateur artistic talents and enthusiasms are mobilized for movement-sponsored events. Beyond this, members indicated that they did have the time and the inclination to engage in a wide variety of spare-time pursuits of one sort or another.

Almost 75 per cent of respondents were involved in one or more social recreations, and among those which members listed were dancing, acting, social gatherings, indoor games, video-making with others, social drinking, pool, billiards, and snooker. Physical recreations commanded somewhat less involvement, with fewer than three out of five engaging in sport, walking, massage, judo, cycling, weight-training, or health exercises. It can be immediately seen that this range of leisure-time pursuits is potentially as diverse as that which might be discovered for the general population, and some of these activities might be undertaken together with non-Buddhists on the basis of shared recreational interest. Nor did more solitary recreations distinguish the membership from the wider public, except perhaps in the higher incidence of those engaged in the graphic arts, creative writing, and music. Other pursuits included photography, gardening, crafts, horses, do-it-yourself activities, reading, and needlework.

As distinct from participation in these various activities, up to 98 per cent of the members were interested observers of recreational performances, in particularly manifesting an interest in culture and the arts, exhibitions, music, theatre, art in general, cinema, and novel-reading. These items predominated, with only 20 per cent taking an interest as observers of sporting contests. Recreation, whether passive or active, is perhaps the area of life in which people voluntarily identify with the wider culture, and the evidence from the Buddhists indicates that they are widely involved in the regular and common pursuits of the general public—probably somewhat more so in artistic and creative endeavour, and somewhat less so in competitive games and feats of physical prowess. But none of these various activities is specifically contrary to the ethos of the religion, and members are free to make up their own minds about what recreational pursuits warrant the expenditure of the time, effort, and money devoted to them. That members should have so wide a span of leisure involvements, given the time which most of them devote to their religious practice, is perhaps surprising, but clearly control of members' time is not, as in some Christian sectarian movements, a device by which members are 'protected' from the allurements of the activities of the wider society. Indeed, members control their own agendas, choose for themselves the times and extent of their chanting, and the number of meetings of the movement which they attend, and so make their own decisions with respect both to the demands of the faith and to how, otherwise, they spend their spare time. They are socially outgoing, culturally oriented, and a little less drawn to physical and spectator sports than might be expected of a relatively youthful cross-section of the population.

As a further indication of the extent to which they were integrated with or insulated from the wider society, members were also asked about their involvement in voluntary associations other than SGI. One out of three respondents was also active in some other voluntary organization. Eleven per cent belonged to each of three different types of voluntary body—service organizations, ecological associations, and political bodies. Among the service organizations were included such groups as : Nightline, the Samaritans, Friends of the Samaritans, The Red Cross, and St John's Ambulance. The ecological bodies included: Whale and Dolphin Conservation Society, World Wildlife Fund, Friends of the Earth, Greenpeace, World-Wide Fund for Nature, the London Wildlife Trust. The political associations included: the Campaign for Nuclear Disarmament, Amnesty International, Stop the Gulf War; while a few were also members of a political party.

These affiliations are all expectable lines of endeavour for those committed to the principles of Nichiren's Buddhism. Sōka Gakkai International is itself a significant agency for the promotion of peace and conservation and, in common with other Japanese religious bodies, endorses the theory that man must function in harmony with, not in exploitation of, the natural environment. The British SGI raised significant funds for the Commonwealth Human Environment

Council (CHEC) by its performances of the musical *Alice*, written, produced, staged, and acted entirely by the membership in the mid-1980s. That event combined SGI's positive espousal of creative arts (costumes, scenery), as well as performing arts, with an explicit commitment to environmental causes for which the whole organization rallied its talents. More recently, SGI-UK sponsored a special conference in association with CHEC in preparation for the 1992 Rio Summit on the environment. The voluntary service organizations give practical expression to the idea of creating value, of life-enhancement by sustaining respect for others and affirming the dignity of human life.

Among other causes which members registered as endeavours that elicited their support were: Oxfam, HANDS, St Christopher's Hospice, and lesbian and gay rights organizations. About 8 per cent belonged to associations that were essentially cultural in their interests—music clubs, amateur dramatic societies, video-workshops; whilst about 1 or 2 per cent were members of a therapeutic programme, a sporting or health club, or a scientific association.

In their moral attitudes, their attitudes to work and to change, and in their leisure pursuits, the British SGI clearly constitutes a distinctive public which differs from the generality. Strongly religious minorities generally differentiate themelves from the main-stream society, whether in its conventionally religious or its more secularized manifestations, but most of them do so by espousing a more rigorously restrictive moral code, and by canvassing interdictions which are an intensification of the normative moral code. This is not the case with SGI. Whilst they profess a stronger concern for compassion, they also proclaim the need for tolerance of differences in moral commitment and comportment. Although committed to proselytizing and recruiting newcomers to their own ethical perspectives, they also accept without censure that the performances of others reflect karmic determinants, which is a virtual acknowledgement that what the conventionally religious might regard as moral deficiency is not really the individual's fault. The Buddha nature which they seek to realize does not preclude moments of anger, hate, fear, and greed, and whilst these emotions and the acts which issue from them are to be transcended, they are also in a sense excused.

This broad liberalization of moral attitudes is, however, not an indication of indifferentism. It is not a consequence of a decline in religious belief which has formerly underpinned moral values.

Rather it is associated with a rededication of religious commitment, but on the basis of a different and—for the Christian and post-Christian British public—unfamiliar set of moral premisses. A different conception of morality is embraced in which certain transcendent and encompassing virtues replace the specifics of a moral code governing concrete performances. The members show themselves as more disposed to endorse what might be termed politicized moral values—the demands for certain moral acts on the part of government and public authorities in the promotion of such causes as peace, disarmament, and ecological conservation—and less disposed towards the regulation of the individual's personal behaviour. They endorse the importance of work, but have often chosen congenial work, or believe that by chanting they may be offered such work, and seek it, to a very considerable degree, within the caring professions and in creative and aesthetic activities. They affirm the need for adaptability, generally embrace the need for change, and regard it with optimism. In all of this they mark themselves off as a radically different sort of minority religion from those found in the traditions of Christian sectarianism. This conception of the relationship between religious faith and moral obligation is associated with a liberal—at times libertarian—attitude to leisure-time pursuits. SGI no more seeks to control its votaries by making specific demands on their time than it does by seeking to regulate their moral conduct. Despite the practice of what, in British experience, is exotic ritual, in terms of their everyday comportment adherents are, in many respects, undifferentiated from the wider public.

VIII

The Involvement of the Members

RELIGIOUS organizations—and today this includes even the established churches which once could rely on blind or even coerced obedience—depend for their viability on their capacity to summon the allegiance of adherents to participate, to give, or perhaps to perform in one way or another. As voluntary bodies, they have little purchase over their following except to urge compliance on normative grounds and by the offer of present reassurance that— here or hereafter—in the experience of the believer, the untoward, however conceived, will thereby be avoided, overcome, or in some measure neutralized. The benefits of believing the required teachings, practising the prescribed exercises, and leading an appropriate life are the constitutent performances by which salvation (or the best help towards it) may be attained, in whatever way salvation is conceptualized. Inducing votaries to commit themselves in these various ways is essential for any movement if it is to survive, and every movement has techniques for sustaining interest, encouraging response, and stimulating performance. Congregationally organized religions such as Christian denominations put their trust in drawing members together as a visible community, and whilst many Christian groups would not make congregational participation into a *sine qua non* for salvation, it is in the congregation that commitment is affirmed and made manifest, even if teachings also emphasize private belief and public behaviour. SGI has its collective occasions, too—in the meetings of its various organizational echelons, and in occasional larger assemblies and rallies—but, following the Japanese model from which its style derives, the *locus* of its crucial activity is within the individual household (supported by meetings of small local groups). The twice daily chanting of the invocation and the recital of the *gongyō* are, in the normal course of events, at most household activities, but they are often undertaken as solo performances by individual members.

Faith and Organizational Commitment

Chanting is at the heart of Nichiren Buddhism. But before indicating the reported incidence of this practice, and the length and level of commitment which it evidences, we may distinguish between this aspect of religious faith and commitment to SGI as an organization. Some of our respondents made this distinction quite explicit, and it is clear that, whilst willingness to contribute time and effort to the organization as such might be induced by fervent belief in the efficacy and the necessity of chanting, none the less the two things, and their purposes, were distinguishable. For many members, this distinction might be almost academic, since SGI was the agency that had disseminated, promoted, and protected the practice, and must, therefore, be supported: for others, these two items were, if linked, still clearly separable. Some members were uncomfortable with one, whilst readily accepting the other.

In any religion, even firm believers sometimes doubt. We asked those whom we interviewed whether they ever entertained doubts, and also, since some members had left, whether lack of belief was a principal reason. Of themselves, some said that they had never doubted. The words of the violin-maker whom we have already cited may be recalled: 'I doubt myself, I think: I don't think I've ever doubted the practice, maybe because I trusted the people whom I met when starting, and whom I continue to see.' But most acknowledged that they had, or had had, doubts, several of them averring that everyone experienced doubts. A surveyor-turned-teacher said he had had doubts 'when I first started—"What am I doing—kneeling in front of a piece of paper—*Gohonzon*. Someone coming in might say, 'What a nutter!'"' I sometimes think it's so incredible, how can it possibly work?' A number of members declared that when they were troubled by doubt they 'chant about it—and always have an answer', as a Caribbean accounts clerk put it. Others saw a positive benefit in doubt; it was a challenge, a way of discovering something about oneself.

Discovering something about oneself, or the trauma associated with it, was what some members believed often induced someone to leave—those who could not face the challenge which practice imposed. The accounts clerk said, 'they give up because they find their true selves [by practising] and they don't want it. It happened to me—I had to realize I was packing away my true self, being selfish.' The surveyor echoed the point: 'When you practise you have to deal with changes in your life. Perhaps there are things too painful to challenge.' The would-be permaculturist maintained that practice caused 'bad karma to come up in front of you', and an accountant/purchasing manager said, 'When you practise obstacles/ problems come up in your life . . . Through practice they [some members] become unhappy about their unhealthy tendencies and so they suffer and give up the practice.' The male musician recalled that '[A friend] stopped, I think basically for fear . . . the practice brings up elements of our character that are horrible . . . you have to change them, and lack of courage may follow, since it is very difficult to continue.' The opera singer, too, believed that chanting was a mirror for one's life, which was uncomfortable, and something which 'people sometimes don't want to see'.

Others emphasized the fact that some people lacked the discipline needed to practise. The art teacher said, 'Some who leave aren't able to organize their lives to chant a.m. and p.m. There is a practical discipline which some people can't cope with—getting up on winter mornings, quite difficult.' The point was reiterated by others. Another theme sometimes volunteered was unhappiness with the organization, and in particular with the service demands. The teacher in the school of occupational therapy thought some could not tolerate leaders' expectations that they would undertake VCG or Lilac service. But the implications of such comments contrasted sharply with the attitudes of other members, who regarded defections as a consequence of karma. The young French widow believed 'they leave because it's their karma. I don't think stopping [practising] is negative . . . Some may have to start in another lifetime.' The community worker who was a headquarters leader was equally relaxed when he said, 'People have a right to leave. The crucial question is the quality of leadership. Without leadership, people can get wrong ideas. Some people have the karma to stop. At the end of the day, there is freedom to choose one's religion as a fundamental human right.'

Members were frank about their uncertainties about the organization itself, even though almost every respondent was deeply and sincerely committed to the actual chanting. Formal structures, authority, the gender divisions of the movement, were the principal focal points about which members had experienced doubts, particularly in the early stages of their acquaintance with Nichiren

Buddhism. Most had come to accept these things and even to value them, but for some, lingering doubts remained. A 36-year old eye surgeon reported:

From 1983 to 1986 the main thing that stopped me practising was NSUK. [I had] personal insights but you are faced by organization. So I had to accept the necessity and value of NSUK. But it is still an issue for me. [There is] a difference between organization which can serve your ends and organization which you have to support to serve its ends . . . You have to come to the insight that practice is impossible without meeting others practising—this is valuable. But it is also uncomfortable—you cannot adapt the philosophy to your own views and prejudices.

Another man, an accountant, who had evolved his own philosophy of life, a 'self-help programme', echoed the same thoughts. It had been a difficulty to give up 'what I had created (my self-help programme) since NSUK was greater. I had difficulty in accepting the organization, I had disagreements with the framework: the different divisions for Men and Women, the fact that meetings were held in a set way, and were not flexible, and fear of authority, having to conform as if I was not in control of myself.'

A free-lance woman journalist dilated on the difficulties that she had encountered: 'The first time it is strange. You take your shoes off . . . At first you feel stupid. You chant at a wall. I felt it difficult to say out loud. A lot of people feel "organization!"—from boarding school to organization. I hate them [organizations]. Also there are a lot of sects, and I went through a stage of demanding of myself if this group was one of those.' She had, however, become reconciled: 'But organization is an important structure. People practising all over the world need structure to have a movement for peace. You see this only later. And teachers don't tell us what to do—they offer support if we ask for it, out of their experience. In fact, it is a democratic organization—everyone is important.' Wariness of organization, of being drawn into a structure, was a recurrent item among a number of those interviewed. A guitar-teacher who had had aspirations to be an actor reported that he began chanting after being introduced by his mother, and did so quite privately:

Quite a long time elapsed before we were taken to a meeting. A member whom we liked as a friend invited us—and because of him, we joined. We both hated organization, and especially organized religion. We went out of curiosity and the trust in the person who introduced us . . . Some things,

I didn't like being introduced to, the structure of the meetings. I didn't like discussion at first. I didn't want to go and talk about my life to strangers. But theirs was honest behaviour. I didn't want NSUK. I was looking for a practice. I wasn't looking for an organization or friends. VCG [Value Creation Group—the service activity undertaken by the Young Men's division] made me feel ill—uniforms. It was boring and anti-what I thought were the ideas of Buddhism . . . What one needs to know is the reality now—and I've yet to be disappointed. Anything I've done for NSUK—the people—very rarely disappoints. I've never regretted being involved in NSUK. There are people I know who've left. They feel pressure. Anyone who stops practising—there is pressure. There's pressure from the leaders, phone calls . . . I've not known anyone stop who doesn't feel the power. It's more organizational things [that cause them to stop practising].

Despite early misgivings, many members had come to have a positive appreciation of the organization. A woman of 49 of Hungarian origin declared, 'I did not want to join [NSUK]. I wanted to do it for myself. I didn't go to meetings. I went only twice. I didn't like organization. I had been in Subud. They had meetings and I was put off. I wanted to do it on my own . . . Now I am a group leader, and I am proud of it.' A 25-year-old woman, married but separated, had

started chanting, but I was against the organization, and practised by myself. When I felt OK with the practice, I went to meetings, and got more and more involved. When I heard of them [the leaders] and the president, I thought of the Salvation Army—higher and lower people. I was thinking that everybody is equal: buddhahood. Then I started appreciating leadership, the president. The philosophy I believe in—master and disciple. So I've lost my negative feelings towards organization, I learned to work as a member of a team.

A woman teacher, married for the third time, saw as benefits 'two things. NSUK organization and . . . the practice. The organization helps you to practise because of going to discussion meetings and exchanging experiences.' Referring to her parents and her marriages, she said, 'It goes back to the security issue; the marriages had come and gone, and they had been my security. With the practice and the organization, I start not to need them in the same way . . . I was a bit worried about being a member of an organization . . . I'd seen my parents give their whole lives [to the Communist Party] and today, at the end of their lives, they are not members any more. Right at the beginning, I didn't like singing songs'—but she had worked through her difficulties. 'I'm sure I'd find it difficult to keep going without an organization. I'd probably not chant so regularly, only when I felt like it.'

Whilst for some, organization as such—meetings, divisions, hierarchy, and even collective occasions for the practice—had been a difficulty, others had found authority, the actual leadership, a deterrent. Not all had become entirely reconciled to the pattern: thus a woman secretary who was a life-long Labour Party member maintained that:

the main difficulty is the organization. I have been in the Labour Party for twenty years, but I am not used to an organization which expects certain obligations, such as [service at] the Richmond Centre, and doing *keibi*. They call the day before [seeking help], and this annoys me. I like to plan my life. They seem to drop everything. Is this general? I do not know—it may be our district leader. I have never met President Ikeda. I find it strange that people worship him. I am not used to that. My socialist views conflict with my religion at times. I have to adjust. It's not a question of dropping out. It's a process I'm going through.

With respect to the occasion of Ikeda's visit to Britain, she said, 'Why so much fuss about it?—about just one person, the emphasis is on "all equals" but they say that, they don't do it. All this fuss about Ikeda, I don't like.' Such thoughts were apparently not so uncommon among new members, as those longer in the movement sometimes acknowledged when recounting their own early ideas and assumptions. Thus a leading member, a community social worker, a university graduate, had 'found it very difficult to have President Ikeda put before me in a master–disciple relation. It took me rather a long time to accept that, and to understand what it really means. In Britain, you come to Nichiren Buddhism with no precedents— one's condition is unaccepting for the need of such a person, or that you have to accept such a relationship.'

Essentially similar points were made by a male musician of 35:

I was a bit wary of organization at first; there are always dangers in organized bodies—stagnation and the danger of getting bureaucratized: they can turn into authoritarian bodies. Most people are wary of organization, but realize it's necessary. We can't all just wander about without a centre of faith to which we can go for guidance and encouragement . . . the first problem was President Ikeda, thinking he was a personality cult figure—that was my prejudice against that sort of thing. I've overcome that and I think that he's a great man, and I've been gradually convinced that he's working for world peace. There's always a danger [of personality cults] but in Nichiren Shōshū ideas like that are laughable . . . the actions of others, the leaders, Mr Causton, and ordinary leaders and members—their power and determination and spirit have really impressed me.

There are of course other members who appear never to have had any problem in accepting either the organizational structure of the movement or the style of leadership. For these members, appreciation is the hallmark of their comments. As one 33-year-old teacher put it, 'Mr Causton is a big influence in my life. We have examples of how to live by living people—President Ikeda and Mr Causton. Ikeda can interpret Nichiren Daishonin's teachings in the light of the twentieth and twenty-first centuries.' Yet even some of those currently enthusiastic about many aspects of the movement had, at earlier times, had misgivings about other features. Thus a woman film, television, and video editor was attracted especially by

the purity of the organization and the leadership . . . I liked the way there was no hierarchy as such. I have great hope and support from the members, and from President Ikeda, who writes incredible guidance. I've learned to trust the organization and the leadership—the experience of the last five years. Whereas at the beginning I would question why (1) uniforms [for the service corps] and (2) [sexually] segregated meetings and things like that, though difficult to start with, the balls get thrown back and you find out why through chanting, and you realize, once trust is established, why these things are so. Opposition has been through my own eyes and small-mindedness.

The gender-based divisions alluded to by this woman had caused problems for others. The art teacher indicated, 'I'm not clear about the Men's division and the Women's division . . . it's a bit sexist. They're explaining why it isn't. I never liked single-sex groups [and am] still reluctant to go to the Men's division. I see these groups trying to provide an answer for those who don't have friends—see them as support groups, therapy groups.' Similar thoughts had once troubled a male community social worker, who had become Men's division headquarters leader, 'I didn't like the idea of Men's division meetings. I didn't feel comfortable with them, but I do now. There are developing relations between men. It's very difficult in our society to have relations with other men, but it's helpful to have better relations with them. It's not inward looking, and it's not free-masonic in style.'

Service to the Organization

As in other religious denominations, the SGI organization itself offers opportunities for practical contributions to its operation, and such support is certainly regarded by many as service which attracts benefit. It is a way of creating value, and hence in one way or another of creating good karma, whilst also furthering the cause of *kōsen-rufu* (world-wide proclamation of true Buddhism)—a challenge which is rarely far from the conversation of Nichiren Buddhists as they contemplate the prospect of the twenty-first century. With these considerations in mind, we asked our respondents about the service that they performed for what was then NSUK, about the responsibility that they had for the movement's activities; as well as about the frequency and duration of their actual practice of chanting. We enquired about any visits that they might have made to the movement's European centre at Trets, in the south of France, where courses are regularly held, and whether they had been on pilgrimage to the head temple of the Nichiren Shōshū sect at Taiseki-ji, in Japan, where the original *Gohonzon* is enshrined—a pilgrimage no longer available to them, now that they are identified not as Nichiren Shōshū believers, but as members of Sōka Gakkai International.

Through its fortnightly bulletin of news and information, the movement makes quite explicit the opportunities that it extends to members to undertake service roles, the young men in the Value Creation Group and the members of the Young Women's division in the equivalent organization, known as 'Lilac'. At the time of our survey, the headquarters reported that there were about 170 of the young women enrolled in the Lilac corps, and about 150 men in the VCG. Older women sometimes serve in the Sunflower group, which is generally active only when there are special women's courses, but they also undertake to distribute the movement's official magazine, *UK Express*, a glossy monthly, and the fortnightly bulletin, which is more an in-house news-sheet.

We have already seen, from incidental remarks about organization, that the idea of such service is not one to which all members have taken at once. One of those we interviewed was of the opinion that some people had left because they were 'unhappy with the organization: there are demands that they cannot tolerate, for example Lilac and VCG service, a conflict with their perception of themselves. Women, many, I know, object to it [Lilac service].' A woman in her mid-twenties, awaiting a place at a polytechnic, had found the service and the gender divisions from which the volunteers were recruited to be a problem:

It was difficult to accept that we have Young Women's and Young Men's divisions: Lilac and VCG. At first, I hated it, it's sexist. Someone encouraged me to do it, so that I might see for myself why I objected, why I expressed negativity. I was against the girls inside serving tea, and the boys outside in the rain [policing the car park, for example]. However, the more I do Lilac, the more I appreciate women to be women, and men to be men, I am glad that men are men and women women. I feel it.

Perhaps SGI members—young, in large part single, enterprising, and in favour of change, as we have seen—are particularly sensitive to what may be seen as sexist orientations. Division of the sexes, adjusting to which quite a number appear to have had difficulty, might have been more easily and naturally accepted in older and more settled religious congregations.

A special type of service which was more demanding required volunteers who were prepared to spend a week at the Taplow Court headquarters, and who, working in teams, undertake to man telephones, act as guides, transport visitors from the railway station to the house, as well as providing at least the auxiliary manpower for such requirements as cleaning, security, and general house-keeping duties. Such special week-long assignments were known by the Japanese name as *keibi*. Those volunteering for this work had their board and lodging provided, but had to pay their own fares to Taplow. The benefits, apart from the intrinsic merit of undertaking work that was deemed to create value, were the availability of special *gongyō* meetings, the opportunity to chant whenever they were free, and experience of the vigorous tempo of life at headquarters. Service was seen not only as intrinsically valuable for the organization, but also as an occasion for learning and acquiring spiritual uplift for those who volunteered. One woman reported, '*Keibi*: incredible work! I wanted to do a good job since NSUK has done much for me, and the members also. I wanted to give something back.' A male accountancy clerk found that doing service had really established his conviction, 'The moment that I really felt this Buddhism was really, absolutely real . . . was when I was doing VCG at Taplow. When *Sensei* arrived I was standing and opening doors for people . . . I felt the organization had the strength to contribute something to change the society/the world.' For the organization itself, of course, *keibi* has been an effective mobilization of resources, and a way of reinforcing the commitment of those members who offered themselves for service.

Some 9 per cent of members did not answer the general question we asked, namely whether they performed any services for the organization. Of those who responded, some 46 per cent said that they were involved in one or another form of service, VCG, Lilac, Sunflower, or another. This is a high proportion of the membership of a religious body, at least when compared with larger denominations. About 17 per cent indicated that they had undertaken *keibi* service, and a further 17 per cent indicated that they had played a part in cultural groups within the organization.[1] Twenty-nine per cent of those answering this question said that they were not involved at all in service activities. *Keibi* and cultural activities were evenly spread over the different age categories, and made up about 28 per cent of each category. Not surprisingly, since Lilac and VCG were respectively recruited from the Young Women's and Young Men's divisions, age had an impact on these groups, and indeed on all kinds of service activities. The younger the people, the more of them were involved in service: 53 per cent of those younger than 30 yeras of age were or had been active. The older the respondents, the less likely it was that they had undertaken this type of service—only 31 per cent of those born before the end of the Second World War. The percentage of those performing no service for the organization was highest in the oldest age category (41 per cent) and lowest in the youngest category (about 23 per cent). Overall, however, it is clear that SGI elicits a high level of commitment from its members, as assessed by the amount of voluntary service that is undertaken.

Some interesting relationships emerged concerning the inclination to undertake service for SGI relative to the extent to which members had friends in the movement. Those who reported that they had no friends in the organization had the highest percentage of those who had engaged in *keibi* service, yet, in sharp contrast, this same group of those who lacked Buddhist friends also had the highest percentage of those who had undertaken no service for the movement. There was also a high proportion of those whose friends were mostly

---

[1] On this subject, see below, p. 165.

non-members who had not performed special services (36 per cent). The case differed with those half of whose friends were members, among whom only 21 per cent had not undertaken service; and those with all or most of their friends in membership, of whom only 18 per cent had not been active in this way. Many members in these last two categories had been involved in *keibi* activities (49 per cent) in contrast to those who had a minority of friends or no friends in the movement (taken together, 38 per cent).[2] We also built up a composite variable based on friends *and* family within the movement —the context of primary relationships. This appeared to have no particular influence on the extent to which members had engaged themselves in service to the movement, from which it may be inferred that it is the fact of having friends in the movement which is the more important association as far as service is concerned. Whether it should be inferred that those who have friends are drawn into undertaking service (perhaps with those friends?), or whether the fact of engaging in service is in itself a way of extending friendships within the movement, it is not possible to say.

A considerable number of respondents, when asked about service undertaken for the organization, mentioned their participation in the cultural activities sponsored by SGI, and it is interesting to note that members saw this as in some sense a service to the organization. Such activities have included the ambitious production of the specially written musical based on *Alice in Wonderland* adapted to the theme of a Buddhist morality tale, and performed for the general public at the Hammersmith Odeon. Another such event was a May Festival in 1990, which included a highly professional performance by twelve actors, backed up by a production team of twelve, of Dickens's *Hard Times*; programmes of jazz, classical music, song, visual arts, a children's day, and dance. Of the dance, the brochure noted:

Because of the wide spread of dancing talent in NSUK, it was difficult to choose between jazz, classical ballet, contemporary, tap, and Flamenco. So we chose them all . . . we created new choreography for each section and set up a punishing rehearsal schedule . . . Chanting was what pulled us through. It saved us in the one area where we lacked experience—Spanish Flamenco. We chanted for help and the next day a troupe of Spanish

---

[2] Kendall's tau-b for age, younger members versus old, and friends in the movement in increasing proportion who do services is twice plus 0.10.

dancers walked into the rehearsal room with their tutor. She volunteered to coach us on the spot. Chanting made it all work.[3]

The mixture of religious concerns, artistic endeavour, and organization also characterizes the annual general meetings of the movement, which are regularly held in the London Palladium. As one neophyte, encountering SGI at such a meeting for the first time, put it, it was 'a combination of the General Synod of the Church of England and "Come on Down"—it was, and is great fun'.

The specialized sections which draw together members with common professional interests constitute a reservoir of skills available to the movement as and when they are needed, whilst at the same time they act as conduits for the diffusion of Buddhist principles into various areas of activity within the wider society. The subdivisions, like the ethnic heritage groups, are not fixed in number, but arise in response to the demands and dispositions of the membership, and add a supportive tier to the whole organization.

Seniority, Involvement and Responsibility

The strong democratic and egalitarian emphasis of SGI-UK is accommodated within a structure of ascending echelons of organization. At the grass roots, there is the local group, usually of eight to ten people, all of whom, before the split between the priesthood and the Sōka Gakkai, had received the *Gohonzon*. Within such a group there are unit leaders who are capable of teaching two or three new members how to perform the basic rituals, in particular how to perform *gongyō*. Just how many groups make up the next tier of organization depends somewhat on the extent to which local membership is geographically concentrated, but normally two or three groups constitute a district, and a district might, for example in London, amount to no more than a neighbourhood, but in other parts of the country where members are more thinly spread a district might be coterminous with a small town. At each of these levels, and no less at higher levels, there is always a leader for each of the four divisions, the Men, the Women, the Young Men, and the Young Women.

District leaders will normally have engaged in practising for four

---

[3] May Festival, 17–28 May 1990, Taplow Court brochure.

or five years, and are considered capable of training and encouraging group leaders, and of conducting short talks on the principles of Nichiren's Buddhism or on a passage of the *Gosho*. In turn, three or four districts constitute a chapter, a level of organization that might cover a borough in London (although some areas with larger numbers of members—such as Camden—might have two or three chapters). The leaders of a chapter are usually men and women with eight or more years of experience, who can give deeper advice and guidance on matters of faith than is available at lower and more local levels. The chapter develops its own programme of activities, particularly in the field of service to the wider community. Thus, in Scotland, a chapter cleaned up a glen in one of the public parks; in Kilburn, London, a chapter gained the approval of the local council to refurbish the flower tubs in a shopping area. The chapters run friendship days, organize picnics, summer garden parties, and so on, to which potentially interested friends are invited, where they have a chance to see that Buddhists are 'ordinary people, leading ordinary lives'.

If chapters are the active core echelon of the denomination, then the next level, (regional) headquarters, is the nerve centre. In 1991, there were twenty centres designated as headquarters in different regions in Britain, and these were seen as the organizational foundation for members in the future. They are regionally based, distributed in accordance with the concentrations of membership. Thus, there are nine headquarters in London. The leaders of the four divisions at headquarters level are people with twelve or more years of practice, and they are responsible for the faith of members and the correct understanding of the teachings. Whilst lower levels of organization do not have physical premises, but operate from the homes of members (usually the local leaders), the expectation is that, in time, headquarters will eventually acquire buildings of their own. None the less, the major activities of SGI continue to take place in the group meetings at various levels. This is the model derived from the parent organization in Japan, where the *zadankai* is the basic pattern for group discussions of a kind that is also familiar in other contemporary Japanese religious movements.

Once a month, the leaders of the various headquarters meet with the national leaders of SGI at Taplow Court, and among these latter there are leaders (one for each of the four divisions) who, between them, take responsibility for one of the five 'areas' into which Great

Britain as a whole is divided. These area leaders are the links between regional headquarters and the central committee of the movement. Thoughout SGI-UK, leaders are appointed rather than elected: up to district level, appointments are made by an appointments board at area level; above that level, that is from the level of the chapter upwards, leaders are appointed by a board of the national leadership, which is regarded as ensuring that those appointed are outstanding in their manifestation of faith.

We asked our sample about the degree of responsibility that they took within the movement, and found that some 41 per cent of them declared that they bore no responsibility for the organization. All the rest carried some charge: 23 per cent were group leaders; 21 per cent had responsibility at district level; 8 per cent were chapter leaders; and 4 per cent had responsibility at regional headquarters. Four per cent did not indicate the hierarchical level of their positions, but mentioned a divisional or sectional responsibility.

Because, as we have mentioned above, leaders will normally have practised for a customary period of years before being appointed to leadership positions at the various levels, there is a predictably high degree of association between the years spent in SGI-UK and level of responsibility.[4] There are, of course, some people with as much as eight years' practice, or more, who have assumed no responsibility within the organization (29 per cent), but this is much more the case with people who have had no more than four years in SGI (61 per cent). Expectably, from the stipulations imposed by the movement, those who take responsibility who have had between four and eight years' experience are found at group and district level, while those with more than eight years' practice who have assumed some responsibility have graduated to upper levels of leadership.

Our findings indicate an association between those who took on some measure of responsibility within the organization and the extent of friendships formed within the movement. About 58 per cent of those all of whose close friends were non-members had failed to assume any responsibilities, and 50 per cent of those with only a minority of members among their close friends had likewise failed to take up any position in the organization. But those not taking any leadership roles amounted to only 33 per cent of those with half their close friends in membership, and only 23 per cent of those most or

---

[4] Kendall's tau-b: 0.28.

all of whose friends were Sōka Gakkai members. It was also those in these last-mentioned categories who had accepted positions of responsibility at both chapter and district levels, respectively 42 and 49 per cent. By contrast, of those with no members among their close friends, or with only a minority, only 16 and 24 per cent had acquired responsibility at district, chapter, or higher levels.[5]

When the figures are controlled for age (see Table 24), this association becomes stronger for those born in 1950 or before. In the age categories of those born in or before 1950, 59 per cent of those who had no friends in the movement had not taken up responsibilities, but of those with most or all of their friends in SGI, only some 22 per cent were *without* some sort of leadership role. About 29 per cent of those in this category had roles at the chapter level or higher, while only 7 per cent of those with no friends in the movement occupied such leadership positions. Among members born after 1950, that is those who were forty years of age or less,

TABLE 24. *Age, friendships, and responsibility in the organization*

Year of birth	No. of friends in SGI membership	Extent of responsibility (%)	
		None	Chapter level and above
1950 or before (Stuart's tau-c: 0.29)	None	59	7
	Minority	46	1
	Half	32	9
	Most or all	22	29
After 1950 (Stuart's tau c: 0.20)	None	58	0
	Minority	52	12
	Half	33	13
	Most or all	24	24

[5] The association is again one of the strongest found in the research—Stuart's tau-c: 0.24. However, these relationships may have been influenced by variations in the intake of new members year by year. SGI-UK reports a significant increase in admissions in 1987 (782) and 1988 (915) over previous years (300 in 1983 and 402 in 1984) and 1,077 for the years 1989/90. New members would probably have fewer friends in SGI-UK and would be unlikely in so short a time to have graduated to leadership positions.

those without responsibility amounted to 58 per cent for those with no SGI friends, falling to only 24 per cent for those most or all of whose friends were in membership. Table 24 shows, for each age category, the distribution of those *not* having responsibility, and those occupying leadership roles at the higher levels.

When the possible impact of friends and family is combined, by creating a scale of what might be described as the influence of SGI members in the primary surroundings of the individual, the picture changes only a very little. The degree of association between the assumption of responsibility by the occupancy of leadership role remains higher for those born in 1950 or before, and lower for those born after that year.[6] In Table 25, we juxtapose for each of the two age categories (those born in or before 1950, and those born after) extreme circumstances—namely, those with no or few SGI members in their immediate environment, and those whose family members and most or all of whose friends were Buddhists. In each case, it is apparent that accepting responsibility at a higher level diminishes in both age-groups for those in whose social context there are few or no SGI members. Of those born in 1950 or before who were without kinsfolk or close friends in the movement, some 58 per cent had not acquired positions of responsibility. In contrast, of those who were surrounded by Buddhist relatives and friends, only 30 per cent had failed to assume leadership positions. The contrast is even sharper in this older age-group with respect to leadership roles at higher levels (chapter level or higher): for those with primary relationships in which SGI members predominate, 27 per cent have such responsibilities, while for those with few or no Buddhist kinsfolk and friends, only 4 per cent are leaders at this level. For those under 40, 63 per cent of those without, or with few, Buddhist friends or relatives do not occupy leadership positions; but only 21 per cent of those with a majority of Buddhists among their kinsfolk and friends lack such responsibilities, and at the higher levels, this involvement in leadership increases from 6 per cent to 23 per cent. For those who maintain a high level of social relationships with other members of SGI, there is no marked increase in the degree of responsibility, since length of time in the movement and in experience of the practice is a decisive factor in the acquisition of enhanced responsibility. Of

[6] Stuart's tau-c: respectively 0.28 and 0.23.

TABLE 25. *Age, social relationships, and levels of responsibility*

Year of birth	Social relationships	Responsibilities (%)			
		None	Group level	District level	Chapter level
1950 or before (Stuart's tau-c: 0.28)	Lowest level: no or few SGI members	58	33	6	4
	Highest level: family and most/all friends in SGI	30	11	32	27
After 1950 (Stuart's tau-c: 0.23)	Lowest level: no or few SGI members	63	17	14	6
	Highest level: family and most/all friends in SGI	21	23	33	23

course, capacity for leadership may be assumed to be an independent variable of differential incidence.

There are other distinctive features relative to the assumption of responsibility in the organization by members with different backgrounds. We have noted the considerable over-representation of people with professions in the media, the arts, and the caring services, amounting, altogether, to almost 50 per cent of our respondents. These occupational categories are somewhat differentially distributed at different hierarchic levels of the movement. Thus, those with special training in the media and the arts were found to be over-represented at the level of the group, of the chapter, and at higher levels: in contrast, those with a special training in the caring professions appeared to be disproportionately represented at district level. Housewives, the retired, and the unemployed were over-represented in the category of members who did not take on any organizational responsibility—some 52 per cent compared to 38 per cent who lacked responsibility among the employed and self-employed.

Thus, people who might be expected to have more free time, or at least to have time not specifically committed to a work schedule, none the less were less likely to have found themselves more fully committed to doing things for the movement. The implication of this finding is that SGI is run more by people who are otherwise busy than by people who have time on their hands, and this undoubtedly reflects in some measure the general ethos of Nichiren Buddhism, and the image of the members as energetic, enthusiastic, vigorous, and outgoing people who are successful in their callings yet able to devote considerable amounts of time to manning the leadership roles of the organization through which their religious beliefs and practice are disseminated. As between the employed and the self-employed, the former are somewhat over-represented at the group and district level of organization, while the self-employed are more conspicuous as leaders of chapters and at levels higher than this. Again, this circumstance appears to reflect the encouragement within the movement for members to take on responsibility, and to accept challenge: their presence in the higher echelons both reflects this ideology and promotes it.

IX

Practising Nichiren's Buddhism

THE core activity for Sōka Gakkai members and for Nichiren's Buddhism is, as members refer to it, 'practising'. They more readily refer to someone as having started to practise, or as having 'stopped practising', than as having become, or ceased to be, a member. Practising is vital to the movement, and, as we have seen, it is normally undertaken as a household or as a purely individual activity. Whilst members appreciate the occasions of group practice at their various meetings, it is individual practice, morning and evening, which is, above all, the basic, staple activity. Practice is the chanting of the *daimoku* and the reciting of *gongyō*, the specified chapters of the *Lotus Sutra*. *Gongyō* takes about thirty minutes of very rapid chanting of the Japanese text, which all members learn. *Nam-myōhō-renge-kyō* is repeated for about ten minutes at meetings, but when undertaken privately it may continue for much longer, according to the disposition of the worshipper. Not infrequently, if people have problems or seek solace, they increase the amount of chanting that they do, and sometimes they may continue for an hour or more: but the regular expectation is much less. The published account of one devotee probably well exceeded the normal expectation. She wrote:

I have a very busy schedule. I get up between 5 and 5.30 to get in about forty minutes *daimoku* in the morning and then at night I go to meetings. By the time I get in it's sometimes 10 p.m.; then I still have to eat and do everything and get to bed by 11 p.m. I normally do chant an hour a day but it's very difficult for me to do more than that because I'm simply not home, normally. So what I do is I 'top up' at weekends [when] I do two hours *daimoku*.[1]

Our respondents told us how frequently they managed to perform their chanting exercises. Some 51 per cent claimed to chant twice

[1] 'Guidelines of Practice', *UK Express*, 249 (Mar. 1992), 13.

TABLE 26. *Length of membership and weekly practice*

Has already chanted for:	Weekly practice (in percentages of membership)			
	Maximum 3 times	More than 3: maximum 7	More than 7: maximum 10	Always or nearly so
More than 8 years	9	9	20	62
5–8 years	6	11	29	54
Maximum of 4 years	9	13	34	44
Total	8	11	28	53

daily, morning and evening, virtually without lapsing, whilst a further 2 per cent admitted an occasional miss. Practising at least ten (of a possible fourteen) times a week was reported by a further 28 per cent. Yet another 8 per cent claimed to practise at least seven times a week. Adding these categories together, we have almost 90 per cent of members who reported practising on average at least once a day, and more than half the total membership who chanted twice a day. Other members failed to maintain this level of performance: some 4 per cent did not chant even once a week; another 3 per cent managed only a couple of times a week; and a further 3 per cent professed to chant at least four times a week.

For members of longer standing, chanting had become a stable commitment. The longer people had been in the movement, the more likely they were to chant faithfully every day. Of more recently recruited members, fewer made this claim.[2] The percentages are set out in Table 26. It appears that, among the group of more recently inducted members, there were those who were not yet totally involved, and who might indeed leave at some subsequent time. Senior members tended to stay on, even if they did not always chant consistently on a daily or frequent basis. A word of caution might however be entered: it is possible that, among those who completed and returned the questionnaire, the most involved members were over-represented, which would, of course, have led to claims of higher practice than might be found among the less committed. The result of 53 per cent of members engaging in daily practice might, in consequence, be somewhat flattering for the organization, but we have no means of checking such a hypothesis. On the other hand, an anonymous questionnaire is an instrument that scarcely admits

[2] Stuart's tau-c: 0.11.

the attraction of overstating responses in order to gain kudos, or, at least, not to lose face. This fact, and the general concern for honesty among the memberships of religious bodies, might be taken as reassuring, and some protection against exaggerated claims by respondents.

The incidence of high levels of performance of *gongyō* and *daimoku* is very much affected by the extent to which people are socially integrated in the movement, as measured by the proportion of their friends who are also members. The social bonding within the movement may be taken to reinforce commitment, and we found a correlation between internal friendships and the frequency of chanting.[3] Thus, in those cases of members who count only 'some' of their friends as SGI members, we found that no more than 40 per cent claimed to undertake daily chanting, a much smaller proportion than in the case of those members a majority of whose friends or all of whose friends were in the movement, where the figure chanting daily reached 63 per cent. Conversely, it was those who had no friends or only a minority of friends in SGI who constituted the bulk of those who chanted a maximum of three times a week—some 70 per cent.

It was possible, beyond these gross results, to control for the influence of age on these findings, and it emerged that these relationships did not hold for those born in 1950 or before, but were evident for those born after 1950.[4] Thus, it is clear that it is particularly among the younger members that practice is strongly influenced by friends. In this age-group, when there were no friends who were in membership, only some 30 per cent chanted daily, a very different result from that for members whose friends were all or mostly within the movement, for whom the figure was 71 per cent engaged in daily chanting. It was precisely those who lacked friends in SGI, those who had no friends among their fellow members, or who had only a minority of them in membership, who made up the majority of those who were chanting at most three times a week (almost 75 per cent).

It is surprising, given the importance of friends as an encouragement to engage in regular daily practice, that the influence of the family does not emerge from our survey, except where there is a combination of friends and family who together constitute the

---

[3] Kendall's tau-b: 0.18.   [4] In this case, Kendall's tau-b rises to 0.23.

TABLE 27. *Age, primary relationships, and the incidence of practice*

Year of birth	SGI members in primary relationships	Practice (%)	
		Maximum 7 times per week	10 to 14 times per week
1950 or before	None or nearly none	31	69
	Some to most	15	85
After 1950	None or nearly none	29	71
	Some to most	14	86

context of primary relationships for the individual.[5]. When controlling our finding for age, we see that what appears is that it tends to be those who lack the influence of SGI members in their primary relationships who practise less frequently (Table 27).

Thus, although Nichiren Buddhism is very much an individual practice, and although, as an organization, Sōka Gakkai is less communal and congregational than most religious bodies, none the less a supportive context of fellow believers and practitioners appears to be of considerable importance in maintaining commitment and performance; this is particularly the case with regard to the support of friends. Those without family in the movement have, in all probability, struck out on their own in adopting a new religion, and such individuals are likely to have come to depend all the more on friends in the absence of direct participation on the part of their kinsfolk. Since we know that most members do in fact become acquainted with Nichiren Buddhism through inter-personal contacts, we may suppose that the possibility of making friends is an important element in the appeal of the movement, and perhaps such friends become all the more significant where there is no shared familial interest in Buddhism.

Courses and Pilgrimage

The routine practice of chanting is obviously the most important index of commitment to this variant of Buddhism. As we have seen, it tends to be associated with seniority of membership and the

[5] Stuart's tau-c: 0.16.

incidence of primary relations in the movement. Yet there are other ways in which SGI members made manifest their faith, in particular by spending time on courses and, as long as the relationship held between the Nichiren Shōshū sect and the lay organization, by going to Taiseki-ji on pilgrimage to worship before the original *Gohonzon*. Of those in our survey, about 27 per cent had paid a visit to Taiseki-ji. One-third of this number (9 per cent of the entire sample) had indeed made such a pilgrimage more than once. Such a journey is an expensive undertaking, and not all members could afford it, even though, at that time, it remained a goal for many. In particular, the unemployed were unlikely to be able to finance such a trip, and this shows clearly in the responses. Only 15 per cent in that category had already made the much-prized journey. The category within which the highest percentage had twice been to Taiseki-ji was that of the self-employed, 13 per cent of whom had undertaken it more than once. They had had the time and the resources to go. Among those whose education had ended before the age of 19 (or who were still students) 78 per cent had not been to Taiseki-ji, compared to 69 per cent of those with higher education.

Understandably, there is a relationship between length of time in membership and the likelihood of having visited Taiseki-ji.[6] But there is no such relationship between that probability and the extent of the individual's involvement in the movement. Thus, the pilgrimage cannot be taken as an indicator of involvement, since to go to Taiseki-ji was a considerable investment, which only a minority could afford. In order to go most members had to save to cover the cost, which normally took some time to achieve.

To visit Trets, the movement's European centre, is a different proposition, however. The point of making a visit is to enrol in a course, and 51 per cent of members had been to Trets, some 22 per cent having been there more than once. Although more women than men had been to Trets (some 51 per cent as against 44 per cent), and more of the members aged 35 to 44 than either the older or younger groups (57 per cent as against 47), these factors had a rather low impact.[7] The extent to which the member has friends in the movement, and the length of time in membership, produce higher coefficients of association.[8] Of those with no close friends in SGI,

---

[6] Kendall's tau-b: 0.41.   [7] Stuart's tau-c: respectively 0.10 and 0.9.8.
[8] Kendall's tau-b: respectively 0.24 and 0.39.

71 per cent had never been to Trets, nor had 60 per cent of those
with only a minority of friends in the movement. Of the rest, some
35 per cent had never been, leaving some 65 per cent who had paid
such a visit. The majority of those with all or most of their friends
in the movement had been twice or even more often to Trets, and
those half of whose close friends were members had for the most
part been at least once.

As between the age-groups, the impact of friends appears to have
been equally strong both for the older group, the over-forties, and
for the younger category.[9] The influence of their primary group
relationships only reinforced what was already evident from the
impact of friends: the greater the proportion of friends and family
who were SGI members, the greater likelihood existed of their
having visited Trets.[10] Similarly, the longer people had been members, the more likely it was that they had been to Trets: 43 per cent
of those who had been in the organization for more than eight years
had been to Trets more than once, 32 per cent had been once, and
only 25 per cent had never been. Of those who had been members
for between five and eight years, 18 per cent had been more than
once, 32 per cent had been once, and 46 per cent had never been.
Of those who had been members for less than five years, only 6 per
cent had been to Trets more than once; 19 per cent had been once,
and 75 per cent had not yet been there.

As might be expected, the various measures of involvement in the
movement were closely linked to one another. Understandably,
there was a high correlation between responsibility in the organization and the incidence of visiting Trets (Kendall's tau-b: 0.49).
Leaders might be expected to have a deeper understanding of the
teachings and so be able to help those to whom they offered
guidance. For them, a course at Trets became an augmentation of
that understanding; it confirmed their existing responsibility, and
opened the way for eventual appointment to a yet higher position in
the organization. Responsibility and service had the lowest correlation (Kendall's tau-b: 0.20), and here it might be presumed that the
one tended to preclude the other: those who had attained high
leadership roles were already fully occupied by the work which their
positions entailed. They were not to be expected to involve themselves in the service roles of VCG or Lilac, acting as guides,

---

[9] Kendall's tau-b: 0.24.   [10] Stuart's tau-c: 0.24.

receptionists, ushers, and the dispensers of tea and soft drinks: they had other things to do. Service was something for the regular rank-and-file members, perhaps a step towards an official leadership position. Trets was more for those already undertaking some measure of responsibility within the organization. Practice was highly associated with responsibility, visiting Trets, and service (Kendall's tau-b, respectively 0.24, 0.29, and 0.32). Those who devoted most time to service and those who occupied leadership roles were those who were most committed to regular, daily practice.

Overall, the study of involvement makes it clear that the longer people were involved, the more extensively they became involved, even though some senior members remained only slightly involved, and some junior members were quite strongly committed. The impact of the circle of close friends remained quite powerful. The more that individuals were surrounded by members in the circle of their close friends, the more involved they tended to be—the more they performed services; the more they took on responsibility in the organization; the more they engaged in daily practice; and the more likely it was that they had been to Trets (sometimes more than once). The family appeared to have less influence on involvement—perhaps reflecting the fact that all our respondents (except one) were converts, thus usually without older relatives in membership. Our respondents were far and away more likely to be the parents within the family groups, than to be children, and hence were less susceptible to the influence of other family members. The fact of primary relationships (family and friends taken together) added little to the impact of friends taken alone, and had no influence on the probability that people would undertake service; this was the same measure of impact as friends had on the likelihood of an individual committing himself to take up a role of responsibility, on the incidence of daily practice, and on the likelihood of having been to Trets. The influence of friends and primary relationships was highest on the extent to which older members had positions of responsibility (those born in 1950 or before). This was not so in the case of practice. Younger members (the under-forties) were more susceptible to friends in the extent of their practice, although the influence of primary relationships in general had no differential impact on the various age-groups.

Different patterns were evident when we controlled for members living as couples or singly in the study of the impact of primary

relationships on the probability that members had assumed positions
of responsibility; the likelihood of their undertaking daily practice;
and the probability of their having been to Trets. Primary relationships had an impact on the responsibility adopted by those who lived
as couples.[11] The more fully a member was surrounded by friends
and family who were also members, the less they shirked responsibilities (63 per cent as against 21 per cent), and the more likely it
was that they had taken up positions of authority at the level of the
chapter or above (6 per cent as against 24 per cent). With regard to
practice, it is those who were living as single people who were most
influenced by their primary relationships. For those who had a
minority of members around them, some 40 per cent claimed to
undertake daily practice. But for those whose close circle included
a majority of SGI members, the percentage was 77.[12]

The matter of visiting Trets offers yet another picture. Both
couples and single people were highly influenced by their primary
relationships with respect to visiting Trets.[13] Those who, within
their families and among their friends, were more fully surrounded
by SGI members were less likely *not* to have been to Trets. For
couples in this category, only 32 per cent had not been there (as
against 78 per cent of those with few or no Buddhists among their
close kin and friends). Of single people surrounded by SGI kinsfolk
and friends, only 23 per cent had not been (as against 66 per cent
of those who lacked the support of family and friends). Going to
Trets is, of course, a group activity: people travel as a party, and it
is likely that the stimulus to go is very much prompted by the
influence of friends who also hope to go, and so group decisions are
common. The single person surrounded by SGI family and friends
was less likely to be unable to go than was the case for those who
were married. The influence of primary relationships clearly operates
as a direct inducement at the social level.

The Rationale of Chanting

If it is appropriate to talk of the soteriological dimension of Nichiren
Buddhism, then one can say that chanting the *daimoku* is the basic

[11] Kendall's tau-b: 0.29.   [12] Kendall's tau-b: 0.23.
[13] Stuart's tau-c: 0.28 and 0.24.

requirement taking the individual towards salvation, or, to put this in more contextual terms, the basic activity leading the individual towards the realization of his or her buddhahood. It is to this end that members chant, and, as we have seen, the majority of members chant daily, and even more of them accept that daily (indeed, twice daily) chanting is the means to reach it. Yet, whatever the philosophical idea, salvation is, in practice, always a divisible experience, precursors, harbingers, or earnests of which might be realized piecemeal. The Buddhists themselves have a keen concept of progress in the attainment of buddhahood, and recognize steps along the way: unlike the Damascus Road model of Christian conversion, it is not a goal that is to be gained by one dramatic act, or in one sudden enlargement of consciousness. Again, apart from the abstract concept of achieving this perfect enlightenment, believers in this as in other religions look for benefits as they move along their chosen path of soteriological exercises. In Sōka Gakkai, such benefit is part of the movement's explicit promise—value creation puts benefit alongside beauty and goodness in a trinity of what is to be realized. Thus, proofs of steps towards salvation, towards buddhahood, include such things as an increase in personal happiness, a better experience of other people, the enjoyment of desired material possessions, and the attainment of stable life circumstances with opportunities to earn a good living, establish a family, and enjoy one's leisure hours.

In a movement in which benefit is so directly promised as a prospect to be realized by faithful practice, it should not be surprising that, at least for some, chanting is seen as practical action towards the acquisition of quite specific desiderata. The movement's English-language organ has expressed the point unequivocally: 'Of course, we need proof of the practice to encourage us to continue. For this reason it is a good idea if we chant with a specific goal in mind, an area of life where we would like to see some specific improvement. Exactly what we chant for is completely up to us, but some sort of goal is valuable in order to help us measure our progress.'[14]

Yet it is also clear that no sophisticated religion, no religion that has sloughed off primitive magical conceptions of automatic or

---

[14] *UK Express*, 230 (Aug. 1990): exactly the same points had been made in the same words in a 'Question and Answer' discussion, *UK Express*, 206 (Aug. 1988), 11.

instant returns for mechanically uttered nostrums, can long subsist on the basis of promising assured material benefits for specific ritual performances. Advanced religions are marked by the supersession of the magical by the ethical. The belief that specific consequences will ensue from set ritual acts, spells, prayers, supplications, gradually gives way to the idea that such acts and prayers will help to bring about a much more diffuse and generalized good. The benefit of ritual performance ceases to be perceived as the peculiar prerogative of the individual ritual performer *vis-à-vis* others, and becomes attributable to the whole worshipping community, and perhaps to a rather wider world beyond. An idea of public good supersedes that of private gain: benefit ceases to be particularistic, and as what is meant by 'religion' advances over what is avowedly 'magic', so that benefit becomes steadily universalized. Associated with this development, the idea also forms that ritual and prayer may achieve their consequences more by the transformation of the subjective orientations than by the realization of a change in specific objective circumstances. Finally, magical ideas are relinquished and replaced as those who undertake (especially corporate) prayer and ritual begin to reinterpret supposedly consequential events, eventually managing to reappraise non-attainment of the specified goals of ritual performances as in fact a better consequence than would have been their achievement, and hence as an evidence of the truth and benignity of faith. Whereas, once, particular good consequences would have been expected, increasingly, *whatever* occurs is held to be good and, in some way, better than any alternative outcome. Consequences are reinterpreted and the failure of particular goals to be realized is rationalized as a kind of success. Thus, religion leaves as a more open question just what constitutes benefit, while magic is stuck with the preconceived notion of exactly what concrete results should occur. As religion has evolved, untoward experience is reappraised and can be often counted as a blessing in disguise. The actual performance of required ritual practice may now be seen as flawed by being undertaken in the wrong spirit, or as unduly impregnated with egocentric ideas and predetermined scenarios, attractive to the supplicant, but not in harmony with the will of God, the dictates of providence, or, in the case of Nichiren Buddhism, with the operation of the universal law.

Given all these possibilities, the criteria by which the effectiveness of chanting is judged cannot always be exactly along the lines envisaged by those who chant. Normal empirical tests are not necessarily relevant in the appraisal of just what chanting has achieved, part of which at least must be the believer's changed perception of the situation. Yet, even though many members of Sōka Gakkai are certainly sophisticated in recognizing, and discounting, any magical connotations of their practice, none the less, there is, as we shall demonstrate below, abundant and diverse testimony to the direct and specific potential of chanting, including many affirmations that in a very direct way the practice has often effected tangible, anticipated, and fully intended results.

We asked members how they conceived of their chanting activities. What was the object of these exercises? Did they chant for the movement as such, for themselves, or for others? Were their goals personal and were the results empirically testable? How did they assess whether the goals of chanting had been achieved? What were the principal benefits that had been obtained? Our questions were more pertinent when addressed to Nichiren Buddhists than perhaps they would have been were they to have been put to Christians with respect to prayer, since chanting more fully constitutes the substance of religious activity for these Buddhists than is the case with prayer in Christianity, and it is even more typically an individual exercise occupying a greater proportion of the time individuals spend in spiritual activities. Whilst supplicatory prayer is certainly directed to ends that can be fairly clearly specified, none the less, those ends, at least on occasions of corporate worship, tend to be expressed in general, often metaphysical terms; and where privately offered, relate perhaps most particularly to the emotional condition of the supplicant. The general prayers for peace, for those who suffer, for the sick are offered as pious hopes perhaps as much as in the expectation of direct divine intervention. They function in considerable part to assuage the feelings of those who pray by giving them a sense of having 'done something' about it, no matter how empirically unrelated to the case at issue. But the Buddhists have a different conception of cause, and a more pragmatic expectation concerning the results of their chanting, which they see not merely as pious invocation, but as an influence at work in the metaphysical economy. Chanting, as they see it, can be directional, aimed at specific circumstances to bring about particular results by changing the force of karma. There is, however, also a subjective element to this interpretation. The SGI members recognize that in chanting they become more conscious of themselves, aware of realities, and capable of acquiring a clearer view of personal problems, but this understanding in no way derogates from the general philosophical view that chanting changes things, has consequences, and might be employed to realize specific results.

Chanting for What?

When a party of the British members visited Taiseki-ji some years ago, on a pilgrimage in which they were to chant before the original *Gohonzon*, the leader of the movement in Britain advised them not to take in with them their 'shopping lists'. The advice, half-facetious, was none the less a recognition that members could easily see the occasion as value-creating in the rather narrow sense of helping to solve their own personal problems and of meeting their own, often material, needs. We asked the respondents to our questionnaire whether they had ever chanted for particular goals, and only some 4 per cent said that they had never done so. What, then, were the goals for which 96 per cent of the members had chanted?

The two most frequent objectives that inspired members to chant were their careers and better relationships: in each case, 52 per cent of the members mentioned these concerns. What was sought in particular was help in finding employment, or in finding better employment, as well as good results in their studies. That this should have been so strong a focus might be expectable of any body of people, but, as already noted, it may have been enhanced in the case of our respondents by the very large proportion who were self-employed, and for whom work might, therefore, be more hazardous than for a population less solely dependent on their own efforts, talents, and good fortune. The fact that many were engaged in the graphic and performing arts and in crafts might also have tended to keep work opportunities in the forefront of the minds of many practitioners.

The concern for better relationships, expressed generally in those terms, and mentioned frequently in interviews, was also a character-istic preoccupation of the members. Although not all of the 52 per cent of members who affirmed that this was a matter about which they chanted regarded relations with their partners as the most urgent concern (some were concerned about relationships with parents, or with colleagues), most typically the reference was to partners. Since a considerable proportion of members were not formally married, but were single or 'living as married', relationships might, in some ways, have been more delicate, or more exposed, than perhaps was the case in actual marriages. If one considers, for comparison's sake, what Christian people pray for, as far as this can be known, it would seem that a better relationship, explicitly stated as such, is probably a much less common object of prayer than it is of the chanting undertaken by the SGI members. This probability may relate to a more pronounced consciousness about inter-personal relations, but may also be affected by the fact that the deliberate act of chanting for better relations may, indeed, have its own influence on those relationships, in keeping in the forefront of the mind that relationships depend to a considerable extent on the individual's own attitudes and mental set. Concern for one's state of mind, and the idea that one can raise one's level of consciousness, are very much more explicit issues in Nichiren Buddhism than in Christianity. Better relationships, and perhaps especially sexual relationships, are much more a preoccupation of the Buddhists and their sub-culture than appears to be the case with any Christian group.

The third most frequently mentioned objectives of chanting among these particular personal goals were a variety of material benefits, for which some 45 per cent of members had been exercised. These varied from immediate material needs, such as help in finding an apartment, to the search for wish-fulfilment of a more general kind. Some had chanted to get a new car; others to win a lottery; and many had simply chanted for money—some of them claiming spectacular results. Perhaps the most dramatic testimony to the power of chanting to produce desired material benefit was provided by the 44-year-old male art teacher, who recounted this episode:

One tends to equate spiritual paths separately from materialism, but it was made clear that if you want something, it will come to you. I chanted for money to begin with, and almost feel guilty about it. I thought, 'What do I want?' First, I wanted money to finish the house. We had the usual mortgage business. We needed a few thousands to finish the extension. Should we re-mortgage the house? I thought, I will enter some competitions. We'd never done that before, but we came up in a DIY store—they offered prizes of gold bars in Texas Homes . . . We entered three times. There was a 'tie-breaker' and you had to say what you liked about it. We won it. M [my wife] was ill, and reluctantly we'd agreed to get a second mortgage. The letter [for the second mortgage] came at the same time as the announcement of the prize. We'd won £7,000 in gold bars . . . We went to the Hilton Hotel in London—had to take a day off! We had chanted for money, and we won. Very quickly, we learned that some people trust in chanting to attain things each day, but the more I chant, the more I see all you've got to do is to chant for what's best for you and your friends. Very rarely will I chant for specific things . . . things happen all the time.

These various material goals—apartments, cars, money, and jobs—were among those which came closest to the magical application of chanting, and the most literal interpretation of the idea of value creation and the experience of benefit as a direct result of invoking the *Lotus Sutra* in order to change one's karma.

Almost as frequently as the application of chanting for material benefits, members recalled chanting for personal health and happiness, which had been the concern of some 44 per cent. These more generalized goals more closely approximate a spiritual as distinct from a magical attitude to the efficacy of chanting, and in their lack of specificity conform to a more ethicized orientation to the search for supernatural power to influence one's circumstances. It is also apparent that the very act of chanting might in itself in some measure achieve the results that are being sought. If chanting is defined as intrinsically effective in promoting happiness and, if not physical health, at least in encouraging a healthy and positive attitude of mind, then such results might readily follow.

Chanting for Change and the Future

All of the foregoing are goals sought for the benefit of the individual himself, and their predominance reflects the extent to which Nichiren Buddhism is a strongly individualistic religious orientation: one takes responsibility for oneself, and chanting has a powerful, albeit not exclusive, role in self-transformation. Realizing one's true identity, transcending one's karma, coming to terms with reality by using the *Gohonzon* as a mirror of one's own individuality—all of these central preoccupations reflect the extent to which Nichiren Buddhism focuses on self-improvement and self-help. The same general characteristic is underscored by the fact that, even on occasions of group worship, when chanting is undertaken in unison, all interaction is between the individual practitioner and the *Gohonzon* (and not among practitioners one with another). Yet not all chanting is directed to one's own condition: it can be directed to the well-being of others. The most general concern for others' well-being was much less commonly reported than were personal goals—less, indeed, than half as frequently—but some 21 per cent affirmed that they had chanted for the welfare of others. A further other-regarding and altruistic goal had commanded the goodwill of some of those undertaking chanting—namely, the health of others. Fourteen per cent had chanted for this goal.

Nineteen per cent of respondents had also chanted for another, essentially personal, goal, namely for a change of their attitudes. This aim, like the search for happiness, might be most closely and subjectively related to the motivations that prompt the individual to chant. The desire to change, the fact of undertaking some actions towards that end, and the satisfaction of having taken such a step might in themselves be sufficient to do much to ensure that change is brought about. That is not to say that the effect of chanting is illusory, of course—an issue on which we should not want to make a judgement—but only to record the intertwined nature of the means and the end in this case. It may well be that, much as the individual might earnestly wish to change his attitudes, he might not, by dint of resolution alone, succeed in doing so. By chanting he takes what appears to be an objective step towards his goal and, if he is convinced that this procedure helps, then it may indeed do so.

One disenchanted woman member, who had hoped for a variety of material benefits, lamented, 'I just realized, as I did when I left school, there was no hope for me now to change. All chanting did was to make me accept things as they are.' A 26-year old nanny had chanted for income, accommodation, and 'always I've chanted to change my relationship, bad, bad, bad karma, a great source of suffering, sobbing, whinging. I chant to respect myself, for compassion, to have a big life and to help others.' She got a job and a place to live

when it seemed impossible. Now to the major issues. The best? Inconspicuous benefits. I'm beginning to see exactly why relationships are beyond me and I'm challenging this in a major way now. I've seen the extent of my self-slander and I'm determined to change this and have an attractive and compassionate life. I'm turning outwards and when this happens there have been flashes of my true potential and what it's like to be really happy despite changing circumstances. Altogether, I'm discovering and building on qualities such as courage and determination—was a watery individual before I practised . . . sorry, going on a bit here.

The corporate concerns of Sōka Gakkai are frequently canvassed in the movement's literature, and these and the goal of *kōsen-rufu* in the twenty-first century are never far from the forefront of discussion. Surprisingly, they are not a strong focus of attention as a goal of chanting: only 18 per cent declared that they had chanted for the movement and its purposes. It may well be that members rely primarily on self-transformation as the basis on which social, political, and eventually global renewal will take place. This orientation, if our characterization is warranted, underlines yet again the significance of the individuation of worshipful concerns and the subsidiary nature of corporate consequences. It may also be the case that, much more profoundly than in, say, Christianity, the organization is seen as merely the vehicle through which truth (faith or enlightenment) is promoted, and as such is less a focus of concern, less a cause to be supported, than are the teachings and the practice which constitute the ideological core of the religion.

Yet, for those most bound into the organizational structure, that structure must be an important concern. Leaders in the higher echelons devote time and energy to servicing the organization, to promoting collective endeavours of one sort or another, to bringing people together for social and cultural occasions. For these leaders, Sōka Gakkai International is not merely a dispensable organizational shell: it has a life and rhythm of its own which is inextricably mixed with the practice and goals of Nichiren Buddhism as such. This stratum within the movement is likely to have the keenest appreciation of the organizational arrangements, and to be most aware of the dependence of Nichiren Buddhism and *kōsen rufu* on these relationships and activities. Thus, it was unsurprising to find that the more responsibility the individual had within SGI, the more likely it was that he would devote chanting to the furtherance of the movement's goals. Those who undertook no special services for the organization were overwhelmingly unlikely to chant for goals of this kind. This was true of 94 per cent of those who performed no services. In contrast, the more regularly members chanted, the higher percentage among them affirmed that they chanted for the movement's goals. This was the case for 23 per cent of those who chanted daily, but of only 2 per cent of those who chanted at most three times a week. Since a heightened degree of involvement, in the ways that we have already assessed it, was associated with a greater percentage chanting for the movement, and since involvement was also greatly influenced by the number of Buddhists among the individual's close friends, so it was that the greater the proportion of Buddhist friends, the more likely it was that such people chanted for the movement.

Chanting and Self-Awareness

Most members had chanted for a widely diverse range of benefits, material, emotional, relational, and spiritual. The quality of their desires, and the extent to which they considered they had been realized, are examined below,[15] but leaving the matter of the effectiveness of chanting to one side, it was clear from both questionnaire respondents and members who were interviewed that chanting fulfilled a variety of purposes, and members interpreted its significance in different ways. Asked what they chanted for, and whether this included particular goals, members offered a range of reflections. An eye surgeon told us that he did not 'chant about specific things or for short-term goals. That does not make sense to me. I do eye surgery: I chant for it, because it is on my mind. Whatever comes into your mind when you chant, you chant about it, but not too specifically.' A psychiatric nurse also rejected short-term goals: 'No. I sort of do sometimes, but it feels like that "fire-engine religion", i.e. praying when you want something, like you dial 999 in an emergency, but don't consider the 999 brigade at any other time.'

Others, although more or less maintaining that chanting was for its own sake and for unspecified benefit, went on to indicate particular goals. Thus, a single woman teacher of 35 said, 'I tend no longer to think when I chant. I concentrate on chanting and chant to have a fulfilling day at work; for the senior management in my school, and to support them; for happiness of my family . . . for the area I live in, the local community. At the beginning, I chanted for material things, for example, a job; for somewhere to live; money for the rent and food . . . Now I chant to understand a situation, or

---

[15] See Ch. X below.

to decide what my next step should be.' A male community worker
with a master's degree declared,

I chant just to chant. You must awaken to mystic truth: I often chanted to
that sentiment. At other times, I chant to [achieve] particular objectives for
that month, that week . . . for things to be done that day . . . at work, at
meetings, for my daughter at school, or for my wife [a nurse] whose job is
threatened by cut-backs. I'll chant for a person going on a course, and as
banal as chanting for the knocking noise in my car—*Nam-myōhō-renge-kyō*
can be a great engineer—for flooring the loft and how to do it; or because
there's an overdraft at the bank.

Chanting 'just to chant' was not everyone's conception of the
practice. As a male lecturer at an agricultural college expressed it,
'there has to be motivation to chant, so you can't chant without some
kind of goal. If the goals . . . were not realized it would not be
possible to carry on chanting.' He and other members were quite
explicit about what they were chanting for. A woman film and
television editor maintained, 'I was told to chant for something
specifically, although I found that difficult to do. I found it difficult
to chant for proof, but it became inescapable when I needed a large
amount of money. I did it, and I gave it a deadline—silly, to do
that—but I couldn't see any [other] way: but the day after my
deadline, I got it. Eight people in the office came to chant with me
next day. That was quite a strong thing. That was at the material
level. (I also felt quite different in myself.)' The young teacher who
had been told not to take his 'shopping list' in to chant before the
Gohonzon at the head temple said, 'We chant for specific goals. So
many things that you want . . . The most important thing is to chant
with gratitude for your life and for *kōsen-rufu*. But there's always the
human element—things one wants for one's life. If I'm practising
sincerely for *kōsen-rufu*, my goals will fall into place quite naturally.'

Members were generally in no doubt about the acceptability of
seeking material benefits, indeed did so sometimes just to 'test' the
system, but they also registered some ambivalence about proceeding
in this way. A twice-married, unemployed woman painter chanted
'for what I want, for example, the right job. I have problems in
chanting for material things such as a car, but I do. By strange
opportunity, I got a nice car—I chanted for a nice car, the right car,
but not with all my being, and I was guided to it. But I also chant
for *kōsen-rufu*, for benefits for me and others.' A young man working

in the Department of the Environment illustrated the goal-oriented nature of some chanting: 'At the moment, I chant for some things—generally, I have something in mind but there are times when I just chant. At the moment, I chant that I shall definitely have a permacultural career ahead of me, that I shall have moved out of [the parental] home and moved in with my girl-friend, do a lot of human revolution and—something I've slipped in as a proof of practice—I want my premium bonds to come up.' For others, chanting is undertaken to give a fillip to tasks in hand. A 47-year-old woman secretary recounted that 'I chant if a difficult situation comes up, to get the best out of it. For example, in fourteen days my mother (she is Church of England) will come. I will chant . . . how to explain it [Nichiren Buddhism] to her. I was teaching a meeting on Friday, I chanted to do it well. [My son] was out of work, I told him to chant for it and he got a job out of the blue. He thinks—though sceptical—there is something in it.'

Emergencies in particular cause members to turn back to chanting, as many instances of chanting for recovery from illnesses illustrate, but the therapeutic benefit of chanting does not exhaust its application. The young would-be permaculturist recounted,

One time, last autumn, I'd been mushroom-picking—you know, magic mushrooms—with a friend and a girl from school, a bit of a hippie person. I assumed that she'd had mushrooms before. All of a sudden, when everyone was happy, she asked, 'What can you expect?' I was surprised she asked me, but she got worried. She didn't know what mushrooms might do to her. She got worked up and we had to call an ambulance. I was walking her about, while I was 'tripping' myself. The ambulance came and they took her to hospital, and I was left on my own, having suppressed the effect of the mushrooms—it all became very worrying, and I began chanting—and all was well . . . I learned a lot from that experience—one example, in time of need your faith can help you through, by *daimoku* in your head. If your head is sorted out, the whole environment can be sorted out.

Chanting for others might occur in less dramatic circumstances, of course. A widowed and later separated woman reported: 'I chant for things, I have a long list—for family and peace, for *kōsen-rufu*, and for people I know who are ill. I'm a singing teacher, and I've developed a method of teaching people to speak who have had strokes. So I chant for them, and for those in trouble.'

Chanting also has the function of increasing the individual's self-awareness, a capacity that is also attributed to the *Gohonzon*, before which chanting is undertaken. A young woman waiting to take up a place in a polytechnic described how, 'when you practise, you can bring up to the surface what is painful, difficult. I started to see awful things in my life. Practice is very demanding on you. You chant for so many things in daily life . . . to do the best possible job; to respect other people's life; to prepare myself for a career, family, marriage in the future. You can chant for anything . . . In doing that, you understand more about yourself.' The point was made more vigorously by the young man going into permaculture: 'Chanting changes your own karma. The more you chant, the more it can materialize, and it looks as if life is going downhill, till you come out on the other side. If you start and then give up when you've brought all this shit out, stored from past lifetimes, then you are left with rubbish and nothing to support you to get over it. With faith, you know you can get over it; if you give up, there's no hope.' In similar vein, a young accountancy clerk found that 'the practice brings up elements of your character which are horrible . . . you have to change them, and lack of courage may follow. When I have problems, it is harder to chant. I can feel when I chant it is changing. It is like losing determination . . . by carrying on and taking action, with the encouragement of other people, I come through. It is horrible when you are low, but you have to carry on.'

The power ascribed to chanting before the *Gohonzon* is repeatedly referred to as looking into a mirror, a tool for one's life. Thus, whilst it is the source of realizing Buddha nature, it has the perhaps initial effect of revealing the distance which the individual has yet to travel to attain it. A young woman whose marriage had broken down expressed it: 'I used to chant alone . . . in the early stages. People gave up when they had to chant with others, because it brings up problems. So I could establish a good relation with *Gohonzon*. I had breakdowns in front of the *Gohonzon*, when I started. I was breaking through unhappiness, sadness, inner attitudes. I had to free myself from frustrations, anxieties of being a single parent.'

The ultimate benefit of chanting before the *Gohonzon* is of course the final message of the movement and of its devotees. As a woman teaching in prisons put it, 'The essence [of Nichiren Buddhism] is my relationship with the *Gohonzon*, which is me, my relationships with the Mystic Law. I mean the *Gohonzon* is not an external object of worship. It is a representation of Buddha nature: we all—everything—has it. Through chanting, I draw out my Buddha nature.' Another woman teacher declared in similar terms that the essence of her religion was

my practice to my *Gohonzon* . . . that is fundamental, and other things come out of that . . . the most fundamental part of my life, the source of my creativity, wisdom. The *Gohonzon* allows me to bring out this source of power [from within the self] and to use it positively. I couldn't do that to the same extent without the *Gohonzon*. I felt, I do feel, it . . . a spiritual experience when I chant. I see my wisdom coming out. I can change my attitudes and bring out my positivity.

It follows from the total faith in the power of chanting, and the importance of this exercise in establishing and maintaining the relationship with the *Gohonzon*, that members are encouraged at all costs to maintain the practice. Members confess to difficulties in this regard: as one woman film and television editor admitted: '[I have had] some difficulty with practice—a great problem of discipline and consistency. Practice makes you examine yourself . . . stop being lazy, negative. That's a struggle sometimes. I don't see it as a crutch: it's quite tough. You're really fighting against your own negativity.' The cost of relinquishing the practice might be considerable, according to the experience of the young man who was a teacher of guitar:

I've stopped chanting at times. I got to a stage of practice—good job in the theatre. I teach classical guitar, I'd chant for students and got ten, and I decided to give up chanting. It was a tool to get on, and I gave my [ritual] bells and apparatus away, and got on my [motor] cycle, and four hours later I woke up in hospital with an injured right arm. Chanting is a way of making sure. I'm taking care of my life—if I'm not chanting, I'm not taking care of my life. It taught me a big lesson. It taught me to be strong and consistent.

The temptation to give up once material needs were met was commented on by a woman teacher, 'People I know who left—some found it too difficult to sustain the practice . . . one or two were using it to gratify their immediate desires, and once achieved they didn't see the point in continuing.' But equally, others might cease to practise because their demands were disappointed, a situation noted by a woman business analyst, who said that some people left 'because of apathy, laziness. They don't have a strong desire to develop their lives. They chanted for material benefits or a boy-friend—if they don't get it, they stop.'

It is apparent from such instances that chanting is assumed to be intrinsically effective, even when undertaken by those who have purely materialistic motives or who seek only personal benefits. Indeed it is sometimes implied that even one utterance of *Nam-myōhō-renge-kyō* is a good cause productive of good effects. Making a strong claim, President Daisaku Ikeda has said, 'When viewed from the long perspective of a whole lifetime . . . the prayers we make based on faith will all be answered without the slightest doubt.' Yet the significant words are clearly 'based on faith'. Whilst he urges members to 'carry out gongyo and chant daimoku with persistence, no matter what', he emphasizes faith, implying that the invocation is not just a formula for success: 'Faith has nothing to do with formality or ritual; it depends on one's heart, one's mind. It depends on one's conviction.'[16]

[16] Daisaku Ikeda, speech at the First SGI Youth Division General Meeting, Tokyo, 9 Sept. 1992, reported in *NSUK Bulletin*, 25 (Sept. 1992), 2.

X

What Chanting Achieved

As the fundamental activity and the focus of belief in Nichiren's Buddhism, chanting epitomizes and encapsulates the teachings of Sōka Gakkai International. Faith in chanting is the indispensable element of commitment. It is time-taking, in itself highly repetitive, and an exacting routine. Members have to believe that it is effective or they would have little reason to remain Nichiren Buddhists. What, then, did members believe that chanting achieved? Of the 96 per cent of the membership who chant for particular goals, only 3 per cent said that those goals had not been realized. Thus, 93 per cent of the entire membership who chanted for particular goals believed that those goals were achieved: chanting proved itself.

Among those who believed that chanting worked, there were, inevitably, some differences in the way in which this was perceived. Some had more direct—even magical—expectations than others. Just what counts as goal attainment is clearly a matter of how situations are interpreted, and so we asked those who affirmed that chanting had brought results in what way their goals had been realized. The majority, some 55 per cent, believed that what they had chanted for had been achieved in a direct way.

The attained desiderata, often referred to in the literature as the 'conspicuous benefits' of chanting (as distinct from less tangible spiritual and psychic gains), were diverse. A supervisor of support staff in the police force had 'avoided going bankrupt; stopped taking drugs (and found Narcotics Anonymous)'; and, in undisclosed ways, claimed to have saved her brother's life. As already noted, the acquisition of money, jobs, promotion, and living accommodation and the achievement of better personal relationships were frequently claimed. One woman, a university lecturer in literature, had chanted for financial help and received a gift of £3,000. A woman goldsmith of 23 had chanted to 'have a quick, easy and painless divorce for all involved [and] to have £300 to give my bank account by Thursday'.

What happened was that 'the solicitors discovered that the marriage certificate was not legally valid [and] my Dad phoned and said he wanted to give me an early Christmas present of some money. I had a cheque from Gran in the next post, and a £300 one-off bonus from work as well as my wages (all by Thursday!).' Thus, as in this instance, immediate needs of a very specific sort have sometimes been the object of chanting as well as more generalized financial, professional, or residential objectives.

Similarly, a free-lance woman market researcher had chanted 'to pass my driving test first time; to not hate my parents and sister; to have my own home; to stop smoking', and claimed 'I passed the driving test first time without being nervous; I stopped smoking; through chanting for gratitude to my parents and sister (my parents are dead) I have a great relationship with my sister. I feel certain my parents have been reborn and are happy and chanting, and I now have a beautiful home of my own.' A woman pensioner listed her objectives in chanting as

1. For my stepfather to recover his health; 2. For the life of a friend who was suicidal; 3. For a life-partner; 4. For my own health; 5. For a beautiful home instead of a grotty bedsit; 6. For a black Pekinese bitch—they cost £300, and I was broke and very sad at the death of my Peke. [The results were] 1. He recovered . . . ; 2. My friend did make a suicide attempt but was found in time—recovered; 3. Not yet; 4. Cured; 5. Have a lovely home and enough money to furnish it; 6. Took three months: she's a retired breeding bitch and was free as they wanted a good home for her. Also became friendly with breeder and frequently visit to be mobbed by Pekes and pups.

A male graduate, an artist and a Labour Party councillor, had chanted to achieve 'my political goals; to have exhibitions and sales; also for an agent . . . plus a gallery. To realize my potential for growth and to help others' Buddhahood.' He had become a local councillor: 'overturned a massive majority. Had a show in a major German art gallery and sold more paintings than I have for years. I also have an agent, but as yet no gallery.' The claims vary from dramatic results with long-term consequences to passing incidents. An example of the former was provided by a woman opera student who was also a singing teacher. Asked if she had chanted for particular goals, she replied, 'Yes. To resolve an unhappy long-term relationships situation and turn it around into something valuable.

2. To become an opera singer in five years (starting from a point of no previous knowledge or experience).' And were they realized?

Yes. 1. The relationship changed completely such that we are now very dear friends. It was the right thing for us both that we split up. He now chants, too! 2. I'm now on the brink of beginning a career in opera, having begun training in 1985, having learned to read music, to sing in Italian, French, and German. Also my teachers are amazed at the vocal progress I've made in such a short time. I've also had incredible support from my environment from day one, to enable me to study, including £6,000-worth of sponsorship for lessons over three years. I know without a doubt that I have been able to achieve these things as a result of my practice to the *Gohonzon*.

In contrast, a free-lance hairdresser recounted that:

when I had no money, I had gone bankrupt, my first goal was to win a pub raffle for seven free pints of beer. I really needed these. I chanted hard and on the seventh draw I won—no one else claimed their tickets—and that was an important first step. My first experience. Shortly afterwards, I built my *butsudan* [shrine] at home with my last £40 in the bank. I chanted that I should not suffer and put my life in the hands of the *Gohonzon*. One week later, I received a cheque in the post for £700 that I didn't even know was owed me.

Momentous gains are sometimes recounted together with incidental episodes which might strike the outside observer as trivial items, but any such experience may readily be regarded by the members as a proof of the validity of the practice. A woman dance animator running a community dance project listed her particular goals as:

1. To increase my income substantially; 2. to be reconciled to a lover who had left me very suddenly; 3. to sort out my personal life, especially a difficult long marriage; 4. to find a flight and accommodation in a favourite resort at short notice in high season. [What ensued was] 1. I got a new job (although I had fewer qualifications than all the other applications) which increased my earnings fourfold. 3. My relation with my husband is much improved, although we will probably part we no longer argue, and have much more respect for each other. 2. The lover returned . . . Although our feelings had not changed, I was no longer prepared to be involved in a deceit. We became good friends again, and although we are no longer in contact . . . it is not causing me pain any more, 4. After being told by numerous agents that it was impossible [I] got two seats on a plane on the day I wanted and a villa for six for the two of us at a reduced rate!

A somewhat smaller proportion of our respondents made less sweeping claims on behalf of the efficacy of chanting, considering that some of their goals had been achieved but that others had not, or they believed that whilst some goals were not yet attained, there were distinct signs of progress. A very small number, amounting to some 5 per cent of the entire sample, did not specify in what ways their goals had been realized, whilst 3 per cent recognized that what had occurred had not been the actual attainment of their aims in the way that they had envisaged it, but had either been a process in which chanting had affected an attitude change in them, or that it had led them to see the need for a change in their goals.

Unexpected Means and Deflected Goals

Some of those members who reported that what they had chanted for had not been realized in the way that they had expected none the less counted the experience as positive. A civil service administrative officer of 22 wrote, 'I've chanted for success as a musician, for a wildly exciting sex life and other similarly greed-oriented things. I'm afraid I can be a bit of a materialist. I've also chanted to improve my relationship with my parents by learning to respect and feel grateful to them, and I often chant for friends of mine to start chanting.' Asked if these goals were attained, he wrote, 'hardly ever in the way I expected, that's the easy answer. As far as I'm concerned, I achieve something even when things don't go according to plan. Let's face it, the odds of my brain's limited ability coming up with the right thing for the universal rhythm of *kōsen-rufu* are pretty pathetic. I've had some good fortune as a musician, my brother and some friends have started chanting, and my parents occasionally seem human. I'll keep you posted on the gonad situation.'

Another male graduate, an artist, acknowledged similar consequences of chanting—the results were different from the expectations, but they were results that he did not doubt were attributable to chanting. He had chanted 'for anything I want to achieve from the success of a Buddhist activity to the happiness of a friend, to making important decisions, everything', and went on to say:

Just about everything that I have chanted for has come about or has begun to change, even if very gradually . . . Very rarely do these goals turn out as one might plan or expect, but almost definitely I have eventually ended where I wanted to be or attaining benefits that I would have never expected. It's a bit like determining to travel somewhere by bus but through an extraordinary set of circumstances ending up travelling to the same place by train (more comfortably and for the same price) or finding yourself in a situation where everything seems to be lost but after reassessing one's attitude finding that this 'terrible' situation leads directly to a very surprising reward.

Similar satisfaction with what appeared initially as goal deflection was reported by a woman graduate craft worker, living in a stable lesbian relationship. Her goals had been: '1. To understand and experience eternity of life; 2. establishing a solid lesbian relationship; 3. develop compassion to help others; 4. establish financial security.' What had been achieved was: '1. impossible to put into words—experience freedom and joy; 2. not with the person I originally thought, but yes, with someone completely different; 3. helped my mother to die peacefully . . . 4. have financial stability in a way I would never have anticipated—Above were all long-term aims and therefore took some time to achieve . . . There is always a result from chanting, not always in the way one originally desired, but in a better way for everyone concerned.' A 33-year-old mother with two degrees and now a student of permaculture design, who described herself as a 'Green anarchist', and who had chanted for money and received a £500 gift, said that her various goals had been realized 'in very different ways outside my thinking capacity. Chanting enables me to let go and not try to control outcomes, and so situations resolve in amazing, unexpected ways; relationships change; support comes from unpredictable sources; and opportunities turn up out of the blue.'

It is not only the means by which goals are realized that are unpredictable, but the very goals themselves may be subject to reappraisal as a result of chanting. Members believe that chanting brings enhanced self-awareness, and hence sometimes the realization that the most treasured dreams and purposes might in the end be undesirable. A temporary office worker of 24 claimed that most of the goals for which she had chanted (a car, jobs, and health) had been realized 'but those that weren't I realized later were not right for my life or me'. The same reinterpretation was made by a woman investment banker with a Cambridge degree, whose numerous goals had largely been realized 'although it depended on my determination/

faith. Of course, if you chant for something which is not really right
for your happiness, then you often don't get it, or how you expected
. . . but then, in hindsight, you may see/understand why you didn't
get what you wanted and get what you do really need to be happy.
There's a difference between what we might want and actually need
to be happy, and chanting helps realize this and achieve what we
need.'

Sometimes, the unanticipated consequences are matched against
the disappointment, with the idea of compensatory gains for failure
of specific goals to reach attainment. A 31-year-old male drag cabaret
artiste had chanted 'for my Mum and Dad to win the football pools,
which they didn't, however my sister-in-law became pregnant,
which was just as good for my parents [as] my sister and I are gay,
therefore my brother's wife is likely to be the only one to give my
parents grandchildren'. With similar logic, a free-lance fashion
journalist declared, 'for three years I chanted to get my ex-boyfriend
back' but 'I never got [him] back, but now it doesn't hurt so much
and I don't feel bitter any more'. A woman primary school teacher
had chanted '1. to get back my husband; 2. for my father when
dying to recover; 3. for good weather for an important community
event in which NSUK was participating—it was pouring at the
time'. She regarded her goals as having been met but

not at all in the way I expected! In 1. eventually I realized that this was not
for the best and we are divorcing—but I feel happy that this is right and
can cope with it; 2. my father did not recover, but the manner of his dying
and the closeness we experienced all had a 'rightness' about them. Even a
year later, I do not feel as though I have lost him. I cannot imagine how I
would have dealt with [these] two experiences without my practice or as the
person I was ten years ago. 3. The rain stopped just as we finished *gongyō*.

An unemployed woman drama graduate was no less convinced
that her aims had been reached, even though what she had chanted
for had been realized 'in totally unexpected ways usually. It sounds
a cop-out but e.g., I have failed in several specific goals, like my
parents' practising, or "knowing for sure" about my relationship
[with a partner], but I have managed to maintain my effort and
determination in spite of logical evidence to the contrary. I am
always satisfied, things improve and most importantly, you can sense
what is needed to *really* make you happy in whatever areas you were
concentrating on, so it encourages you to carry on toward your

goals.' Another unemployed woman graduate of 23 felt some of her goals had been attained, others not, 'which leads me to conclude that it could all be based on coincidence (that is, when things do happen they are coincidence, not the result of chanting)'—for committed members a most unusual conclusion.

A small percentage of the respondents to our questionnaire indicated that they were still chanting for their objectives, or that in chanting for one thing they had in fact achieved something else which they regarded as the result of their chanting; or they suggested that they had achieved their goals not solely by chanting but by also employing other means. As one female flower-stall holder, who claimed various achievements through chanting, put it, 'It really is too long a subject to go into in a short space without sounding "flip" or mumbo-jumbo-ish. It's like anything in life, it has to be worked at, and chanting is for me a great "bonus" in that respect.' For a manic depressive who had suffered for many years, getting the right diagnosis rather than the direct cure was the benefit. 'Three years ago eventually I was diagnosed and put onto the right medication, I have made a fantastic recovery from manic depression—although I still take a preventative drug.' A 33-year-old male script-writer, when broke and in debt, had chanted for financial stability, a good relationship with his father, to visit Taiseki-ji (once he had paid off his debts), and to become a professional writer. He had re-established a relationship with his father, and 'all of the other goals listed . . . have come about through chanting to the *Gohonzon* for the wisdom and courage to achieve them, and over a period of time, in some cases, years. No magic, you see.' A male teacher in his twenties saw the attainment of his aims, generally 'in ways I hadn't foreseen: I would chant about the particular goal and take whatever action I thought might help me to achieve it.'

The Goals of Health and 'Relationship'

In contrast to such passing instances of compromise, equivocation, or the recognition that results credited to chanting had been facilitated by the employment of other means—which were evinced by a very small proportion of members—some 87 per cent of respondents were confident that chanting was the sure way to move towards the realization of their personal goals. The remainder saw chanting as an indirect means to such achievements. There were two particular concerns in which, in the philosophy of members, objective goals were to some extent potentially dependent on subjective dispositions: health and relationships. Inevitably, personal health is a prime target of chanting for many people, whether that of the individual practitioner or of family or friends, and a number of members testified to having recovered from illness through chanting. Nor were all such cases of a psychological nature. Whilst depression featured in several instances, and asthma and eczema in others, at least six respondents claimed to have been wholly or partially cured of cancer, five of epilepsy, other individuals of rheumatoid arthritis, breast abscesses, and multiple sclerosis, and several of drug addiction and alcoholism.

A female civil service officer with a master's degree had 'chanted to recover my health and overcome depression and suicidal tendencies' and had 'now recovered my health and eradicated depression'. A widow of nearly 70 had 'had cancer three times, including liver cancer nine years ago, which was inoperable. I literally chanted for my life. After three months, no tumours could be found.' A woman teacher, currently self-employed in greeting-card design, 'chanted to be free of alcohol addiction. It took a while and a lot of *daimoku*, but not totally free of it. I chanted to have another child—when I had endometreosis (a disease which causes infertility)—and that too was realized.' A carpenter had sought 'the good health and peace of my 91-year-old mother who was very ill, immobile, and going senile, and is now sharper in mind and more active every week'. A general manager, living in 'a deep and meaningful gay relationship', had chanted for 'the ability of my partner (when alive) to cope better with his very debilitating illness—he was diagnosed with AIDS' and reported that 'my partner developed an ability psychologically to live very effectively with his life-threatening illness to the point of dying very happily with no recriminations and nothing left undone'.

Relationships, particularly with husbands and partners, featured even more commonly than health among the objectives of chanting. A woman who took summer work in the holiday industry 'chanted for my marriage to rekindle the love and friendship that it had during the early part of my marriage' and claimed that it had 'brought back into my life the depth of feeling that I had put aside and taken for granted would always be there. My marriage is now the happiest it has ever been, after nineteen years.' A woman artist of over 60 years had chanted, among other things, for 'a man in my life'. What then followed was that 'A man I met at age of 16, American, did not see or hear of again after one year, wrote me forty-odd years later, when I chanted for a man. I chanted for us to be together (he, an American, no money, in California); after one year of chanting we were reunited by the *Sun* newspaper via Cilla Black programme. I find it hard to know what to write—the list is endless.' A woman medical receptionist had 'often chanted for material things, but the biggest benefits have been chanting to create a harmonious marriage, and overcome hatred and fear towards my father'. She and her husband had 'both realized we have to face the same direction in life and take responsibility for ourselves. I have been able to overcome fear and hatred towards my father who was a violent person, and gradually create a father–daughter relationship.'

Through chanting, even tragic situations sometimes appear to have redeeming features. A woman community worker wrote of her objectives, 'To chant for my ex-husband's happiness even though I was wishing him dead for all he was putting me through at the time of our divorce.' She believed her chanting had led to a situation in which 'my ex-husband and I enjoy a good relationship, and his girl-friend and I are close and our daughter and her son are very good friends, so much so that our daughter feels glad of the opportunity she has had in meeting G., my ex-husband's girl-friend's son, which is unlikely to have happened if we hadn't broken up.'

Prospective partnerships have been no less a focus of some members than the repair and rehabilitation of existing relationships. A woman party-plan manager (selling goods in other people's homes) chanted 'to find a *kōsen-rufu* partner' and 'to respect myself after a failed marriage (which, of course, I thought was my fault)'. Later she 'married a man who loves and respects me in every way (which before I never thought possible)'. A woman solicitor by chanting 'got the answer in my heart not to continue in [a] bad relationship . . . I am chanting to know who my *kōsen-rufu* partner is by a specific date next year.'

The Subjective Effects of Chanting

The realization which many members claimed of the need to change their attitudes was among the more emphatically inconspicuous benefits of chanting. The woman solicitor just mentioned had come to 'understand my anger . . . I have chanted for terrible things to happen to people I have had bad problems with, and my attitudes have changed to them: the "terrible" things did not happen!' A female student on a BA course, who had chanted 'to feel calm and generous about someone I hated', confessed that 'I was practically choking as I forced myself to chant for him but I knew it was the only way to stop feeling so bitter. Things are still not perfect, but I'm no longer destroying myself with hatred.' Another woman, a civil servant, had, by chanting, 'started to understand about my unhappy childhood . . . [and] also chanted about a relationship problem at work which was distressing to cope with'. She added,

I now realize, through chanting, about karma: I now know that I chose to be born to my parents, and I understand how much my father suffered as an alcoholic. I realize now that in the situation he was in and the way he was brought up, he did the best he could for me; and I can now think of him with love and respect. (He died when I was still in my teens and I used to hate him because he made my mother and my brother and sisters as well as me all suffer.) I now offer special prayers twice a day for him, I resolved the problem at work after suffering for about a year. I really chanted to respect a colleague who I despised. It really worked and the situation became one of absolute respect on both sides and it is now a pleasure to go to work.

A woman deputy-manager of a science museum had experienced renewed challenges about jobs and money, but her attitudes were now different: 'you know what you have to do to achieve change— no point wasting time complaining (although it will be a struggle to overcome this) but basically get down to it.'

Although there were no significant differences between the more and the less involved members in the way in which they thought about the connection between chanting and the attainment of goals, it was possible to identify those who were sceptical about the effect of chanting. Those members who were not engaged in performing services for the movement, and who were not undertaking responsibilities, and those who were practising relatively little (at most three times a week), were the very people who doubted or rejected the idea that chanting was effective in the attainment of particular goals. Of course, we cannot, from such a correlation, determine whether scepticism was itself a result of lack of achievement, or alternatively whether, because they were sceptical, they gave so little time to chanting. It appears likely, however, that limited credence or lack of credence in the *Gohonzon* might be responsible both for the failure to chant and for limited involvement in the movement.

Whatever they thought about the possibility of attaining particular goals, the vast majority of SGI members regarded chanting as the agency by which so-called inconspicuous benefits of all kind were produced. Chanting was the motor-power of their faith, the activity in which they manifested their commitment, and from which they derived their sense of Buddhist identity and, indeed, claimed their identity as individuals. How, then, were they disposed to articulate the spiritual and psychological benefit which they claimed to derive? They used a wide variety of terms, many of them synonymous or readily congruous one with another. Some 39 per cent saw the benefit as an increase in self-confidence, courage, strength, stability, or self-respect, adding to these terms self-control, self-determination, self-improvement, the capacity to take charge of one's life, and the ability to deal with its problems.

That objective change was well-expressed by a 44-year-old art teacher: 'What I notice is that, if you have a period when you commit yourself, something happens to you that other people notice. Children at school say "You're high" or "happy". They sense it. You've had a lot of good chanting . . . it's like you're charged for a few days . . . The more I chant, the less I judge people and situations . . . I become detached, and I don't know what's going on inside me. Your growth is accelerated. I feel a bigger person than I was last night.' The themes of self-confidence, self-control, and a sense of responsibility recur. A 22-year-old administrative officer in the civil service wrote, 'I've become more tolerant of most people. Some people have suggested I've become rather more balanced and less inclined to get angry or to take evasive action when things get tricky. I certainly find my life more stimulating than I ever did before. Buddhism has shown me that if you really want to enjoy life, you've got to grapple with it. This no longer fills me with dread— quite the reverse.' A 50-year-old twice-divorced American band leader dilated:

Benefits of practice are happiness, awareness that my life is the Mystic Law, also the lives of others, confident that I am in control of my life, and able to respect all living beings . . . I have learned to control my desires which got me into trouble. Although I could pursue these desires, if they don't create value for myself and others, it is no good. Desires are my weakness—

I have a sexual karma, an affectionate love for the ladies. But since this practice, I have been able to control it, although I had many opportunities. I asked what is this great change in my life (they are not bad these desires, they are karma). So I was able to supplant it for buddahood. And it is not the result of getting older or lack of opportunities. Now I can deal with it through this practice.

A 36-year-old woman, embarking on a musical career, saw the benefit of her practice as 'Completely changing my ideas about why I have experienced difficulties in my life, i.e. taking responsibility for my actions. This has definitely helped me to see clearly where I have gone wrong and has enabled me to change direction relatively painlessly.' A 32-year-old male dancer also emphasized 'a much greater sense of responsibility . . . much stronger self-control—I led a fairly hedonistic life-style, careless towards myself and others', in addition to which he had acquired an 'ability to recognize self-destructive tendencies—use of drugs, depression, self-deprecation, and to have the means to combat them'.

Clearly, for the sizeable proportion of members of whom the foregoing cases are illustrative, chanting is more than merely an expressive act. It is not, in the conventional sense, simply an act of worship, in which gratitude, obeisance, and devotion are manifested. The activity is conceived of as more of an interaction with the *Gohonzon*, in which chanting releases competencies of an objectively observable kind. For these devoted adherents, chanting was as much a therapy as an obeisance. It was a way of claiming a birthright, of realizing potency, of becoming part of the supreme force or agency of the universe. It was the opposite of declaring one's dependence or of making supplication for favour; and the virtues it epitomized were assertive and self-generated.

That not everyone drawn into SGI could testify to the therapeutic benefits of chanting is no more than might be expected, in this case as in that of any religious system, and even though our respondents were taken from a list of those who were members, there were, none the less, dissentient voices. Seven of our respondents indicated that, for one reason or another, they had ceased to be members, and most of them (though not all) had ceased to chant. One male student who had stopped declared that since doing so he had 'lost to a degree' the 'belief that I can control my environment'. His goal in chanting, 'to achieve a happy relationship with a member of the opposite sex', had not been realized, but he did not directly indicate whether this was why he had ceased to chant. A retired state-registered nurse, who, despite having lapsed, testified to various benefits from her earlier practice, such as an increase of energy, clarity of thought, and 'strength to speak up for myself', had also effected improved relationships with her husband and children, even though her husband had objected to her chanting. A male teacher of 40, who had stopped practising altogether, regarded its main benefit as having been ' a form of relaxation', and the original attraction as having been no more than that of 'belonging to a group'. A project controller had joined only 'to humour my wife' (who was Japanese). A 50-year-old decorator and builder still chanted once or twice a week, but no longer considered himself a member. He had been attracted by hope and had chanted to overcome depression, which he had not achieved.

The most trenchant of the lapsed members was a young woman law student who, on the strength of her experience, rejected the idea that there were benefits from chanting. She wrote:

My experiences with Nichiren Shōshū were certainly not the positive benefits I had originally hoped to receive. I am afraid that I consider that I fell for a marketing image of the organization which did not materialize in reality . . . I wish I had not been so convinced it could work for me. I do not think it is suitable for everyone, as I have seen other members experience similar repercussions after taking up the practice . . . The repercussions were quite devastating and began immediately I began the practice, so I knew it was not 'coincidence' as some Buddhists have suggested. I suffered health problems of a nightmarish quality, affecting my mental health, and finally I became worse off. I was unable to solve the latter because of the problems I was experiencing with panic attacks and delusions as well as severely disturbed sleep patterns. It got to the stage where I could not even work properly, and I gave up my job. Other people noticed my distressed state and thought I was suffering as a result of the chanting. They told me to stop (these were non-Buddhists). The Buddhists told me to carry on and it would get better. It was suggested that I had some particularly heavy karma to expiate from 'previous lifetimes' in keeping with their beliefs in reincarnation. I went along with this [but] what proof does one have of previous existences? You cannot prove it. I did not feel it alleviated stress, which I had been experiencing, as much as other tech- niques such as TM (Transcendental Meditation] which I now practise. I also found it far too time-consuming and impractical with a busy life-style, particularly since I discovered I was neglecting some important things in order to practise . . . there was not enough support or help from other

Buddhists who did not understand what I was going through. They did not suggest that I cease practising as I felt I should in the end and I gave up abruptly, feeling it was not helping me at all. Also I considered many of the older members fanatical and unbending in their approach. In the end it just became a machine into which I was plugged the whole time—there seemed no middle way. I do not think that the organization is as wholesome as some of the organizers would have us believe. Certainly to my knowledge people have become worse off emotionally, suffering some of the problems I encountered (i.e. life turning upside down), for others it seems to work very well indeed. I only wish I had been one of those. I eventually had to seek help in extricating myself . . . I felt the 'brainwashing' had sunk in quite far and I felt I could not manage without it. It became addictive. I eventually got help from a medium who told me that I was too sensitive to cope with added stimulus from the chanting because of my nature. I am already psychic and the Buddhism made me super-sensitive.

It is something that I can well do without. Also I disliked the fanaticism and the coercive elements/tactics used by some members encouraging people to chant more than they should at the beginning. They thus experience the problems I encountered and many leave the practice after a short time because of side-effects. In some ways it smacked of a cult religion where 'brainwashing' techniques are used.

This negative reaction was certainly an unusual case among members, but as an account it also presented what were regarded as objective consequences of chanting, even if, in contrast to the vast majority, in this case those effects were seen as detrimental. Other members, some 20 per cent, who made fewer claims or claims to less objective consequences (all of them beneficial) emphasized a more subjectivist interpretation of their experience. Claiming less of a transformation of ability, they saw chanting as producing a change of attitude, a way of acquiring optimism, hope, and a sense of purpose. They saw it, as indeed all committed members surely would, as the path to the realization of Buddha-nature, but the emphasis was on chanting as an agency working an inner change in the self, not so much the conferment from without of particular talents or capacities.

There were many responses illustrative of this appraisal. A 35-year-old woman teacher declared:

Nichiren Buddhism has transformed my life. My attitude to life changed. The main aspect is that I want to contribute to life, rather than to take away from it. It has taken away a feeling of helplessness. I feel I can do something positive in situations rather than being a victim. For example, in the Gulf

War—lots of people were upset but powerless. It was easy to see the lower state of people coming out—animality (kill and destroy) anger. Being trapped, they lash out. However, that doesn't help in the long run. By chanting to resolve the situation . . . I help [to create] peaceful surroundings.

A swimming and judo woman teacher declared herself to be 'happier: I look upon difficulties with a positive attitude, believing I can overcome them. My relationship with my husband has improved 100 per cent. I am less irritable and easier to live with.'

In very similar vein, a 35-year-old musician said,

I've changed a lot of negative attitudes towards myself and others . . . I've realized my responsibility for my life, to have a good life, and my responsibility to others . . . All spheres have benefited from from a more positive approach. People have said you can do this with positive thinking—it helps—but in the end you have to act. Positive thinkers can be victims of external circumstances, but Nichiren Shōshū stands this on its head—circumstances are part of *your* responsibility. You can change them: responsibility lies with me first and foremost.

A temporary secretary saw the benefit to her as 'Hope . . . giving up all forms of drugs (except nicotine). Knowing that however bad things seem, I will be able to overcome them if I carry on practising: having true friends, being able to listen to people.' And another temporary office worker said simply, 'I find I worry less if I have problems. Instead of worrying I chant about them.' An unemployed sales manager had gained 'a sense of purpose and identity, and big improvement in the emotional, subjective quality of my life', while a senior editorial accountant from St Lucia declared that she had 'learned to be more tolerant'.

These two themes were brought together by a Caribbean female accounts clerk, who said,

It [Nichiren Buddhism] made me more open . . . opened my eyes tremendously. I was living at home and always felt the police were prejudiced because they used to come and take away my brothers . . . I'd run when I saw a policeman. When I started chanting, I saw everyone has a function. I realized not everyone was racist—they're not. It made me broaden my views—homosexuals and gays, I see they're people like me . . . My relationships have changed. I'm a very loving person, but you can be over-loving. I'd give my evening to sitting with my boy-friend, now I know that you must have a balance, not giving up what I want to do . . . I am not jealous now of my boy-friend. A relationship is just a stage . . . you move on. I see so much talent in different guys, but I can have them as friends, I don't have to have them as lovers.

The Proofs of the Practice

It would be making too fine a point of these differences in emphasis about exactly what members saw as the primary benefit of chanting to attempt to correlate them with other variables among the membership. The differing ways in which benefits were assessed did not amount to a calculated rejection of alternatives, but only to an ordering of individual priorities: few members would have wanted to put forward their own appraisal of such benefits in opposition to others. The belief of members in general was that chanting achieved all manner of benefits, and whilst the members of longer standing tended to have grown in their appreciation of the so-called inconspicuous benefits, they were far from denying that chanting might also yield material gains of the widest variety of sorts. Proofs were acknowledged as important, and proofs were more easily acknowledged in the case of the realization of concrete goals than in the matter of changed subjective states. For the conscientious practitioner of the rituals, benefit of both kinds—indeed, of all kinds—should accrue.

There were still those who saw objective benefits as primary, and who recounted these in terms of increased physical energy for particular undertakings; in physical as well as in psychological health; in matters of fortune and good luck; and benefits which including successful marriage, and the ability to overcome problems. Better health was claimed by a 39-year-old teacher in a school of vocational therapy:

I was unwell, working so hard on my house, drinking too much [at the time of being introduced to Nichiren Buddhism]. I lost sight: I didn't have a balanced view. Chanting gave perspective, so I didn't work myself to death any more. Also, something else happened. Generally, I have memory and concentration difficulties. They were cyclical, every ten to fourteen days, a kind of depression, and I became introverted. I became that again when [temporarily] I wasn't chanting. It started again during the six weeks' lapsing. Since I practise, I haven't had it any more. My mind works better and I have better concentration . . . the biggest gain of practice. I went through several years to counselling. And it worked, but money was tight (two children and a house) and chanting was cheaper than counselling. Chanting was healthy. I felt good so. I had no memory lapses. I felt powerful, centred . . . also, we had our son and he would wake me upon the middle of the night. With chanting, I was able to be an adult. Before, I felt horrible and angry. I might have smashed his head against the wall or put a pillow over his head—making him cry more, since my anger was not controlled and I would have passed it on to him. I had strength to cope with my children only after a week of chanting.

A woman arts administrator recounted that 'I used to get depressed two weeks out of four, and now I rarely get depressed.' A woman teacher of 42 said, 'Initially, it enabled me to overcome alcoholism totally'. A professional dancer and model engaged as an aerobics instructor, who had acquired self-discipline, claimed also to have acquired 'perfect health, improving sex (you know, the usual)'. A male community social worker 'had severely destructive tendencies. I am not saying I am particularly stable, but I'm more so than when I started. I have changed my tendencies: they were based on anger. Ego had quite a strong hold, I'm aware of the ego and the way it can restrict or distort one's life, and I don't always win over it.'

There were also claims to have experienced special protection. A free-lance woman journalist had 'changed my karma over the years. I always felt protected. In vulnerable situations, it was fine. I moved from a basement flat and a young lady moved in—she had three burglaries. I did not—I was protected by the *Gohonzon*—if I need extra protection, it works. I left my car windows open in the middle of Bristol. It was the following morning—nothing was broken or stolen.' The young Caribbean woman accounts clerk recounted a more dramatic episode. She had, reluctantly, gone to see off a group of members going on pilgrimage (*tozan*) to Japan, but afterwards felt good about having done so. Later, she went to see her boy-friend, but alighted from the underground having failed to hear a warning announcement (she was wearing a walkman) and found herself on a platform full of National Front supporters with knives and bottles. 'I walked through them chanting in my head. I kept saying, "Know you're protected." They threw bottles and pushed and shoved me. I kept walking and this guy came up—blond and wearing a jacket just like mine, and said, "Hello darling—where shall we go and eat tonight?", and took me up the station platform, escorted me out: then, suddenly, he'd disappeared. He was a *shōten zenjin*, a Buddhist god, protecting me. It was all because I'd seen the party off at Heathrow.'

Others claimed a variety of reassurances, including the acquisition of a sense of harmony in life, peace of mind, the experience of joy, and a sense of balance. Some 12 per cent of respondents mentioned these consequences, typified by a 62-year-old woman artist, now engaged in caring for elderly people: 'I am out of the poverty trap I was in for twenty-five years. I am working. I am happy. I can communicate with others. I know now, life is eternal. I have no fear of death, will die with no regrets, knowing I shall be reborn over and over again.'

Ten per cent of the sample maintained that they had experienced intellectual benefits, particularly in the matter of self-understanding and the growth of insight. Although describing the benefit as 'emotional', a 36-year-old eye surgeon went on to express it in intellectual terms:

I feel comfort from knowing you can have faith in something. From my background, faith and belief are difficult concepts, opposed to reason. Beliefs equal a loss of reasonable thought . . . I feel there is something to have faith in and you don't have to drop cultural ideals, or to deny scientific progress. From a philosophical point of view, it makes paradoxes easier: subject/object, observer/observed. It is a relief to have a religion that allows you to deal with it: it allows for the reasonable and the emotional . . . Nichiren Shoshu covers my needs . . . to me, religion is a defence mechanism to protect yourself from everyday affairs.

The Caribbean accounts clerk contrasted Buddhism with her previous Christian experience, expressing her intellectual satisfaction with her new religious affiliation:

The doctrine of Nichiren Shōshū I can understand. Other Buddhisms I don't understand, but Nichiren was all set out for me . . . I was brought up in it like a child [not literally], taught what doctrines meant and how to relate them in everyday life. I was never on my own. I could always go to the district leader and say, 'I don't understand'. They would explain and everything would fall into place. When I used to go to church, I used to sit and listen to the preacher, what he said he used to lose me . . . I never found myself there—if there was something said in church that I didn't understand, it was 'Don't ask questions, I'm preaching now'. But in Nichiren Shōshū, you can ask and no one would say, 'Be quiet!' I've always had an answer to my questions.

A small number of respondents—just 3 per cent—listed a number of virtues that they had acquired and which they regarded as distinct blessings, including altruism, compassion, and enhanced regard for others. These changes of orientation and disposition had usually come about incidentally, not by any means necessarily as a consequence of a conscious search for their acquisition. Just 1 per cent of the sample related chanting to the increase of group support, making new friends, and the improvement of relationships. An accountant, who had had many different kinds of employment, said, 'members have helped to support my life emotionally when I have been in difficulty. I was often in a state of confusion: at that time, the support was there.' A male swimming instructor who was 'starting to build my life at 42—after the break-up of my second marriage' had benefited from 'the wonderful people who gave me support when it's needed'. Such support had also been forthcoming for a woman secretary, when she benefited from 'establishing better relationships with everybody, a wider circle of friends whom I would never have met, since there would have been nothing in common. We struggle together, support each other, chant together.' Chanting brings about the attitude of mind which welds the members together, and thus produces these apparently incidental benefits of group support, since without the common cause of chanting, many would not have found much to bind them with others who had come to SGI. A woman restaurant owner had seen benefit from 'the fact that through participating in meetings, etc., I removed myself from an unhealthy environment, namely, one of heavy drug use'. These appreciations of group activity were relatively few, and, of course, the support of fellow believers might be experienced in any of those religious bodies which demand a high degree of commitment. On other evidence, there is no doubt that, for many, sharing experiences in group meetings was an important aspect of their religious life, functioning for those who had problems as a type of group therapy. More generally, perhaps many members would have acknowledged group support as a gain, but these respondents did so in the context of responding to a question specifically about the benefits of chanting. Overall, some 82 per cent of our respondents related chanting to change in their own personal feelings and dispositions, but only some 4 per cent referred to social benefits as such as a consequence of chanting.

In Nichiren Buddhism, chanting fulfils functions that are analogous to those subserved by both prayer and ritual enactments in Christianity. There are, of course, also significant differences:

prayer is sometimes likened to conversation, and certainly it is addressed to a being, and it takes on more diverse forms. It is also explicitly directional. It may be formalized pious utterance in set formulas. Or it may be spontaneous supplication, thanksgiving, or exhortation (exhorting, at times, the deity, at times, those praying, and, at times, a wider public who are neither auditors nor observers). The *daimoku* and *gongyō* most closely approximate formula prayer. Whatever supplicatory or directive elements are mentally attached to such chanting, as when, in *daimoku*, members pursue particular goals, they are not specifically articulated. Chanting is thus closer to ritual than it is to prayer as generally conceived in Christian terms, and this even though this ritual chanting is most frequently a purely private performance.

Yet chanting differs from many ritual performances, in that it is not presented as a symbolic act which produces socially recognized specific consequences. Many rituals are declamatory acts—solemn enactments are performed, their symbolic significance asserted, and changes of quality, status, or relationship are then affirmed to have been achieved.[1] So it is with baptism, marriage, confession, and absolution as sacramental performances (as well as with the naming of ships, the opening of bridges, and other like inaugurations). The cognitive phenomena remain the same, but the 'spiritual' condition, as represented in the emotive and evaluative elements of a situation, is proclaimed to be (and believed to be) transformed. Statements are made regarding the intrinsic condition of participants ('received into the faith'; 'declare you lawfully wedded man and wife'; 'thy sins are forgiven'). In so far as these statements are believed—by participants and by the wider society—the ritual has 'worked'; a change has been wrought because, by uttering these performances, perceptions and evaluations have been transformed; and sometimes the force of law is employed to reinforce and consolidate these changed estimations of status or relationship. Chanting, although highly formalized in context, duration, and frequency of performance, makes no such claims to effect specific and symbolic transformations of this kind. Yet chanting is, as we have seen, credited by its votaries with great

[1] What have been termed 'declamatory acts' have been observed as ritual religious performances by others who have used other designations for them: J. L. Austin, *How to Do Things with Words* (Cambridge, Mass.; Harvard University Press, 1961), 5, called them 'explicit performances'; John Skorupski, *Symbol and Theory* (Cambridge: Cambridge University Press, 1976), 93 ff., writes of 'operative acts'.

intrinsic power. The point of invoking the *Lotus Sutra* in the *daimoku* is to improve the individual's karma—to reduce the effect of bad karma and to help the practitioner to better his own present and future prospects. Chanting is deemed to act automatically, operating in accordance with the law of cause and effect, which is the basic philosophical premises of Nichiren Buddhism. Though it is claimed that ultimately chanting benefits the world at large, it is not initially so much concerned with the condition of the wider public, but rather with the circumstances of the one who chants. Only when sufficient people commit themselves to chanting will they, as more enlightened individuals, realizing progressively more and more of their Buddha natures, gradually produce the effect of transforming the character of social institutions and the structure of society.

Chanting is the fundamental of Nichiren's Buddhism. The religion stands or falls by what chanting achieves. The members of SGI-UK make bold claims for it, and offer manifold instances of what they regard as proofs of validity of those claims. Unlike Christianity, and, indeed, unlike other variants of Buddhism, the implicit theodicy that they invoke does not rely on benefit postponed into an indeterminate hereafter. Such benefit may occur there as well—in future incarnations. But the emphasis is on benefit here, and, if not always benefit now, then, at least, benefit soon. Yet a considerable part of the effectiveness of any religious belief is in its capacity to change subjective dispositions, in disseminating confidence and hope, and reinterpreting quotidian experience into the terms of an alternative conspectus of life and its meaning. In these respects certainly, Nichiren's Buddhism, as the British members of Sōka Gakkai present it, may well claim manifest success.

Epilogue

So extensive has been the incursion into British society (and other Western societies) of new religious movements since the early 1960s that a rather general analysis is often taken as an adequate level of explanation of the emergence and growth of any one of them. To the public at large, SGI-UK is, on the face of it, simply one of a number of new movements of exotic provenance to which such general theories apply. These explanations invoke the earlier breakdown of indigenous patterns of belief and practice; the increased scepticism regarding traditional religious institutions and ideologies; the spread of scientific (and often scientistic) thinking; and the fragmentation of what were, at least notionally and ideally, coherent and integrated moral and cultural systems. These circumstances facilitated the acceptance of these many new forms of spirituality which were, for the first time, widely and easily available. The mass media, much increased international travel, and the accessibility of other cultures stimulated the taste for the exotic, even if they also eventually transformed what was initially exotic into something less alien and more familiar. More fundamentally, there was the transformation of social structures—the enhanced mobility of modern society, the changing patterns of work, and the new conceptions of authority and processes of democratization which had been occurring in the previous couple of generations, and which challenged both traditional political arrangements and ecclesiastical structures.

Such factors clearly help to explain the spread of all or any of the new religions, but to appreciate the actual mechanisms of growth, and the basis of attraction, recognition of such broad historical processes of change needs augmentation. To explain the spread of any one movement (or of a cluster of movements that have certain salient features in common) requires more refined analysis of the life circumstances, relationships, motives, and encounters of those involved. The search for a fuller explanation must lead to consideration not only of movement policies and decision-making but also of the entire network of communication among individual believers.

Our study has aimed not so much at a complete historical account of SGI-UK, but rather at illustrating the typical processes of encounter and attraction, the ways in which commitment was stimulated and sustained, and among what sort of people. All of these issues have been examined in relation to the types of spiritual experience which these people reported. We have, thus, considered the movement less in terms of chronological or historical analysis than by reference to patterns of typical social response. This individualistic mode of analysis is related to wider sociological considerations by the statistical information which our survey yielded, but it is appropriate at least briefly to indicate the relationship of the research to some more general, if more tentative considerations about the wider social context in which Sōka Gakkai has had to operate in contemporary Britain.

The decades in which the movement has grown have been a period of relative affluence in a society in which material wealth has increased, and in which the economic emphasis has shifted markedly from that of a typical producer society of the late nineteenth and early twentieth centuries to one dominated by consumerism. The ethic of the producer society, of early and developing capitalism, was geared towards capital accumulation, the endeavour to provide the work order with more capital equipment and, incidentally, to make the process of production, as economists have put it, 'more roundabout'. Such goals demanded a moral order in which the work ethic had a central role, in which people had to be induced to postpone economic gratification by devoting themselves to production and by minimizing consumption. Self-restraint and the acceptance, perhaps even the acceptability, of scarcity was the rule, and thrift, and, where possible, saving, were the rationale of economic and indeed moral behaviour.

That the Christian ethic that had informed Western society underwrote just such orientations is clear. It was an ethic which had grown out of conditions of scarcity, of deprivation, want, famine, plague, and war. It put forward principles which helped men to accommodate to such perilous circumstances. It taught forbearance, restraint, patience, long-suffering, commitment to duty, including commitment to work, which in itself came to be upheld as intrinsically ennobling. Obedience, willingness, respect for authority, and diligence in one's calling were part of the explicit Christian canvass, while the reinforcement of patterns of social status, order, and control were always its latent, and often its manifest, functions for the wider society. Asceticism was at the heart of Christian moral counsels as the appropriate preparation for the afterlife. Whilst this world was a vale of tears, gratification of desire would come only in the life hereafter. The soteriological scheme was a model for that postponement of gratification and self-indulgence which fitted well the needs of burgeoning capitalism in societies bent on the enhancement of production.

Restraint was not only the virtual touchstone of moral order in the life of the individual, it was also the requirement of society itself, as organized in the political state. As Marx and other radicals saw it, the state was an agency of repression, organized to keep citizens under control, prescribing standards of conduct and proscribing a wide variety of behaviour. The state under Christian guidance evolved into a refined instrument for the maintenance of order and the discouragement of self-indulgence, dissolute conduct, lasciviousness, and the prohibition of every sort of social disorder and sexual irregularity. The paternalistic state was the more pliant and benign manifestation of this concern for the corporate good, social cohesion, and value consensus. (The extreme and exaggerated form found expression, by resort to coercive rules, and by basing its social probity on biological or ethnic premises, in Nazism). The decline of statism, the loosening of social authority, and the abandonment of policies which sought to maintain control over people broadly coincided with the shift from production-oriented to consumption-oriented economic regimes. The producer society, even in the incipiently capitalist West, had a command rather than a market economy, as Henry Ford's dictum—that customers could have a car of any colour, as long as it was black—sharply epitomizes. The shift to a consumer economy demanded the abandonment of the regulation of personal comportment as consumer choices became the basis for a market economy. The development of *laissez-faire* economics inevitably brought in its wake a *laissez-faire* morality. As moral regulations of one sort and another fell into desuetude, so a positive philosophy enhancing freedom of choice evolved—permissiveness. (In its exaggerated manifestation it became libertarianism, of course—the abandonment of all moral regulation.)

Clearly, the old ascetic ethic of Christianity, with its role model of austerity, single-minded devotion to duty, seriousness of purpose, and the recognition that time, effort, and other resources were all properly employed only when in the service of the divine, was ill attuned to the new economic order. Consumerism existed by stimulating demand, inducing self-gratification, urging people to buy, and to buy *now*. Asceticism was alien to the ethos on which the economic well-being of society itself had come to depend. The new order required the legitimization of consumption, an ethic which promoted hedonism, self-indulgence, and the unending pursuit of pleasure. In the advertising and entertainment industries it found vehicles to promote exactly such a value system. These agencies were themselves instrumental in undermining the message of traditional Christianity, and became, in not too long a time, far more powerful than the churches in their capacity for persuasion and in their control of the media of communication. New generations found the age-old message of indigenous religion incompatible with their life experiences and expectations. Encouraged to believe in the right to choose and the right to please oneself, they found the preaching of restraint, decorum, patience, and the need to postpone gratification increasingly alien to their inclinations. Ideals of duty to the state, or action for the corporate good, were subordinated to the search for personal fulfilment and the desire to enjoy life to the full. As belief in an afterlife (whether of rewards in heaven or punishments in hell) diminished, so the disposition to get out of the present life all that was available became a transcendent preoccupation. In such a context, where there has developed a strong belief that only in this world is pleasure available, the desire to perpetuate or repeat earthly life has made conceptions of reincarnation increasingly congenial.

Congruent with these developments has been the persisting decline of belief in a personal God, as revealed by numerous surveys conducted in all Western countries in recent decades. In its stead, the idea of an impersonal life force or spirit has become increasingly acceptable to modern thought. For many, especially for better-educated people, the anthropomorphic model of deity has become in itself an anachronism. Scientific interpretations of life and the universe, invoking abstract principles and empirical evidence, have rendered time-honoured explanations less and less plausible in advanced society. Systems have replaced persons as the operative agencies in so much of contemporary social life that it is scarcely surprising that similar trends should have affected the spiritual sphere and, together with the shifts in popular morality, these currents have caused an accelerating erosion of traditional beliefs, structures, and relationships.

These then, briefly adumbrated, are aspects of the social context into which the new religions emerged in Western society from the 1960s onwards. Not all of those movements marched with the new times. Some sought a reassertion of the old discipline, albeit with a new spiritual rationale. Such were the Unification Church and, outside the Christian tradition, the International Society for Krishna Consciousness. They continued to call for self-sacrifice for some transcendent cause; preached asceticism, self-denial, discipline, and the realization of oneself by dedicated service to some higher being. But many others embraced the brave new world, abandoned moral codes and the call for ascetic exercises, and endorsed the search for pleasure, happiness, and fulfilment in this world. Widely divergent movements endorsed such goals. Some, such as the various human potential movements and the advocates of systems of positive thinking, did so in at best only quasi-religious terms, and urged their pursuit by methods claimed to be essentially rational. Others, also disclaiming religious status—such as the purveyors of meditation techniques—canvassed more mystical means towards very similar goals of attaining perfect fulfilment. Yet others—Rajneeshism would be an example—did so by reference to ancient patterns of disciple-ship which conjoined licence for hedonism with certain demands for service and sacrifice.

Sōka Gakkai International, whilst drawing on ancient scriptures, none the less has a message which claims special relevance for our own times, perceived in its own terms as the Latter Day of the Law. That relevance is manifest in the convergence of the general contemporary climate of economic and social permissiveness with Sōka Gakkai's relinquishment of moral codes and its espousal of general abstract ethical principles which leave adherents free to discover their own form of 'taking responsibility'. Its permissive ethic, its endorsement of the search for personal happiness, and its emphasis on personal fulfilment are a virtual espousal of the secular ethos of post-Christian Britain. That its members should so largely be drawn from those engaged in the mass media, or in the entertainment industries, and from artistic pursuits, where personal freedom and the demand for self-expression are all at a premium, reinforces the impression of a movement in which a new ethic confirms the experiences and meets the needs of those who join. The work experience of such members differs radically from that of those engaged in the extractive and manufacturing employments of producer societies, and participates much more in the ethic of expressive consumatory concerns. It would be remarkable if people engaged in the media, advertising, and entertainment were to endorse asceticism: it is altogether expectable that they should espouse the expansive values of the permissive society.

SGI-UK is thus a movement in tune with the times in its stance regarding personal comportment. It shares this moral posture with other new religious and quasi-religious movements that are of quite different provenance and which present themselves in quite different philosophical terms. Thus, Werner Erhard of the *est* movement (later called Forums Network) made 'taking responsibility' a basic demand by which the individual would achieve mastery of his life, by recognizing that he himself was the source of all he might do, and all that might be done to him. The assertion that the environment reacts—indeed responds—to the individual's chanting is at the core of Nichiren philosophy. The individual is held to be totally responsible for his circumstances by having made causes in the past which predicate his present condition. To alter his karmic state he must chant, and in so doing he takes control and influences not only his subjective dispositions but also what appear to be external objective forces. As long as he chants he need not be a victim, and must not perceive himself as such. There are clear echoes here, too, of the promise made by Scientology, that its graduates should be 'at cause' over their external circumstances, and of similar claims by the movement, Exegesis. Just as Erhard has proclaimed that meditation is a means by which people might accept and welcome 'the demons which arise from the unconscious', so Sōka Gakkai maintains that evil states of mind can be externalized and transcended by contemplation of the *Gohonzon* and by chanting before it. The human potential movements, like SGI, also renounce the disposition to make evaluative judgements, to attribute blame, or to indulge feelings of shame or guilt.

These powerful moral orientations are further reinforced by the ontological theories espoused by the Sōka Gakkai. The general congruity of Buddhism with the formulations of modern science has been claimed by Buddhists of many varieties, and although the concepts of karma and reincarnation go far beyond anything that science can validate, the general theses which Buddhism offers to explain everything from the material world to human psychology can be represented as much more easily compatible with rationalistic science than is the case with the Christian interpretations of man and nature, underwritten as they are by reference to arbitrary actions of deity and dependence on nature-defying miracles. The principle of cause and effect is as fundamental to science as it is to the Buddhist interpretative scheme of things. It may not be easy in Buddhism to establish specific links—indeed the time-scale of karmic influences goes beyond such a possibility—but there is a similar invocation of abstract principle and allusion to empirical instances (however arbitrarily these may be chosen). Karma links the individual to others and to society, and purports to 'make sense' in certain terms of perennial questions about identity, chance, fate, and destiny. It claims to be an encompassing explanatory device, available at all levels, but one which is subject to modification by conscientious effort. By invoking the *Lotus Sutra*, the Sōka Gakkai adherent believes that he can control karma, can come to be in charge, take responsibility for his own life and circumstances, and realize his buddhahood—and all this through the meritorious act of chanting.

Given these similarities of disposition, it can be no accident that movements as different in religious doctrine and intrinsic ritual as are Sōka Gakkai and various of the human potential movements, such as Scientology, *est*, and Exegesis, should emerge and flourish in recent decades. Nor are the similarities of orientation confined to the common disposition to eschew the realm of personal morality. These movements all display a greater or lesser measure of concern for trans-personal and politicized moral programmes. Some of the human potential movements claim to promote various social causes—drug rehabilitation in the case of Scientology, the hunger project for the Forums Network, and the assertions made on behalf of Transcendental Meditation that a vital by-product of its adherents' activities is the improvement of general civic well-being in the reduction of crime and other forms of social pathology. But in such matters, Sōka Gakkai perhaps far outstrips other contemporary new movements—in its promotion of concern for world peace,[1] ecological issues, refugee relief, and educational and cultural programmes. Thus, although personal moral norms are regarded as no longer appropriate for modern times, the so-called 'Latter Day of the Law', commitment to what might be termed political morality exemplified in such concerns as these is a strong focus of concern. Again, the movement shares a convergence of sympathies with those of many, especially younger, people in discriminating between matters of personal comportment and these social and political global issues.

Sōka Gakkai also differs from other contemporary movements in its insistence that chanting is more than a passive mode of seeking to be 'in tune with the infinite', as early versions of positive thinking expressed the goal. It is more than mere relaxed meditation and the affirmation of a mantra as in Transcendental Meditation. It is seen as a more interactive involvement with an objective agency—a universal law—than is the case with the 'boot-straps' philosophy of the human potential movements. For many Sōka Gakkai members, chanting is no mere routine or mechanical act. These members at least did not regard it as a magic formula, a ritual which automatically put things right. Indeed, the practice may be perceived as a conscious and deliberate endeavour to establish a relationship with the *Gohonzon* which virtually amounts to a form of induced psychotherapy. The more deeply grounded members sometimes commented on the enhanced self-awareness that was achieved by chanting to the *Gohonzon*. They realized how they had tended to give free reign to the lower states of consciousness, indulging themselves in anger and animality, and how they had suffered accordingly. The more alert practitioner recognized how by his performance he had come to 'externalize his rottenness', bringing to consciousness the least attractive sides of his nature and facing up to them. Some members made it plain that chanting could be an exacting, indeed searing, experience, and a reason why at least some initially found it possible to practise only when alone, in case the experience of facing up to things was too traumatic to countenance when others were present. Yet, such experience, were it to occur frequently or to persist, might be insupportable were members regularly to

---

[1] For an account of the movement's efforts in peace education by book publishing and the promotion of exhibitions depicting the horrors of war, see Daniel A. Metraux, 'The Sōka Gakkai's Search for the Realization of the World of *Risshō Ankokuron*', *Japanese Journal of Religious Studies*, 13/1 (Mar. 1986) 31–61.

practise entirely in isolation, or to lack the type of sympathetic support and explanatory counselling which the movement makes available.

Such support comes in two forms: in the meetings of the various echelons of the organization, and in the guidance available from leaders at each level. Meetings, as we have observed, serve to provide group support for members. They are occasions of mutual sharing of experience, testimony, and, in a sense, confession. They are relatively informal occasions, loosely structured, and offering every encouragement to all present to make themselves known, and to tell their own stories—including the uninitiated and casual guests. Such occasions, under unconstraining leadership, effect a translation of each individual's experiences—both subjectively before the *Gohonzon*, and objectively in negotiating the everyday world—into the argot of the movement. Incidental events and 'accidents' are reinterpreted and given meaning in the light of karmic philosophy, and a shared understanding of how the (Buddhist) world works is communicated, shared, and mutually reinforced. Even severe experiences of self-examination induced by chanting may now be put in context, normalized, and effectively handled.

Guidance is, in many ways, the watchword of SGI. As a concept, it owes much to Japanese culture—to the conception of a master-disciple relationship, which is a pattern that extends from the relationship between a convert and the member responsible, by *shakubuku*, for converting him. In SGI, the hierarchy of such relations is institutionalized in the tiered echelons of the organization. Leaders are people usually of longer standing in the faith than those whom they lead, and they are available both to guide discussion in meetings and to counsel individual members. In general, the need for confidence in leaders is well articulated in the movement, even though it might be going too far, in any strong sense of the term, to talk of 'a charismatically infused leadership hierarchy'.[2] As we have seen, in Britain, some members found it difficult to respect local leaders, although admiration was not infrequently expressed for the General Director of SGI-UK

---

[2] This description is used by David A. Snow, 'Organization, Ideology, and Mobilization: The Case of Nichiren Shōshū of America', in David G. Bromley and Phillip E. Hammond (eds), *The Future of New Religious Movements*, (Macon, Ga.: Mercer University Press, 1987), 157.

and, although with exceptions, more emphatically for Ikeda, the international president.

Whilst some of our respondents spontaneously expressed their admiration for their chapter or district leaders, and whilst the initial attraction of SGI was, for a considerable proportion of members, the style, comportment, or personality of members whom they encountered, none the less, criticism, disenchantment, and disapproval of leaders at various levels was sometimes voiced. Guidance may often have been sought or, in group circumstances, freely given, but not all those charged with its provision evoked unqualified respect. Thus, whilst in some respects some leaders might act as role-models for members, in conformity with the master–disciple principle, the pattern was by no means universal, and less apparent in Britain than has been suggested is the case in the United States.[3] The measure of equivocation of British members regarding the role of disciple may exempt the British SGI from the charge (which has sometimes been levelled against the movement in Japan) of being unduly regimented and disciplined.

None the less, the emphasis on guidance ensures that there is in place a systematic diffusion of certain values throughout the entire organization. Leaders at each level—in a way reminiscent of the monitoring arrangements of nineteenth-century schools—are charged to guide those who have been less long in membership. This system has the advantage of conforming to the ideals of democratic practice whilst reinforcing authority within a hierarchic lay structure. Leaders at each level constitute a chain, and behind the guidance of each one stands the authority of the entire movement, its president, and ultimately the teachings and counsel of the Nichiren Buddha and the universal law that he expounded.

In practice, guidance functions often to reconcile members to their experience, to reinterpret both untoward living realities and the misgivings, uncertainties, and subjective doubts that may arise from practice before the 'mirror' of the *Gohonzon*. Those doubts might relate not only to lack of self-confidence, but also to the actual effectiveness of chanting. Some members openly expressed their doubts, asking whether a specific effect was attributable to an actual cause or was rather a matter of coincidence. Leaders might deal with

---

[3] Considerable importance is attached to leaders as role-models in the American branch of the movement (then known as Nichiren Shōshū of America) by Snow and Phillips, 'The Lofland–Stark Conversion Model', 442.

doubt by urging members to further chanting, although intellectual doubt was perhaps a more difficult issue to resolve than was the experience of untoward events in everyday life. Adversity may be re-evaluated as the opportunity for growth and rededication, and as an occasion to demonstrate resilience, and confidence in the power of chanting. The doctrine of karma facilitates such transvaluations, and provides a near-perfect theodicy.[4] The message of SGI is very much that by altering subjective states of mind, attainable through chanting, so situations and events can be effectively changed for the good. From the range of possible responses to the adversity which is the common experience of everyday life—frustration, embitterment, resignation, practical action, or reinterpretation—Sōka Gakkai, whilst by no means eschewing practical action, enjoins reinterpretation, and leaders' guidance is often vital to effect the shift in subjective orientation which creates in the member a more positive attitude in the management of his or her daily affairs.

It would not be inappropriate to regard SGI—no doubt alongside a variety of other religious and therapeutic movements—as one of those emergent associations which, since the time of Alexis de Tocqueville and Émile Durkheim, have been recognized to be spontaneous structures mediating between the individual and the increasingly impersonal wider society, particularly as manifested in the state itself. Those who are likely most acutely to feel the need for supportive associations that confirm the individual's worthiness are found in those sections of society which are least enmeshed in structured relationships and least constrained by conventional institutional arrangements. That such a high proportion of SGI members should be self-employed people, artists, individual entrepreneurs, small business people, professionals, or independent agents of one sort or another, and that many appear to have experienced broken marriages and disruptive relationships, tends to suggest the functions which the movement fulfils. SGI may also attribute its apparent success in holding its members not only to the practicality of its supportive counselling, but to the fact that this

---

[4] Of Buddhism in general, Max Weber wrote, 'The most complete formal solution to the problem of theodicy is the special achievement of the Indian doctrine of *karma*, the so-called belief in the transmigration of souls . . . Each individual forges his own destiny exclusively, and in the strictest sense of the word.' Max Weber, *The Sociology of Religion*, trans. Ephraim Fischoff (London: Methuen, 1965), 145 (originally published as *Religionssoziologie* (Tübingen: Mohr, 1922)).

measure of pragmatism is combined with a superordinate meta-physical system from which the movement claims its legitimization. In this it has an advantage over the human potential movements, even though some of those movements are sometimes capable of eliciting strong allegiances, particularly from those whom they recruit to their administrative staff. SGI conjoins an ancient religious wisdom, and the attitudes of reverence which such religions have traditionally sought to awaken in their votaries, with a positive—as they would see it, 'life-enhancing'—ethic which vigorously canvasses its claim to thoroughly practical applicability.

The structured provision of guidance and the schedule of local meetings at various levels serve to bind together the members of what might otherwise be an amorphous body of believers (perhaps one should more appropriately say 'practitioners'). Nichiren Shōshū Buddhism lacks an articulated congregational structure. There are no rites which *must* be collectively performed. The concept of priesthood itself differs from that implied in the sacramental role of the Christian priest, and, more important as far as Western branches of SGI are concerned, the Nichiren Buddhist priests, even before the schism of 1990–1, were relatively remote agents who operated only in Japan, and who, at least in Britain, rarely visited and performed no indispensable rituals (such as funerals and post-humous naming ceremonies which, in common with priests of other Buddhist sects, Nichiren Shōshū priests have traditionally performed for adherents—until recently, including Sōka Gakkai members—in Japan). The organization which the movement has adopted is the creation of Sōka Gakkai, not of Nichiren Buddhism as such nor of the Nichiren Shōshū sect. Given this inheritance, an important function of guidance, built on the parent–child model widely characteristic of Japanese social organization, has been to provide cohesive bonding for the movement, and to reinforce the tiered echelons of formal organization.

As was evident from the responses of some members, and is certainly warranted by Nichiren's teachings, the philosophy of *Nam-myōhō-renge-kyō* is that chanting is in itself effective, even without a copy of the *Gohonzon*. Some members chanted—apparently effect-ively and with results that were at least to their own satisfaction—before they knew anything about SGI (or NSUK, as it then was). One or two more sceptical adherents indicated that, whilst they were sincerely committed to 'the practice', they were much less enamoured of the organization. Several advanced the information that they had not been looking for any sort of organization and had accepted it only reluctantly. One hazard for religions in which all professional intermediaries are dispensed with, and in which the individual is enjoined to 'work out your own salvation' and is regarded as fully capable of doing so, is that belief and practice become independent of formal organized structures which may in such a context come to be perceived as otiose. The point has been well expressed, relative to Nichiren Shōshū of America, by David Snow, who wrote:

Movements that promise individuals the realization of personal benefit or gain in their everyday lives if only they engage in some seemingly magical ritual such as chanting Nam-Myōhō-Renge-Kyō . . . run the risk of creating a pool of 'free-riders' within their ranks. After all, why help the movement attain some larger goal, such as world peace, when that goal constitutes . . . a 'public good' . . . and when recitation of some mantra within the confines of one's home is sufficient to yield a continuous stream of physical, material, and spiritual benefit? Movements such as NSA are thus confronted with the task of convincing members both of the need for collective action and the utility of their participation in that action.[5]

Despite the tenuous aspects of the relation between practice and organization, SGI appears to have suffered few 'free-riders', although in the nature of individual private belief and practice such people may be difficult to discover. On the other hand, a number of members had undergone a conversion from attitudes of hostility towards organization to acceptance of, enthusiasm for, and commitment to SGI, and had acquired a keen appreciation of what they saw as the indispensability of structure and collective order in religion. There were many who were more than willing to devote their time and energy to the organization as such and, from their evidence, it would appear that SGI had gone a considerable way to solving the problem of 'free-riders' by providing both service and support to those who chanted as well as opportunities for them to serve the organization.

As a religious body, SGI represents a new type of structure which signally differs from conventional Western preconceptions concerning the relationship of religious ideology and organization. The ideology of Nichiren Buddhism has readily adapted to the

---

[5] Snow, 'Organization, Ideology, and Mobilization', 162.

individualistic orientation that it has acquired in its modern form under the auspices of SGI, although the assumptions of Nichiren himself must have been for the continuance of traditional Japanese temple allegiances and priestly officiation. The schism between Nichiren Shōshū and Sōka Gakkai indicates how readily the ideology might become independent of its original structural support, and how effectively it might be sustained by a more modern, rationally devised, and co-ordinated organization. Perhaps of necessity, a formal organization like SGI adopts public goals which, whilst easily related to chanting (and the achievement of which is held to be at least partly the result of members' chanting), may also be seen as independent objectives—such as world peace, ecological conservation, and the promotion of culture and education. Without such corporate ends which bind members in commitment to higher purposes, and which add a social dimension to the purpose of chanting, it is arguable, *contra* Snow, that the movement might not hold together at all. After all, it is not inconceivable that the practice as such might have spread as an autotherapeutic procedure for which nothing was needed except perhaps a rosary, and for which any sort of elaborate organization might have seemed superfluous. Clearly, the *Gohonzon*, when new copies were available, functioned to legitimize chanting as an authentic practice, while copies of the *Lotus Sutra* provided intellectual justification for faith. These were elements which authenticated the movement and conferred upon it specific identity, but such artefacts could have been distributed without the facilities of an organized, cohesive movement with its centralized, rational, hierarchic structure. We may see how limited was the impact of these items on organization, when one observes that, since the schism, new members chant without receiving a personal replica of the *Gohonzon*.[6] Looser patterns of diffuse association suffice for

---

[6] Given the centrality of the *Gohonzon* to the practice, SGI-UK has sought to clarify the position now that the High Priest has refused to grant further replicas to new members. In a series of comments on the situation, the Vice-General Director affirmed, 'revealing Buddhahood is not impossible without the Gohonzon, for we can conjure up the image of the Gohonzon in our minds;' 'although many members know theoretically what the Gohonzon is that they have enshrined in their homes, they still tend to regard it almost like some magic object. They look for the power of the Gohonzon outside themselves and somehow in the scroll of paper itself. They don't realize that the Gohonzon is an instrument to draw out the Buddhahood that already exists within their own lives. So it can be a benefit to practise first without the Gohonzon and discover, through actual proof, that in fact the Gohonzon exists within yourself;' 'Ultimately, everything in this practice depends on your attitude—the

such spiritual bodies as the Spiritualists, New Agers, paganism, Druidism, and, not too far removed, the vegetarians, and Alcoholics Anonymous. Yet SGI—whilst it fails to conform to the defining specifications of a Western sect—is a more coherent, structured, and organized body than any of these diffuse associations. It is in its espousal of the public good, its commitment to practical social action, as well as to private ritual performances, that SGI acquires its special resilience, not as an agency providing access to magic but as a religion. Chanting is lifted from purely private preoccupations to being an agency through which members express and reinforce their commitment to clearly defined social goals. It becomes analogous to prayer in affirming purposes and aspirations that transcend the personal and sometimes petty supplications of individuals in search of benefits—significant as these might be in inducing members to chant in the first place.

What SGI has succeeded in doing has been to maximize lay participation whilst retaining a firm system of central control. The ordinary lay member can feel that he is doing something—for himself, for his relationships, for the movement, and for the world. Chanting is held to affect all these things. Members not infrequently extolled the democratic and egalitarian character of their movement, in accordance with their belief that Buddha nature was available to all. Paradoxically, outsiders have sometimes seen only authoritarianism in every aspect of the movement, from the attitudes of reverence accorded towards Daisaku Ikeda to the disciplined service provided on public occasions by the uniformed stewards and stewardesses (VCG and Lilac volunteers). Yet the regard for Ikeda and the enthusiasm for service are certainly uncoerced and spontaneous, even if, as in all religious movements, there is a strong normative expectation of just such conformity of response. Both dispositions appear to reflect the felt needs of members: there is satisfaction to be had from contributing to the cause, and a sense of security in trusting a leader whose prestige (not to say charisma), although carefully protected and projected, is undoubtedly a consequence of the strong devotion offered by the greater part of his following. These organizational features are to be acknowledged no less than

sincerity of your faith—not whether you physically possess the Gohonzon.' Kazuo Fujii, 'How to get the Most from your Practice without the Gohonzon', *UK Express*, 258 (Dec. 1992), 12–13.

the more obvious functions—material as well as psychological—that are recognized as attributable to chanting.

Ideologically and organizationally, then, the SGI has found ready resonance with the changing course of wider currents of thought in contemporary British society. The decline in the credibility of an anthropomorphic deity; the sense that traditional, formal religious institutions have in some sense become hollow representations of conceptions of worship that are superseded; the emphasis on the private nature of belief and practice—all open the way for less formal, less institutionalized patterns of faith. The desuetude, and perhaps the abandonment, of prescriptive moral codes; the rejection of an ascetic ethic as an agency of salvation; the emphasis on letting individuals please themselves in respect to all matters of personal comportment; and the general espousal, without a sense of shame or guilt, of hedonism as both a legitimate philosophical orientation and an attitude to everyday living—are characteristic features of contemporary Western values to which SGI supplies a spontaneous echo. Personal autonomy, the cultivation of a sense of personal responsibility, and dependence on one's own efforts (whether practical or therapeutic) all fit into the enterprise culture flourishing in what appears perhaps to be a post-socialist world.

In all these and perhaps other ways, Nichiren Buddhism, as promoted by SGI, easily converges with the aspirations of today's younger generation and with their perception of things. In presenting an ancient faith in modern form it offers legitimization for many of the dispositions of today's young people. Innovation is backed by tradition. When thirteenth-century scriptures are given twentieth-century relevance, the mystery of the sacred invocation readily accommodates the pragmatism of everyday life. Contemporary cultural themes are allied to antique parables, and the burning issues of our times are addressed both in age-old rituals and by practical modern methods. Well may dedicated members affirm that SGI is a faith whose time has come—a time to chant.

APPENDIX A

The 1990–1991 Schism of Nichiren Shōshū and Sōka Gakkai

New movements in religion tend, in the nature of things, to be the product of lay initiative. They have often arisen as responses to what have been perceived as deficiencies in the clergy, and often as a challenge—expressed or implicit—to priestly dominance. In effect, that challenge has usually been a demand for opportunities of more open access to spiritual resources, accompanied by distrust of complicated liturgies and elaborate doctrines which the priests alone are permitted to claim fully to understand. The lay impulse has been to seek more immediate spiritual help with less of the manipulative apparatus in which priestly classes tend to invest. Consciously or unconsciously, the lay movement seeks a reorientation concerning the vital focus of spiritual endeavour (for example, by an emphasis on faith rather than on ritual performances). Priests seek to preserve orthodoxy and become custodians of sacred objects and places. They mark off their purported piety by distinctive means of training, by tonsure, dress, and ritual routines, all of which lead them to distance themselves from ordinary people and everyday affairs which not infrequently they see as mundane, and perhaps even as a source of pollution. In such circumstances, laymen are sometimes prompted to seek new means by which to acquire protection from the untoward and for new sources of reassurance about salvation (in whatever form salvation may, in their culture, be conceived). Such a growing divergence of orientation is likely to be exacerbated if a priesthood—purporting to offer indispensable service for laymen, and exercising a monopoly of such putative spiritual power—in itself becomes cynical, corrupt, and self-indulgent. A process of this kind leads a disenchanted laity either to have recourse to competing agents who claim to offer assistance towards salvation, or to take spiritual affairs into their own hands.

The process outlined in the abstract applies to various historical instances, conspicuously to the history of Protestantism. The Reformation, whilst not an initially lay movement, met, with its doctrine of the priesthood of all believers, the aspirations of the laity, whilst subsequent dissenting and schismatic movements sought more direct access to saving grace, and wider opportunities for lay spiritual experience. Such struggles between priests and laity are by no means confined to Christian history: they have occurred in various religious contexts.

It can scarcely occasion surprise that tension should have arisen between a newly spawned, vigorous, rapidly growing lay movement and an ancient religious sect, controlled by a priestly caste on to which the lay movement was engrafted. Many of the priests were such by hereditary succession and they monopolized certain functions and ministrations of importance for 'salvation'. Initially, each party appeared to have much to gain from the other. The *quid pro quo* lay in the legitimization of the spiritual practices of Sōka Gakkai members (and, incidentally, of other non-Gakkai lay believers) by providing members with copies of the *Gohonzon* and by the performance of funeral, memorial, and posthumous naming ceremonies (typically provided by priests of the various Buddhist sects in Japan), in return for which Sōka Gakkai provided funds and donated buildings to the hitherto decrepit temples of the Nichiren Shōshū priesthood. Such mutual interdependence did not, however, eliminate the inherent tensions arising between two contrasting modes of religious organization, each bearing the marks of the cultural influences of the social conditions prevailing at the time of its emergence. The priesthood was a conservative body, small, secluded, and with horizons narrowly circumscribed by the centuries of Japanese insulation from the external world. Sōka Gakkai was a movement of revitalization, adapted to modern conditions, pursuing from the outset a policy of expansive growth, and quickly acquiring an international clientele and orientation. The priesthood was characteristically authoritarian, status conscious, and hierarchic: the lay organization was populist, egalitarian, and unwilling to concede the sort of status differences which were endemic in conceptions of priesthood. The history of the schism—which can be only lightly adumbrated here—illustrates precisely these underlying dispositions.

Friction between the Nichiren Shōshū priesthood and the Sōka Gakkai occurred almost from the very beginnings of the lay movement. Differences arose when the wartime Japanese government required all Buddhist priests and lay believers to accept a Shinto amulet, which the Sōka Gakkai leaders Makiguchi and Toda refused, but which, to appease the authorities, the priests accepted (as well as establishing a Shinto shrine at Nichiren Shōshū headquarters at Taiseki-ji). This *trahison des clercs* rankled with some Gakkai members, who could uphold their own first two presidents as more ardent than the priests in protecting the true faith. In 1943, for disobeying the government's edict, Makiguchi and Toda were put into prison where, in 1944, Makiguchi died. In 1952 some Sōka Gakkai members humiliated a once-excommunicated but now reinstated Nichiren priest who had worked to manœuvre the priesthood into the acceptance of the Shinto amulets as required by the government's decree. Following that incident the priesthood threatened Toda with the loss of his post as senior lay representative in Nichiren Shōshū and deprivation of the right to visit the head temple. Even at this time, the issue for the priesthood was the extent of lay power and their felt need to preserve the superior status of priests.[1]

Events became more complex in another outburst of friction in 1977–9. This was a period when Sōka Gakkai followed what the priesthood called 'the line of 77'. The priesthood objected to ideas articulated by the SG President Ikeda in speeches made in November 1976 and January 1977, which were subsequently published as a book in 1977.[2] (Following protests from Nichiren Shōshū, the book was later withdrawn). In that work, Ikeda had quoted the *Gosho Zenshu* on the definition of the functions of priests and laymen which had led him to conclude that 'the Sōka Gakkai is an organization that carries out the function of both the priests and the lay believers'.[3] He went on to assert that inner heart and attitude, not the shaven head and the robe, determined who was to be regarded as the true priest. Everyone who had determined to help the common people to overcome their sufferings, 'regardless of whether they are members of the clergy or lay believers' and irrespective of outward form, 'has renounced the secular world in spirit'.[4] He quoted the *Daishōgon Hōmen Sutra* to the effect that not by putting on the clerical robe but by working to free sentient minds from impurities was how one achieved renunciation of the world.[5] He claimed, citing scriptures, that not only priests but any layman who was devoted to the law might receive alms. He went on to conclude, specifically for Sōka Gakkai, 'we are the true *shukke*, or clergy of today. Lay believers and clergy members are in fact absolutely equal in rank, as indicated by High Priest Nittatsu Hosoi of the Head Temple of Nichiren Shōshū in the following remark, "Regardless of whether their heads are shaven or not, all those who chant *Nam-myōhō-renge-kyō* before the *Dai-Gohonzon* in the High Sanctuary constitute a single religious community in which lay members are absolutely equal in rank with those of us who are members of the clergy".'[6] Ikeda went on to say that the community and training centres of Sōka Gakkai were the 'temples of the present',[7] adding in more conciliatory vein, 'We must not forget that the actual temples of Nichiren Shōshū play very important roles as centres where the solemn religious rites appropriate to ordination, funerals, and memorial services are carried out. But it is only when these centres of formal worship are combined with the Sōka Gakkai centres where the emphasis is on *kōsen-rufu*, that a truly progressive and vital religion, one that is open to all, can be made to flourish.'[8] He condemned the passive approach of conventional religions as too conservative and static, which was why Sōka Gakkai was 'creating a new type of organization'.[9]

---

[1] Nichiren Shōshū of America, Handout, 'Supplement to the Cover sheet of Information', Packet no. 1.
[2] Daisaku Ikeda, *A History of Buddhism* (Tokyo: 1977).   [3] Ibid. 13.
[4] Ibid.   [5] Ibid., 14–15.   [6] Ibid. 18.
[7] Ibid. 22.   [8] Ibid.   [9] Ibid. 22–3.

The 1990–1991 Schism 235

This then was the mood of the increasingly successful Gakkai movement, in which bold claims were made for a new dynamic approach to spirituality, challenging the staid and settled style of the clergy of Nichiren Shōshū, and setting forth a programme in which modernity was set over against antiquity, faith against ritual, and rational methods and procedures against traditional custom. It went too far and too fast for the clergy who, despite Ikeda's citation of High Priest Nittatsu's comments, could not but feel threatened by this bold claim to have created a new 'third order' of votaries who regarded their own status as equal to that of the religious professionals. Were they to go further and assume the functions of ritual performances, the priesthood might find themselves deprived of both special status and livelihood.

The Gakkai leaders subsequently wrote of this period,

The period after the Shō-Hondō's completion [the Great Main Temple built with Sōka Gakkai donations for Nichiren Shōshū at Taiseki-ji] was considered the second chapter of kosen-rufu. The Gakkai made a fresh start in introducing Nichiren Daishonin's Buddhism more widely and deeply, enabling it to permeate every aspect of Japanese society . . . We did this because we were confident that we could better protect Nichiren Shōshū from the problems of the outside world through our efforts to develop Sōka Gakkai and expand propagation by unfolding the second chapter of kōsen-rufu. The issue of the so-called '77 Agreement stems from the fact that the Nichiren Shōshū priesthood had increasing doubts about the Gakkai without correctly understanding the true intent of the Sōka Gakkai's designation of the second chapter of kōsen-rufu. The priesthood developed the erroneous idea that the Gakkai's efforts to develop community centres to apply the Daishonin's Buddhism more flexibly to society and to solidify the organization as a legal entity were efforts to strengthen the Gakkai's independence from Nichiren Shōshū. This caused friction between the conservatism of the priesthood and the progressivism of the Sōka Gakkai, which wanted to openly apply the Daishonin's Buddhism to society for the sake of kōsen-rufu.[10]

The priesthood saw these developments differently, declaring (subsequently) that the intention of the Gakkai had been to become master and make the priesthood into followers.[11] They believed that the book *The Human Revolution*, a hagiographic account of the early activities of Sōka Gakkai, and in particular of the struggles of the second president, Jōsei Toda, was being canvassed as 'the modern Gosho'; that a separate Sōka Gakkai Buddhism was being introduced; that various eulogistic terms were being applied to Daisaku Ikeda, and the idea promoted that Sōka Gakkai was directly descended from Nichiren and the *Gosho*. They objected to the

---

[10] *Issues between the Nichiren Shōshū Priesthood and the Sōka Gakkai*, v (n.p.: SGI Headquarters, 1992), 159–60.
[11] *Dai-Nichiren, The Circumstances Surrounding the Sōka Gakkai Problem* (Nichiren Shōshū Bureau of Religious Affairs, cyclostyled, [no place or date of publication given]), 2.

way Sōka Gakkai centres were being equated with temples, and even alleged that Gakkai leaders were conducting weddings and memorial services.[12] Some priests were vigorous in condemnation, and, after rumbling on, the dispute led to admonitions being issued by High Priest Nittatsu. Thereafter, in 1978, the Sōka Gakkai leaders acknowledged certain 'errors' which in conciliatory (and subsequently published) speeches they retracted. Thus, Hojo, the General Director of Sōka Gakkai, declared:

in the past few years we pursued the establishment of the Gakkai's individuality and foundation in society so much that we came to disregard the premise the Sōka Gakkai must live up to as a lay organization of Nichiren Shōshū. And thus, Nichiren Shōshū's traditional doctrines dimmed in the Sōka Gakkai . . . we delved into an aspect of laymen's religious role in view of the mission of religion in modern times. By this we intended to evaluate the unprecedented rise of a laymen's organization in contemporary times. Unfortunately, however, the result was that we only added momentum to slighting Nichiren Shōshū and its temples and priests . . . Now to summarize. . . . we have no choice but to frankly admit that we have been lacking in consideration towards Nichiren Shōshū's traditions, its interpretation of Nichiren Daishonin's teachings and its legitimate formalities.[13]

Hojo promised that Gakkai members would be encouraged to go to temples, and would cease to arrange cultural centre activities at times coinciding with temple activities. Vice-President Tsuji of Sōka Gakkai apologized because Sōka Gakkai had 'carelessly allowed' several wooden *Gohonzon*, which had been authorized by High Priest Nittatsu, to be transcribed without the proper accompanying documentation, and acknowledged that the strong respect that had developed for successive Sōka Gakkai presidents had led to members 'excessively expressing . . . admiration for the presidents'.[14] The Sōka Gakkai Study Department staff professors' conference agreed in mid-1978 to publish guidance on various matters on which they had been admonished by the High Priest (although they did not admit that these items had ever been authorized). Thus, they affirmed that, in future, they would view the use of expressions asserting a direct connection with Nichiren through the *Gohonzon*, or the fusing of oneself with the *Gohonzon*, as arrogance, since the connection was necessarily through the High Priest. They would henceforth avoid any suggestion that the enlightenment attained by President Toda was the equivalent of that of Nichiren, or that he was the founder of a form of Buddhism other than Nichiren's. Nor did Sōka Gakkai seek to assert that its president was the true Buddha or 'the eternal master'. There was no intention to create a

[12] Ibid. 24–5.
[13] Hiroshi Hojo (General Director of Sōka Gakkai), *World Tribune* [official organ of Nichiren Shōshū of American (NSA), American branch of Sōka Gakkai] (5 Feb. 1979). [14] Takehisa Tsuji (Vice-President of Sōka Gakkai), ibid.

Buddhism separate from that of the priesthood. They retracted the earlier assertion that there were precedents for lay members receiving offerings.[15]

Responding to these retractions, in the spring of 1979 High Priest Nittatsu also made some conciliatory statements, acknowledging that friction had led to disturbances. He was glad that Sōka Gakkai had made new determinations to change tack. He added, 'still young . . . many of Nichiren Shōshū priests may lack important capability in leadership. So you, as believers, have felt discontented from time to time. But . . . both priests and temples can develop themselves soundly only when they receive their believers' support, understanding, and consideration'. He chastized laymen for slandering temples, conceded that 'in thirty years Sōka Gakkai has made astounding progress, bringing about the unprecedented rise of Nichiren Shōshū. This is a historical fact. The glorious accomplishments of the Sōka Gakkai will definitely shine in the history of Buddhism. But please remember that there were always the unanimous support and cooperation by the priesthood behind the spectacular advancement of the Sōka Gakkai. True, the structure of Nichiren Shōshū was not at that point perfectly advanced enough to keep up with the developing rhythm of the Sōka Gakkai.'[16] Clearly, the High Priest saw the structural sources of tension between a large, dynamic movement operating in mass society, and the semi-cloistered priesthood operating according to ancient procedures and an entirely different rhythm.

Despite these emollient gestures and retractions by Sōka Gakkai, there remained the endemic competition for control of ideology, control of believers, and control of offerings. The friction persisted, eventually causing Daisaku Ikeda to resign as its president and as *sokoto*—leading representative of lay believers—in April 1979. The High Priest Nittatsu died in July of the same year, but his attempts to conciliate the more extremely anti-Gakkai priests failed, and in August 1980 some 201 of them defied orders and demonstrated against Sōka Gakkai, calling for Ikeda to be ousted from his new position as president of Sōka Gakkai International.[17] They even challenged the legitimacy of Nittatsu's successor Nikken, and for this these so-called *Shoshinkai* priests were defrocked and excommunicated. Japanese newspapers fanned the flames of the dispute, reporting the criticisms of dissident Sōka Gakkai officials, who averred that Ikeda behaved as if he were a reincarnation of Nichiren, repeating the charge that Sōka Gakkai had ordered the carving of wooden copies of the *Gohonzon*, and suggesting that members of Sōka Gakkai had even little awareness that they were followers of the Nichiren Shōshū sect[18] (this last assertion despite the fact that, for

[15] 'Basic Questions of Study', 10th Staff Professors' Conference of the Study Department [of Sōka Gakkai], ibid.   [16] High Priest Nittatsu, ibid.
[17] *International Herald Tribune* (18 Nov. 1980).
[18] *Asahi Evening News* (4 Dec. 1980).

the *Gojukai* ceremony and to receive the *Gohonzon*, members had had to go to their local temples and register as lay believers).

That tensions did not cease is evident from retrospective mutual criticisms made once matters had come to a further head in 1990, but in the intervening years, for many Sōka Gakkai members, relationships appeared to have been resolved: certainly this was the impression of rank-and-file members in Britain. In November 1990 (just at the time when the survey for this research was in final preparation), the biennial *Gojukai* ceremonies were held in London, and were given headline treatment in the *NSUK Bulletin*. They were described by the British General Director as 'profound and immensely important for your life' and he thanked the High Priest for permission to arrange them.[19] It was currently affirmed that 'all members of NSUK must receive it [the *Gohonzon*]'.[20] Yet there were contemporaneous voices indicating the boundaries of the priestly role in Nichiren Shōshū—a faith through which the individual could directly bring out his buddhahood from the first day of practice: 'This directness is in contrast to some other religions where the clergy occupies an intermediary position between the adherents . . . and their object of worship.' The role of the priesthood was to maintain the purity of the teaching of the *Gosho* and to conduct *Gojukai* and other ceremonies. It was 'because of their support and devotion over centuries that the Sōka Gakkai could be founded sixty years ago'[21]—an echo of a point made in the accord with the High Priest in 1979.

The new outbreak of mutual recrimination between the priesthood and the leadership of Soka Gakkai in December 1990 cannot here be followed in detail. It began when the General Administrator of the Nichiren Shōshū head temple accused Ikeda of making heretical remarks in a speech to the 35th Headquarters Leaders' meeting on 16 November 1990, of which the leading priests claimed to have a tape recording.[22] To these initial charges were added retrospective allegations of critical disrespect (identified in the movement as 'slander'), bad temper, and heated arguments expressed in earlier recent meetings between the leaders of the two organizations. Nichiren Shōshū later admitted errors in the transcription of the tape, and some of the charges which Nichiren Shōshū initially brought it subsequently withdrew,[23] but by then the die was cast and steps had been taken that implied an irrevocable breach between the priesthood and the movement which embraced the vast majority of lay believers.

The principal charges levelled against Ikeda and Sōka Gakkai were of rather diverse kind, some trivial and some inherently improbable, but all of them testifying to the priesthood's deep-seated distrust of the Sōka Gakkai leadership, and eventually leading also to the expression of the laity's

[19] *NSUK Bulletin*, 60 (9 Nov. 1990), 1.   [20] *UK Express*, 232 (Oct. 1990), 12.
[21] *UK Express*, 234 (Dec. 1990), 35.   [22] *Dai-Nichiren, Circumstances*, 11–15.
[23] Ibid. 22.

discontent with the performance of the priests. The first explicit charges relating to Ikeda's speech were that Ikeda had been critical of the High Priest. It was alleged that he had denied the validity of the doctrine of the four dicta (the principle of refuting the teachings of other Buddhist sects) by comparing Nichiren with Shinran (founder of the Jōdo Shin Shū sect). In having exhorted his followers to sing Beethoven's 'Ode to Joy', with its allusions to God, he had acted in a way tantamount to praising non-Buddhist teachings. It was said that he had relegated *shakubuku* as the appropriate form of proselytizing in favour of the gradualist method of *shōju*.[24]

The charges relating to the four dicta and the question of *shakubuku* were retracted, but not before the Nichiren Shōshū Council had acted swiftly to revise the rules governing lay representation in its deliberations, which had the immediate effect of removing Ikeda from his position of *sokoto*—head of all lay organizations attached to the sect—and other Sōka Gakkai leaders ceased to be *daikoto* (lay representatives on the council).[25] New charges were also advanced, one a criticism by the head of the Study Department of Nichiren Shōshū of the publication in one of Sōka Gakkai's scholarly periodicals of a photograph of the robes of the English Order of the Garter (which were on show at an exhibition of *Robes of the Realm* at one of Sōka Gakkai's art museums), because he thought that the cross emblazoned on the robe was an emblem of Christianity.[26]

The specific original charges were quickly overtaken by escalating recriminations and the imposition of sanctions. In the early spring of 1991 Nichiren Shōshū withdrew its recognition of President Ikeda as the sole person charged with the guidance of overseas members and revoked its existing policy of not recognizing any organization of overseas followers other than SGI.[27] The head temple dispatched missionary priests abroad to establish the so-called *Danto* (believer) movement, and some British and other European members defected (including the leader of Sōka Gakkai in Spain).[28] Announcements from Nichiren Shōshū appeared in the Japanese press on 5 June 1991 indicating that henceforth SGI would no longer be permitted to organize pilgrimages to Taiseki-ji: those wishing to visit would be able to do so only by registering with a local temple as *Danto* members. The effect was quickly felt, however, and the temple itself was held to be expecting only 5,000 in the eighteen-day pilgrimage season in July, as against more than 100,000 who would otherwise have been expected.[29] (In

---

[24] *Issues*, i. 11.   [25] Ibid. i. 12, and *Dai-Nichiren, Circumstances*, 3–5
[26] *Sōka Gakkai Reply Dated January 1st, 1991 to Questions Raised by the Head Temple Regarding the Content of the Speech Made by Sōka Gakkai International President Ikeda at the 35th Headquarters Leaders' Meeting on 10th November, 1991* [sic], cyclostyled circular 'd' (1991), 12.
[27] *NSUK Bulletin*, 68 (22 Mar. 1991), 2; *Issues*, iii, p. xxv.
[28] Private communication, 12 Apr. 1991.
[29] *Far Eastern Economic Review* (11 July 1991), 17.

November it was reported that the conflict had caused the collapse of profits of a local transport company, and in February 1992 reports said that the number of visitors (to Taiseki-ji) had fallen so dramatically that bus services to and from the train station in Fujinomya had gone out of business.[30])

In July 1991 Sōka Gakkai was reported as having in May 'announced that it would conduct its own funeral services for members'[31] and in November it was further reported that Sōka Gakkai had 'started to break Nichiren rules by holding weddings and funerals without Nichiren monks in attendance'.[32] In that same month the head temple decided to advise Sōka Gakkai to dissolve itself,[33] and there was speculation that it might take steps to excommunicate Ikeda, whilst reports a few days later indicated that the Gakkai would 'campaign to oust the chief priest of the Nichiren Shōshū sect'.[34] At the end of November, a notice of Sōka Gakkai's excommunication from Nichiren Shōshū was authorized by the priesthood, on the grounds that the movement had gone against Nichiren Shōshū teachings.[35]

Older issues were raised again, particularly the charge that Ikeda was guilty of something approaching *lèse-majesté* in declaring the *Shō-Hondō* (the cost of which Sōka Gakkai had borne) to be the *Kaidan* prophesied for the days of *mappō*. The response of Sōka Gakkai was to quote in justification a pronouncement made at an earlier date by High Priest Nittatsu to precisely the same effect.[36] A new turn of events occurred when certain dissident priests joined the chorus of criticism of the head temple, the High Priest, and the regime that functioned there. High Priest Nikken was accused of having erected an elaborate tombstone at a family burial site administered by a temple of a rival Zen sect, and having made offerings there. He was also alleged to be planning the building of an expensive house for himself. Priests were accused of devoting their time to golf and to night-clubs.[37] Later additions to the list of charges emanating from dissident priests included the charge that Nichiren Shōshū discriminated among priests by family lineage, in assigning those who enjoyed prestigious family links to temples with favourable circumstances, while those without found themselves in remote areas.[38] Others alleged that Nichiren Shōshū had 'intentionally caused the current dispute'.[39] A Belgian, Claude Wouters, who had trained and been ordained a priest at the head temple, wrote of 'hurried

[30] *Nikkei Weekly* (30 Nov. 1991); *International Herald Tribune* (11 Feb. 1992).
[31] *Far Eastern Economic Review* (11 July 1991), 17.
[32] *Financial Times* (12 Nov. 1991).
[33] *Nihon Keizai Shimbun* [Japanese Economic Journal] (7 Nov. 1991).
[34] *Japan Times* (10 Nov. 1991).   [35] *NSUK Bulletin*, 84 (6 Dec. 1991), 1.
[36] *For Information of NSUK Members*, cyclostyled (Taplow, 18 Nov. 1991).
[37] Ibid.   [38] *NSUK Bulletin*, 90 (6 Mar. 1992).
[39] *NSUK Bulletin*, 91 (27 Mar. 1992), 4.

gongyōs' sometimes conducted by intoxicated priests, spiritual laxity, priestly cynicism, and outbursts of temper by High Priest Nikken.[40]

Throughout the year a trickle of priests defected from Nichiren Shōshū, at first mainly those who belonged to Sōka Gakkai families; but later defections were of priests unconnected with Sōka Gakkai, some of them distinguished, including the son of former High Priest Nittatsu. In addition, other priests who remained in the sect formed an association for the protection of the law, a body by implication opposed to Nikken. In October 1992 their number was reported to approach 500 (of a total understood to be about 1,300).[41] With priests, some temples also disaffiliated, and by February 1993 twenty-five temples were reported to have done so.[42] Meanwhile, a further discreditable episode unfolded. A Sōka Gakkai member in Seattle reported that, years before, whilst conducting for new members the first *Gojukai* ceremonies ever held overseas, Nikken had become involved with the police about his refusal to pay for the services of a prostitute. Nikken had declared the member disclosing this information to be a liar, and the member had then started a libel action against him, which was now pending.[43]

In a petition demanding that Nikken resign, his critics quoted, as an illustration of hypocrisy, the eulogy of Ikeda which Nikken had included in his New Year message for 1991, since this message was uttered at the very time when, it was alleged, senior priests, including Nikken, were plotting to overthrow Ikeda. Nikken was himself now accused of heretical teachings, and of seeking to declare himself as infallible and essential, whilst allowing priests to state in formal lectures that earlier High Priests, and even the teachings of Nichiren himself, were to be regarded as merely 'provisional'.[44] The petition, which had the support of some fourteen million Japanese and over two million people overseas, recalled that Sōka Gakkai had contributed to Nichiren Shōshū not only for the *Shō-Hondō*, but two other significant lecture and reception halls at Taiseki-ji and facilities for the temple grounds, as well as some 350 local temples. At this time, too, Sōka Gakkai members were reminded, or informed for the first time, that in March 1990, without prior discussion, the priesthood had sought to raise the pilgrimage fee for Taiseki-ji. They had also doubled the fee for memorial tablets (*tōba*). In response, it was now revealed that as early as July 1990 the Sōka Gakkai leaders had requested that the priesthood refrain from living extravagantly.[45]

[40] *NSUK Bulletin*, 106 (11 Dec. 1992), 6.
[41] *NSUK Bulletin*, 102 (9 Oct. 1992), 1–2; 104 (6 Nov. 1991), 1.
[42] *SGI-UK Bulletin* [successor to *NSUK Bulletin*], 108 (12 Feb. 1993), 6.
[43] *NSUK Bulletin*, 104 (6 Nov. 1992), 3.
[44] *For Information of NSUK Members*, 2.
[45] *NSUK Bulletin*, 83 (22 Nov. 1991), 4.

The question of *tōba* now became an important issue for the Japanese membership. The president of Sōka Gakkai, Einosuke Akiya, said that hitherto 'we lay believers chose to be reticent regarding problems involving the priesthood'. Drawing parallels with Martin Luther, Akiya mentioned indulgences, and said, 'Following the same pattern, the Nichiren Shōshū priesthood has been saying that if one purchases a sufficient number of *tōba* . . . the sins of the deceased will be expunged. Thus, throughout Japan, they indiscriminately go around telling people that they must erect *tōba* . . . for each family member that passed away, people are urged to purchase as many as eight *tōba*. After you erect a tablet, the priest will tell you that it appears that all the sins of the deceased have been expiated, but this is nothing but a tool for making money'.[46]

In their reappraisal of events, the Sōka Gakkai leaders concluded that the temple authorities had, from July 1990, contrived a policy, designated as 'Operation C', to bring about the downfall of Ikeda, and to assert their direct authority over the laity.[47] The core issue was the relative status of priests and lay people. Sōka Gakkai declared them to be of equal significance—a claim which Nichiren Shōshū priests regarded as arrogant and destructive of the unity of believers, and of the three treasures of Buddhism. Sōka Gakkai, however, contended that the priesthood was determined to 'establish itself as a necessary intermediary between the *Gohonzon* and lay believers' and to this end they promoted 'services designed to make the offices of priests indispensable to believers',[48] hence their concern with *tōba* and other observances, on which much of their income depended. They noted, too, that the attribution of cause for the schism had shifted from the objections made against Ikeda's speech of 16 Nov. 1990 to the affirmation that he had made in 1968 concerning the identification of the *Shō-Hondō* as

---

[46] *NSUK Bulletin*, 104 (6 Nov. 1992), 4. *Tōba* were only one of the sources of priests' income. Another was the conferment of posthumous names. According to one authority, the most famous urban temples charged several million yen for giving a posthumous name: the practice—a unique Japanese custom—was related to ancestor worship and had no basis in Buddhist literature, but developed in the Edo period, when a system of certificates of conversion to Buddhism was developed. The priesthood contended that the giving of posthumous names had been a custom in Nichiren Shōshū since the time of Nichiren, who had given such names to his own father and mother. Hiromi Shimada, in *Weekly Economist* [in Japanese] (31 Dec. 1991 and 7 Jan. 1992). Opposition to this lucrative priestly monopoly had occurred in the wider context of Nichiren-derived Buddhism before the founding of Sōka Gakkai. Nishida Toshizo (1850–1918?), whose thought had influenced other lay movements in the Nichiren tradition, held that posthumous names should not be denied for lack of money and 'that it was immoral for priests to encourage mistaken ideas about the matter'. Helen Hardacre, *Lay Buddhism in Contemporary Japan: Reiyukai Kyodan* (Princeton, NJ: Princeton University Press, 1984), 14. Nishida, although a layman, also took it upon himself to inscribe posthumous names for the dead who lacked descendants to worship them. Hardacre, *Lay Buddhism*, 15.

[47] *Issues*, iii, pp. xv-xviii.   [48] Ibid. iii, p. xxxiii.

the High Sanctuary of True Buddhism. This issue Sōka Gakkai now regarded as totally spurious, since they could establish that Ikeda was only echoing a similar identification that had been made by High Priest Nittatsu, and, indeed, one that had also been affirmed at earlier times by Nikken (statements which he, Nikken, had since decided to reconsider).[49]

Akiya now regarded the Gakkai's conciliatory policy following the disruption of 1977 and President Ikeda's resignation as induced purely to avoid a split from the priesthood: 'The Gakkai chose to apologize and alter its way of explaining . . . Buddhism only to protect the great movement of kōsen-rufu.'[50] Now the Gakkai leaders retracted some of their earlier apologies and concessions. In particular, they affirmed that there had been nothing wrong in transcribing eight paper *Gohonzons* into wooden ones, claiming this to have been done with the approval of High Priest Nittatsu, who had held that such transcriptions were 'a common practice'.[51] Various retractions were made from the document *Basic Issues of Study* published in 1978, which was now seen as having been produced only because of priesthood intimidation and the Gakkai's strong desire to maintain unity.[52]

Whatever the rights and wrongs of the complex and tortuous process of charge and counter-charge which has marked this schism, the underlying issues remain apparent. Sōka Gakkai is a mass movement, outgoing, lay in spirit, and dedicated to making Nichiren's teachings effective and practical in the everyday modern world. The Nichiren priesthood is essentially locked into an ancient ritualistic and quasi-monastic system, concerned to preserve its authority and jealous of its monopoly of certain sacred teachings, places, and objects. It has inherited many attributes of traditional Japanese Buddhism, including the incorporation of aspects of ancestor reverence, giving rise to the emphasis on funeral and memorial objects and ceremonies, and readily incorporating these phenomena into its putative indispensable services for laymen. The priesthood has distrusted the very modernity of Sōka Gakkai, has looked somewhat askance at the cultural mass events which that movement has promoted, and the social and political concerns it has espoused. For its part, the Gakkai has—until lately—stifled whatever criticism its leaders may have felt for the excessive expense of the traditional Japanese practices encouraged by the priests for funerals and in honour of the spirits of the ancestral dead. The distrust and criticism of the conduct and comportment of priests, occasionally if discreetly expressed in leadership meetings in time past, have now become open charges, and some of the bedrock assumptions of Japanese religion have been exposed in what at times has come close to echoing a Marxist critique of the clergy. Certainly, the thrust of the challenge has been to bring Sōka Gakkai more directly into

---

[49] Ibid. iii. 123–69; iv. 3. [50] Ibid. v. 162. [51] Ibid. v. 168.
[52] Ibid. v. 175.

tune with a more secular society, somewhat de-ritualizing and th
revitalizing the religious tradition to which it is attached.

For British members of Sōka Gakkai International, who took :
initiate the necessary legal procedure to change its old name of N
SGI-UK in 1992, the priesthood was never a vital or conspicuou
their experience of Buddhism. The full paraphernalia of fur
memorial services have not been exported from Japan, and the :
Nichiren Buddhism in Britain, and elsewhere in the West in count.
the priesthood is not established, has been freed of such cultura
concerns. If the sacramentalist and sacerdotal claims of the priesthoo
challenged in Japan by Sōka Gakkai's insistence on the equality of pn
hood and laity, such claims scarcely received expression—the occasion of
Gojukai apart—in Britain. The British members were kept informed of the
dispute by their in-house bulletins, and explanation was offered for what
was, for some, a disturbing experience. The British leadership explained
that the issues were not new, but went back 'for some hundreds of years',
and were endemic in Japanese religion, 'not only a problem within Nichiren
Shōshū but rooted in the history of Buddhism in Japan'.[53] Nichiren
Buddhism in the West was already adjusted to a more secularized mode of
operation, as the British leader commented: 'Here in the UK, we see very
little of the priests . . . we have little understanding of the functions and
methods of operation of local temples . . . We do not encounter, as our
Japanese friends do continuously, their incessant demands for contributions, or the aloofness and sometimes arrogance of their attitudes towards
their "followers".'[54]

The one outstanding service of priests for lay people in the UK was the
performance of *Gojukai*. That had not always been an indispensable ritual
as a prerequisite for membership of the movement, but it had become an
occasion for legitimizing that affiliation, even though, by the standards of
ritualistic religions, the performance was brief and unadorned by elaborate
ceremonial procedures, vestments, or essential paraphernalia. Since the rift,
membership in SGI has been authenticated by the issue of a certificate—a
conspicuous shift from sacred performance to rational procedure, and in
itself a token of a measure of secularization.

The ceremony could be superseded: there remains only the difficult
question of the *Gohonzon*. The replicas which new members had formerly
received had been issued under the authority of the High Priest, inscribed
by his sacralizing hand, from which copies were printed by a wood-block
process. Only he was empowered to make such copies. With the schism, no
further copies of an authenticated *Gohonzon* would be available to those
who, as members of SGI, had severed their relations with the Nichiren
Shōshū priesthood. Yet the *Gohonzon* was at the heart of the practice, it was

[53] *NSUK Bulletin*, 68 (22 Mar. 1991), 1–3.   [54] Ibid. 2.

the agency by which the individual realized his own buddahood, the mirror in which, through chanting, he could review his life and become acquainted with his own mind. Whilst chanting alone, anywhere, was always recognized as in itself efficacious, the *Gohonzon* had always been a vital element of complete religious performance. It will, of course, still be available to older members, and new ones will become acquainted with it at meetings and at the movement's centres. It has served to legitimize the practice, and it is difficult to see that it could in any sense be superseded or lose its central place in Sōka Gakkai devotions. Yet, it is perhaps to be expected that there will be a reassertion of the importance of faith and attitude of mind. British members have been reminded that in Nichiren's day 'many believers did not have the *Gohonzon* at home', and whilst it is recognized that, 'Of course, it would be better if members could continue receiving the *Gohonzon*' it is also contended that 'Ultimately, unless you have faith, even having the *Gohonzon* at home would be meaningless. Most important is one's faith itself. Our faith will remain steadfast even if we are denied the *Gohonzon*.' The importance which Sōka Gakkai continued to attach to its faith in Nichiren's Buddhism and to the *Gohonzon* was manifested in December 1991, when 16,249,638 members from all over the world submitted petitions to High Priest Nikken demanding his immediate resignation.

APPENDIX B

Questionnaire

The information which you provide on this questionnaire is confidential and remains anonymous: please do not write your name on the sheet. In answering, please circle the appropriate number if categories are provided.

1. At what date did you first encounter Nichiren Shōshū?

2. At what date did you first start chanting?

3. Are you now a member?

   If Yes—when did you actually receive Gojukai?

4. How did you first encounter Nichiren Shōshū?

   Through: 1. My (future) spouse
   2. A member of my family
   3. A work colleague
   4. A friend
   5. A casual acquaintance
   6. At an exhibition or concert
   7. By literature or publicity
   8. Some other means (please specify)

5. If you first encountered Nichiren Shōshū through an individual, was that individual Japanese?

6. Before joining Nichiren Shōshū did you regard yourself as belonging to any religious movement or organization?

   If yes—which?

7. Even if you did not belong to any other faith before joining Nichiren Shōshū, would you say that you were then a religious person?

   If yes—how would you describe your religious inclinations?

8. Before becoming acquainted with Nichiren Shōshū had you encountered

   a) Any other form of Buddhism? If Yes—which?
   b) Any other form of Eastern religion? If Yes—which?

9. Before becoming acquainted with Nichiren Shōshū had you any particular interest in Japan or things Japanese?

   If Yes—please indicate the form(s) which that interest took by circling the appropriate category(ies)

   1. Language
   2. Literature
   3. Graphic Arts
   4. Films
   5. Martial Arts
   6. Cuisine
   7. Other (please specify)

10. Are any of your close relatives members of Nichiren Shōshū?

    If Yes—please circle the relevant category(ies)

    1. Wife/Husband (Girl/Boy Friend)
    2. Father
    3. Mother
    4. Brother(s)/Sister(s)
    5. Father-in-law
    6. Mother-in-law
    7. Brother(s)/Sister(s)-in Law
    8. Other relatives

11. If you have children over 18 years of age, are any of them members of Nichiren Shōshū?

    If Yes—please indicate how many out of how many.

12. Do you find it possible to undertake special service for the movement?

    If Yes—in what capacity?

13. Do you hold any position of responsibility in the movement?

    If Yes—what position do you hold?

14. Apart from the teachings, can you say what originally attracted you to Nichiren Shōshū?

15. Is the original attraction still the most significant aspect of Nichiren Shōshū for you?

    If No—what is NOW the most attractive feature of the movement?

16. What proportion of your close friends are members of Nichiren Shōshū?

    Please indicate the number; out of how many close friends?

17. Do you find it possible to practise every morning and evening without fail?

    If No, can you estimate how many times a week you normally practise?

    1. At least *ten* times a week
    2. At least *seven* times a week
    3. At least *four* times a week
    4. *One, two or three* times a week
    5. *Less often* than once a week

18. What would you say have been the principal benefits to you from practising?

19. Have you ever chanted to realize particular goal(s)?

    If Yes—please give some examples?

20. Were the goals for which you chanted realized?

    If Yes—in what way?

21. Have you experienced any difficulties or negative reactions from relatives and friends because you belong to Nichiren Shōshū?

    If Yes—by whom? and in what circumstances?

22. Have you ever visited Taisekiji?

    If Yes—when was that?

23. Have you ever attended a course at Trets, the European Centre?

    If Yes—when was that?

24. Please indicate your main recreational activities by circling the appropriate categories (*multiple responses are possible*):

    (*a*) in which you are an *active participant*

        1. Graphic Arts
        2. Music
        3. Dancing
        4. Acting
        5. Creative Writing
        6. Sports
        7. Walking
        8. Social Gatherings
        9. Indoor Games
        10. Photography
        11. Video making
        12. Other (please specify)
        13. None

(b) in which you are an *interested observer*

    1. Exhibitions
    2. Music
    3. Theatre
    4. Cinema
    5. TV
    6. Videos
    7. Novels
    8. Spectator Sports
    9. Other (please specify)
    10. None

25. Do you belong to any voluntary associations?

    If Yes—please indicate by circling the most appropriate category(ies)

        1. Political
        2. Cultural
        3. Social
        4. Voluntary Service
        5. Other (please specify)

    It would be helpful if you could list the actual organizations

26–31. Please say for each of the following, how important it is in your life by circling the appropriate number in each row:

	Very Important	Quite Important	Not very Important	Not at all Important
A) Work	1	2	3	4
B) Family	1	2	3	4
C) Friends & acquaintances	1	2	3	4
D) Leisure Time	1	2	3	4
E) Politics	1	2	3	4
F) Religion	1	2	3	4

32–41. Do you think it proper for religious bodies to speak out on:

    A) Disarmament
    B) Abortion
    C) Third World Problems
    D) Extramarital Affairs
    E) Unemployment
    F) Racial Discrimination
    G) Euthanasia
    H) Homosexuality
    I) Ecology and Environment
    J) Government Policy

42. If someone said that individuals should have the chance to enjoy complete sexual freedom without being restricted, would you tend to agree or disagree?

    1. Tend to agree
    2. Tend to disagree
    3. Neither/It depends

43–44. Why are there people in this country who live in need? Here are some possible reasons. Which one reason do you consider to be most important? (*Circle one number under A below*): and which reason do you consider to be the second most important? (*Circle one number under B below*):

	(A) most important	(B) second most important
Because they are unlucky	1	1
Because of laziness and lack of willpower	2	2
Because of injustice in society	3	3
It's an inevitable part of modern progress	4	4
Other (please specify)	A	B

45. Here are two statements which people sometimes make when discussing good and evil. Which one comes closest to your own point of view?

    A) There are absolutely clear guidelines about what is good and evil. These always apply to everyone, whatever the circumstances.
    B) There can never be absolutely clear guidelines about what is good and evil. What is good and evil depends entirely upon the circumstances at the time

        1. Agree with Statement A
        2. Agree with Statement B
        3. Disagree with both

46. Overall, how satisfied or dissatisfied are you with your home life? Circle your degree of (dis)satisfaction on the scale (*1 being most dissatisfied and 10 most satisfied*):

1	2	3	4	5	6	7	8	9	10
Dissatisfied									Satisfied

47. In political matters, people talk of 'the left' and 'the right'. Generally speaking, how would you place your views on this scale (*1 being most to the left, and 10 most to the right*)?

1	2	3	4	5	6	7	8	9	10
Left									Right

48–53. What should be the aims of this country for the next ten years? Below are listed some goals to which some people give priority. Would you please say which one of these you yourself consider the most important? (*Circle one answer only under A below*): And which would be next most important? (*Circle one answer only under B below*):

	A first choice	B second choice
Maintaining a high level of economic growth	1	1
Making sure the country has strong defence forces	2	2
Seeing that people have more say about how things are done at their jobs and in their communities	3	3
Trying to make our cities and countryside more beautiful	4	4

If you had to choose, which of the things on the list below would you say is most important? (*Circle one answer only under A below*): What would be the next more important? (*Circle one answer only under B below*)

	A first choice	B second choice
Maintaining order in the nation	1	1
Giving people more say in important government decisions	2	2
Fighting rising prices	3	3
Protecting freedom of speech	4	4

Here is another list. In your opinion which one of these is most important (*Circle one answer only under A below*): And what would be the next most important? (*Circle one answer only under B below*):

	A first choice	B second choice
A stable economy	1	1
Progress towards a less impersonal and more humane society	2	2
Progress towards a society in which ideas count more than money	3	3
The fight against crime	4	4

54–60. Here is a list of various changes in our way of life that might take place in the near future. Please say for each one, if it were to happen, whether you think it would be a good thing, a bad thing, or do you not mind?

	Good	Bad	Don't mind
A) Less emphasis on money and material possessions	1	2	3
B) Decrease in the importance of work in our lives	1	2	3
C) More emphasis on the development of technology	1	2	3
D) Greater emphasis on the development of the individual	1	2	3
E) Greater respect for authority	1	2	3
F) More emphasis on family life	1	2	3
G) A simple and more natural life-style	1	2	3

61–73. Please look at this list and tell us, *for each item listed*, how much confidence you have in them: is it a great deal; quite a lot; not very much; or none at all? (*Please circle the appropriate answer for each item*)

	A great deal	Quite a lot	Not very much	None at all
A) The Churches	1	2	3	4
B) The Armed Forces	1	2	3	4
C) The Educational System	1	2	3	4
D) The Legal System	1	2	3	4
E) The Press	1	2	3	4
F) Trades Unions	1	2	3	4
G) The Police	1	2	3	4
H) Parliament	1	2	3	4
I) Civil Service	1	2	3	4
J) Major Companies	1	2	3	4
K) The Social Security System	1	2	3	4
L) The European Community	1	2	3	4
M) Nato	1	2	3	4

74–76. We now ask some questions about your outlook on life. Each item has two contrasting statements on it. Using the scale listed, where would you place your own view? 1 means you agree completely with the statement on the left; 10 means that you agree completely with the statement on the right, or you can choose any number in between

1	2	3	4	5	6	7	8	9	10

A) One should be cautious about making major changes in life   You will never achieve much unless you act boldly

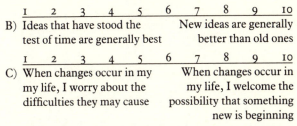

B) Ideas that have stood the test of time are generally best — New ideas are generally better than old ones

C) When changes occur in my my life, I worry about the difficulties they may cause — When changes occur in my life, I welcome the possibility that something new is beginning

We should now like to ask you some questions about yourself. We emphasize again that the information is confidential and that you remain anonymous.

77. Please indicate your sex.

78. Please give the year of your birth.

79. In which country were you born?

80. Are you: 1. Married
              2. Living as married
              3. Divorced
              4. Separated
              5. Widowed
              6. Single
              7. Other (Please specify)

81. What is your occupation or profession?

82. Please specify your actual job.

83. Are you: 1. Employed
              2. Self-employed
              3. Housewife not otherwise employed
              4. Retired/pensioned
              5. In full-time education
              6. Unemployed

84. At what age did you complete full-time education?

85. Please list any diplomas, degrees, or professional qualifications that you possess (*please write these out in full rather than using abbreviations*)

Thank you for your co-operation

APPENDIX C

The Interview Schedule

Interviews were loosely structured occasions when respondents were encouraged to talk freely about their experience of Nichiren Buddhism. The following schedule was used to prompt discussion of particular aspects of experience if these were not spontaneously forthcoming.

Tell us about how and when you joined NSUK.

Was that the time at which you first started chanting?

What were your circumstances at that time [your job; whether you were living at home; whether you were actively seeking some solutions for particular problems]?

What had been your previous religious experience?

Had you belonged to other organizations, tried other churches, new movements, or quasi-religious movements?

Were you still practising your former religion when you met NSUK?

How were you first brought into touch with NSUK? (Friends, partner, etc.?)

If you were not religious before, how is it that you became religious?

Was NSUK something entirely un-looked for, or were you very much open to spiritual experiences?

What was it about NSUK that attracted you?

If previously religious, were you consciously dissatisfied with your previous religion? If so, in what way?

What have been the benefits of belonging to NSUK?

Were there any difficulties for you in joining and accepting Nichiren Buddhism? [intrinsic—elements of doctrine, practice, membership, etc.; or extrinsic—opposition from kinsfolk, relatives, etc.]

Have you ever had any doubts about Nichiren teachings?

What would you say most convinced you of the truth of Nichiren Buddhism?

Some people who join NSUK subsequently leave: why do you think that is?

How often do you find that you chant?

    Were there periods when you chanted less? If so, why was that?

Do you usually chant alone or mainly with others (family or friends)?

What do you chant for—for someone, or yourself, or more generally?

Do you find it possible to undertake any service for NSUK?

    Why do you do this, or if not, why not? What kind of service?

Do you undertake *shakubuku* of others?

How has being a Nichiren Buddhist affected your way of life?

Have you retained former friends since you joined NSUK?

Have you acquired new friends?

What would you say was the essence of your religion—beliefs, ritual, ethics, the organization itself?

What do you see as the essential differences between Christianity and Nichiren Buddhism?

Have you encountered any of the many religious and therapeutic movements that are active in Britain today?

What does Kōsen Rufu mean to you?

Have you been living very long in your present place? Are you settled there?

Are you trained for any particular profession or occupation?

What is your actual job?

Are you married/single/living as married/etc.?

At what age did you complete full-time education?

What is the highest qualification that you have acquired?

What do you like to do in your free time?

Do you watch TV or videos? If so what sort of things appeal to you?

How do you spend your vacations? [Abroad? Alone?]

Do you read a particular newspaper? Which? Or periodicals?

What is your taste in music and the arts?

What do you regard as the most important things in life?

Is there anything that you would like to achieve in particular?

Can you give me an approximate idea of your age?

GLOSSARY

bonnō soku bodai desires of ordinary life are at the same time enlightenment

butsudan Buddhist altar

Dai honorific sometimes prefixed to *Gohonzon*

daikoto lay representatives on the Nichiren Shoshu council

daimoku an invocation—in this case of the *Lotus Sutra*

Daishonin honorific title attached to the name of Nichiren

Danto literally 'believer', the name for believers in Nichiren Shoshu attached directly to the temples

eshō funi the oneness of life and its environment

Gohonzon the sacred scroll inscribed by Nichiren, and the object of worship

Gojukai ceremony at which new members receive the *Gohonzon*

gongyō recital of two chapters of the *Lotus Sutra*, a ritual undertaken morning and evening

Gosho the collected writings of Nichiren

Kaidan the sanctuary in which the *Gohonzon* is housed at Taiseki-ji

kanjin no honzon an object of worship for observing one's mind or life

keibi special service

Kōmeitō Clean Government Party

kōsen-rufu world-wide proclamation of Nichiren's Buddhism

mappō the Latter Day of the Law (namely, the present age)

Nam-myōhō-renge-kyō the invocation of the *Lotus Sutra*

ninpō ikka the oneness of the person and the law

pāramitās six ways of salvation—by alms; obedience; forbearance; assiduity; meditation; attainment of wisdom

sanshō shima obstacles that obstruct the path to enlightenment

Sensei literally 'Teacher'—the title accorded to Mr Ikeda

shakubuku literally 'break and subdue' [false teachings]—the vigorous method of proselytizing *shitei funi* master–disciple, two yet not two

Shō-Hondō the great main temple (the status of which as the *Kaidan* of the age of *mappō* was disputed)

shōji soku nehan the suffering of life and death are nirvana (or enlightenment)

shōju the gradual method of proselytizing, without refuting other teachings

Shonin honorific sometimes attached to the name of the High Priest

Shoshinkai dissident party of priests who disavowed Nikken for his failure to discipline or expel Soka Gakkai in 1979–80

shōten zenjin Buddhist beneficent gods

shukke renunciation of the secular world

Sōka Gakkai Value Creation Society

sokoto leading lay representative on the Nichiren Shoshu council

sokushin jōbutsu same body, same Buddha

tōba memorial tablets

tozan pilgrimage—to Taiseki-ji

zadankai small discussion group

zui hō bini the adaptation of the precept to the locality (justifying the acceptance of local cultural conditions)

SELECT BIBLIOGRAPHY

BABBIE, EARL T., 'The Third Civilization: An Examination of Sōka Gakkai', *Review of Religious Research*, 7 (1966), 101–21.

BENZ, ERNST, 'Buddhism in the Western World', in Heinrich Dumoulin and John C. Maraldo (eds), *Buddhism in the Modern World* (New York: Collier, 1976), 305–22.

BETHEL, DAYLE, M., *Makiguchi the Value Creator* (New York: Weatherhill, 1973).

BOCKING, BRIAN, 'Reflections on Sōka Gakkai', *Scottish Journal of Religious Studies*, 2 (1981), 113–30.

Buddhism and the Nichiren Shoshu Tradition (Tokyo: Nichiren Shoshu International Centre, 1986).

CAMPBELL, COLIN, 'The Cult, the Cultic Milieu, and Secularization', *A Sociological Yearbook of Religion in Britain*, 5 (1972), 119–36.

CAUSTON, RICHARD, *Nichiren Shōshū Buddhism: An Introduction* (London: Rider, 1988).

COWAN, JIM (ed.), *The Buddhism of the Sun* (Richmond: Nichiren Shōshū of the United Kingdom, 1982).

DATOR, JAMES A., *Sōka Gakkai: Builders of the Third Civilization: American and Japanese Members* (Seattle: University of Washington Press, 1969).

ELLWOOD, ROBERT, S., *The Eagle and the Rising Sun: Americans and the New Religions of Japan* (Philadelphia: Westminster Press, 1974).

HOURMENT, LOUIS, 'Transformer le poison en élixir: L'Alchimie du désir dans un culte néo-bouddhique, la Sōka Gakkai française', in Françoise Champion and Danielle Hervieu-Léger (eds), *De l'émotion en religion: Renouveaux et traditions* (Paris: Centurion, 1990), 71–119.

INOUE, NOBUTAKA, 'NSA and Non-Japanese Members in California', in Kei'ichi Yanagawa (ed.), *Japanese Religions in California: A Report of Research within and without the Japanese–American Community* (Tokyo: Department of Religious Studies, University of Tokyo, 1983), 99–161.

Issues between the Nichiren Shōshū Priesthood and the Sōka Gakkai, 5 vols. n.p.: SGI Headquarters, 1991–2.

METRAUX, DANIEL, 'The Sōka Gakkai's Search for the Realization of the World of *Rissho Ankokuron*', *Japanese Journal of Religious Studies*, 13/1 (Mar. 1986), 31–61.

—— *The History and Theology of Sōka Gakkai* (Lewiston, NY: Edwin Mellen Press, 1988).

MORGAN, PEGGY, 'Methods and Aims of Evangelization and Conversion to Buddhism, with Particular Reference to Nichiren Shōshū Sōka Gakkai', in Peter B. Clarke (ed.), *The New Evangelists: Recruitment Methods of New Religious Movements* (London: Ethnographica, 1987).

SNOW, DAVID A., 'Organization, Ideology, and Mobilization: The Case of Nichiren Shōshū of America', in David G. Bromley and Phillip E. Hammond (eds), *The Future of New Religious Movements* (Macon, Ga.: Mercer University Press, 1987), 153–72.

—— and PHILLIPS, CYNTHIA L., 'The Lofland–Stark Conversion Model: A Critical Assessment', *Social Problems*, 27 (1980), 430–47.

SHIMAZONO, SUSUMU, 'The Expansion of Japan's New Religions into Foreign Cultures', *Japanese Journal of Religious Studies*, 18/2–3 (1991), 105–32.

SHUPE, ANSON, D., 'Militancy and Accommodation in the Third Civilization: The Case of Japan's Sōka Gakkai Movement', in Jeffrey K. Hadden and Anson D. Shupe (eds), *Prophetic Religion and Politics* (New York: Paragon House, 1986), 235–53.

WHITE, JAMES, W. *The Sōka Gakkai and Mass Society* (Stanford, Calif.: Stanford University Press, 1970).

INDEX

abortion 130, 131, 134, 135
afterlife 218, 219
Agreement of 1977 235
Akiya, Einosuke 242, 243
alcohol 23
    addiction 31, 202
alcoholism 202, 211
Alice [in Wonderland] 19, 55, 59, 65,
    153, 165
altruism 65, 213
Arapura, J. G. 86 n.
armed forces 139–42
ascetic ethic 31, 219, 231
asceticism 2, 218, 220, 221
attraction 49
    characteristics of organization as 56,
        64, 68
    ethical 59, 67, 68, 69
    initial 49–64
    intellectual 59
    moral freedom as 57
    personal happiness as 59, 64, 68
    practical benefits as 55, 64, 67, 68, 69
    quality of membership as 53, 60, 64,
        67, 68, 69
    social 59
Austin, J. L. 214 n.
authority 216, 225
    doubts concerning 157, 160
    of Nichiren 8
    over laity 242
    respect for 144–6, 218
    structure of 14, 146

Baha'i Faith 92
Bainbridge, W. S. 45 n.
Barker, Eileen 45 n., 50 n., 97 n.
benefits 9, 21, 23, 56, 86, 127, 162, 181,
    186, 190, 205
    of chanting 24, 66, 93, 193, 210
    of group support 213

material 193
    practical 55, 67, 69, 83
    therapeutic 191
    unrealized 207
    see also conspicuous benefits;
        inconspicuous benefits
Benz Ernst 12 n.
Bethel, Dayle M. 9 n., 10 n., 11 n.
brainwashing 208
Bromley, David G. 97 n., 224 n.,
    225 n., 228 n., 229 n.
buddhahood 22, 222
    attainment of 5, 6, 7, 8, 32, 71, 181
    availability of 86
    chanting for 196
    compared with God 87
Buddha nature 6, 37, 192–3, 208
    availability of 230

Campbell, Bruce, F 12 n.
Campbell, Colin 52 n.
capitalism 217, 218
Causton, Richard 28, 32, 59, 71, 149
cited 5 n., 6 n., 18 n., 21 n., 22 n.,
    23 n., 30 n., 36 n.
    leadership of 161
change, attitudes towards 146–7
chanting 8, 36, 56, 155, 173
    age at commencement 45
    benefits of 66
    centrality of 98
    compared to prayer 183
    death and 34
    doubt and 35
    duration of 109
    effectiveness of 24, 182, 194, 227
    encounter and 46–8
    family and 175
    frequency of 173–5
    friends and 175, 213
    Gohonzon and 25, 26, 37, 201, 229

Index

Index